"Skloot has created a luminous yet brutally candid memoir. From its uppercut of an opening . . . through the author's careful, scrupulously non-self-pitying catalog of his mental deficits and on to a chronicle of his early family life that makes you smile even while it's breaking your heart, this book possesses a gravity and immensity that belie its brief length."—Julia Keller, *Chicago Tribune*

"While the early descriptions of his condition are fascinating, by far the more vivid part of the book is the latter two-thirds, where he gives us distant and recent memories of his family. . . . Earlier he had spoken of writing as a way of facing down the 'insult' of his injury. This whole book is an instance of that, and a tribute to the creative spirit."—David Guy, *Washington Post*

"Never self-indulgent, the book is a clear-eyed investigation into our powers of recall . . . and a look at how we never stop trying to make something transcendent of our disturbing memories. . . . Skloot's essays add up to a profoundly moving tale of emotion triumphing over the analytical."—Bernadette Murphy, *Los Angeles Times*

"What will amaze readers . . . is the poise—and even humor—with which Skloot turns personal catastrophe into literary reflection. These reflections convert neurological fact into poignant insight on how brain failure at once imperils and reveals the human essence. . . . A remarkable literary achievement."—*Booklist* (starred review)

"An unusual and engrossing memoir written with intelligence, honesty, perception and humor."—*Publishers Weekly*

"A harrowing, yet inspiring story."—John Marshall, *Seattle Post-Intelligencer*

"His meditations collapse voyeuristic distance on the brain damaged and lead us beyond empathy to answer our shared fate with an eloquence that may help prepare us, even for ultimate change."—Steven L. Glazer, *Literature and Medicine*

"Skloot's candid, concise and poetic prose provides a remarkably unsentimental look at the ways our lives can change in an instant or a day, and the amazing adaptability that can result."—Marc Mohan, *The Oregonian*

"What makes this collection compelling is the fact that the story is told from inside the experience, rather than from the perspective of a doctor or scientist. . . . Despite the ways his illness has slowed him down and made even the simplest tasks seem suddenly complicated, in this book, Skloot has managed to convey a life story that is at once pared down and rich with possibility."—Jennifer Lee, *Pittsburgh Post-Gazette*

"The first essay begins, 'I used to be able to think.' Yet he has put together this collection of measured, lucid, often funny essays cataloging his own dementia. He tells us that one essay—'A Measure of Acceptance'—took him a year to write, in 15-minute segments, putting his thoughts together like a verbal collage. The essays

D0197272

prove to us what a doctor told him: 'Inefficiency in mental processes is not stupidity.'"—Adair Lara, *San Francisco Chronicle*

"Floyd Skloot is not simply one of the wisest, wryest, and most interesting essayists I've ever read, he is also among the funniest. *In the Shadow of Memory* taught me as much about myself and my brain as it did about Skloot's battle to regain a semblance of the life he once led. It's a tale that is honest, insightful, and—in the end—profoundly moving."—Chris Bohjalian, author of *The Buffalo Soldier* and *Midwives*

"Over the past decade, Floyd Skloot has developed into one of the finest essayists we have. His strong, subtle, exquisitely truthful and often very funny writing testifies to an impressive humanity and maturity. *In the Shadow of Memory* is Skloot's best book, and can stand comparison with any personal essay collection by anyone in recent years."—Phillip Lopate, author of *Portrait of My Body*

AMERICAN LIVES *Series editor:* Tobias Wolff

Floyd Skloot

In the
Shadow of
Memory

University of Nebraska Press

Lincoln & London

Acknowledgments for the use
of previously published material
appear on pages xiii–xv.
© 2003 by Floyd Skloot

First Nebraska paperback
printing: 2004

Library of Congress
Cataloging-in-Publication Data
Skloot, Floyd.
In the shadow of memory /
Floyd Skloot.
p.   cm.—(American lives)
ISBN 0-8032-4297-2 (cloth:
alk. paper)   1. Skloot, Floyd.
2. Authors, American—
20th century—Biography.
3. Brain-damage—Patients—
Biography. 4. Creative ability.
I. Title. II. American lives
(Lincoln, Neb.)
PS3569.K577 Z47   2003
362.1′97481′092—dc21
[B]   2002020316

ISBN 0-8032-9322-4
(paper: alk. paper)

For Beverly

Contents

Preface

In the Shadow of Memory is a first-person account of living with brain damage. In December 1988, most likely on a plane trip from Oregon to Washington DC, I contracted a virus that targeted my brain. Details of this event and its aftermath will be described later; at the outset, I want to suggest that my book is about the experience of sudden and enormous personal change.

You don't have to be brain damaged to know what this is like. Illness, devastating loss, unanticipated alteration in circumstances: so many of us go through catastrophic life changes that our experience often seems defined by a radical unpredictability. I am hardly alone. The letters and calls I've received as these essays have appeared in print make that clear. We are all riding "the ever-whirling wheel of Change" that Edmund Spenser wrote about, a wheel from "which all mortal things doth sway."

But brain damage intensifies the meaning of sudden personal change by affecting the very organ with which we define who we are. The brain, where mind and body come together, where Self originates, is transformed in an instant. Not just how we see or speak, how we feel or think, what we know or recall, but who we are is no longer the same. Without warning, without choice, we are Other.

Usually, books about brain damage are written by physicians, psychologists, research scientists, or caregivers. *In the Shadow of Memory* comes from the other side of the examination table. I wrote the individual essays slowly, in small and scattered increments, sometimes spaced over the course of a year or two, depending on my health and ability to think. I misused words, got tangled in abstract thoughts, forgot what I was saying. I left blanks to fill in later and discovered over time how shards of thought might fit.

The book begins with "Gray Area," five essays that explore the science, meaning, and personal implications of living with brain damage. One essay is about thinking with a damaged brain and another about the way brain damage changes emotional life. One focuses on the experience of having a riven memory system and another on the loss of balance. The last essay deals with going out into the world as a brain-damaged person, traveling to a place where memory is embedded in the land itself, and practicing techniques to improve my functioning. Though the five essays in "Gray Area" begin and are deeply rooted in my personal experience, they also reflect more than a dozen years of research and contemplation because, like most people in my situation, I've been driven to learn everything I can about what has happened, what is being done to treat it, and what the experience suggests about my own and others' lives.

Part Two, "The Family Story," deals with efforts to recover what has been lost. It reconstructs key aspects of my personal past, putting pieces together, testing myths, examining stories, trying to figure out who and what I am by reassembling the fragments of my history. It's something we all do; in my case, it was being done with urgency and outside the customary frame of reference. Going over my past at a time when my mother was beginning her slide into age-related memory loss and my brother was dying from complications of diabetes made the whole process even more tenuous. But it also provided an opportunity for renewal, for a fresh view of my history and the world in which it took place. Memory is personal, but it is also familial and cultural. The assembling of my personal story became an act of both private and public reclamation.

The final group of essays, "A Measure of Acceptance," moves toward reconciling the private and public sides of my experience. As I write in this second year of the new millennium, in the fourteenth year since I got sick, I see that my experience has been one of new beginnings as well as mounting losses. I may seem shattered, but there are many ways in which I am better than ever, ways that are not obvious or flashy, not what I expected of myself in the year 2002. Slowed down, living quietly with Beverly in rural isolation, learning how to think and write in new ways, I feel reborn, hopeful, looking at the coming years with genuine astonishment at all I thought would be important.

Acknowledgments

The essays in this collection originally appeared, sometimes in slightly different form, in the following publications:

The Antioch Review: "The Family Story."

Boulevard: "Dating Slapsie," "Kismet," "Reeling through the World: Thoughts on the Loss of Balance," "Tomorrow Will Be Today," "The Watery Labyrinth," and "The Year of the 49-Star Flag."

Creative Nonfiction: "Gray Area: Thinking with a Damaged Brain" and "A Measure of Acceptance."

Mississippi Review: "Jangled Bells: Meditations on *Hamlet* and the Power to Know."

The Missouri Review: "Wild in the Woods: Confessions of a Demented Man."

Northwest Review: "The Painstaking Historian" and "What Is This and What Do I Do with It?"

Open Spaces reprinted "In the Shadow of Memory."

Southwest Review: "In the Shadow of Memory" and "Living Memory" (under the title "A Wild Place").

Tikkun published a portion of the preface.

The Utne Reader reprinted a version of "Gray Area: Thinking with a Damaged Brain" under the title "Me, My Brain, and I."

Virginia Quarterly Review: "Counteracting the Powers of Darkness."

Witness (Special Issue on American Families): "Zip."

"Counteracting the Powers of Darkness" was named among "Other Notable Science and Nature Writing of 2001" in *The Best American Science and Nature Writing 2002* (Houghton Mifflin, 2002).

"Dating Slapsie" was named a Notable Essay of 2001 in *The Best American Essays 2002* (Houghlin Mifflin, 2002).

"Gray Area: Thinking with a Damaged Brain" was reprinted in *The Best American Essays 2000* (Houghton Mifflin, 2000) and in *The Best American Science Writing 2000* (Ecco Press, 2000).

"In the Shadow of Memory" was named a Notable Essay for 1997 in *The Best American Essays 1998* (Houghton Mifflin, 1998) and was cited for Special Mention in *Pushcart Prize XXIII* (Pushcart Press, 1999).

"Kismet" was reprinted in *The Anchor Essay Annual/Best of 1999* (Doubleday, 1999), was named a Notable Essay for 1998 in *The Best American Essays 1999* (Houghton Mifflin, 1999), and was cited for Special Mention in *Pushcart Prize XXIV* (Pushcart Press, 2000).

"Living Memory" (under the title "A Wild Place") was cited for Notable Travel Writing 2000 in *The Best American Travel Writing 2001* (Houghton Mifflin, 2001).

"The Painstaking Historian" was named among "Other Notable Science and Nature Writing of 2000" in *The Best American Science and Nature Writing 2001* (Houghton Mifflin, 2001).

"The Watery Labyrinth" was named a Notable Essay of 2000 in *The Best American Essays 2001* (Houghton Mifflin, 2001).

"Wild in the Woods: Confessions of a Demented Man" was named among "Other Notable Science and Nature Writing of 1999" in *The Best American Science and Nature Writing 2000* (Houghton Mifflin, 2000).

"The Year of the 49-Star Flag" was cited for Special Mention in *Pushcart Prize XXV* (Pushcart Press, 2001).

I would like to thank *Southwest Review* for honoring "In the Shadow of Memory" with its 1997 McGinnis-Ritchie Award for Nonfiction in 1997. Thanks to *Creative Nonfiction* for honoring "Gray Area: Thinking with a Damaged Brain" with its Creative Nonfiction Award for Best Essay about the Brain and for giving "A Measure of Acceptance" the Walter V. Shipley Best Essay Award, sponsored by JP Morgan Chase. I am also grateful to the Oregon Arts Commission, which provided an Individual Artists Fellowship in Nonfiction, and to Oregon Literary Arts, Inc. for a writer's grant during the time that some of these essays were written.

Several editors have been kind and helpful in their attention to my work with these essays. I would like to express my appreciation to Richard Burgin, Lee Gutkind, Elizabeth Mills, and John Witte for their personal involvement, commitment, and friendship.

My agent, Louise Quayle, has been a steadfast supporter of this book. I am fortunate to have had her advice and resourcefulness.

My daughter, Rebecca Skloot, through her love, determination, and skills as a writer, has been an inspiration, superb critic, and graceful editor. She took the time from her own burgeoning career as a nonfiction writer to bolster my work, and she never wavered in her support or her candor. I am blessed.

My wife, Beverly Hallberg, is this book's soul and the love of my life. She read everything first, helped me be clear and honest, and understood what I hoped to do in writing about my experience with brain damage. Talk about being blessed!

What we refer to as mind is a natural consequence of complex and higher neural processing. Clearly brain injury or disease can severely compromise the mind.

John E. Dowling, *Creating Mind*

In a dark time, the eye begins to see,
I meet my shadow in the deepening shade;
I hear my echo in the echoing wood—

Theodore Roethke, from "In a Dark Time"

In the
Shadow of
Memory

1

Gray Area

1

Gray Area:
Thinking with a Damaged Brain

I used to be able to think. My brain's circuits were all connected and I had spark, a quickness of mind that let me function well in the world. I could reason and total up numbers; I could find the right word, could hold a thought in mind, match faces with names, converse coherently in crowded hallways, learn new tasks. I had a memory and an intuition that I could trust.

All that changed when I contracted the virus that targeted my brain. More than a decade later, most of the damage is hidden.

My cerebral cortex, the gray matter that MIT neuroscientist Steven Pinker likens to "a large sheet of two-dimensional tissue that has been wadded up to fit inside the spherical skull," is riddled instead of whole. This sheet and the thinking it governs are now porous. Invisible to the naked eye but readily seen through brain imaging technology are areas of scar tissue that constrict blood flow. The lesions in my gray matter appear as a scatter of white spots like bubbles or a ghostly pattern of potshots. Their effect is dramatic; I am like the brain-damaged patient described by neuroscientist V. S. Ramachandran in his book *Phantoms in the Brain:* "parts of her had forever vanished, lost in patches of permanently atrophied brain tissue." More hidden still are lesions in my Self, fissures in the thought process that result from this damage to my brain. When the brain changes, the mind changes—these lesions have altered who I am.

Neurologists have a host of clinical tests that let them observe what a brain-damaged patient can and cannot do. They stroke his sole to test for a spinal reflex known as Babinski's sign or have him stand with feet together and eyes closed to see if the ability to maintain posture is compromised. They ask him to repeat a set of seven random digits forward and four in reverse order, to spell *world* backward, to remember three specific words such as *barn* and *handsome* and *teach* after a period of unrelated conversation. A new laboratory technique, positron emission tomography, uses radioactively labeled oxygen or glucose that essentially lights up specific and different areas of the brain being activated when a person speaks words or sees words or hears words, revealing the organic location for areas of behavioral malfunction. Another new technique, functional magnetic resonance imaging, measures increases in brain blood flow associated with certain actions. The resulting computer-generated pictures, eerily colorful relief maps of the brain's lunar topology, pinpoint hidden damage zones.

But I do not need a sophisticated and expensive high-tech test to know what my damaged brain looks like. People living with such injuries know intimately that things are amiss. They see it in activities of daily living, in the way simple tasks become unmanageable. This morning, preparing oatmeal for my wife, Beverly, I carefully measured out one-third cup of oats and poured them onto the pot's lid rather than into the bowl. In its absence, a reliably functioning brain is something I can feel viscerally. The zip of connection, the shock of axon-to-axon information flow across a synapse is not simply a textbook affair for me. Sometimes I see my brain as a scalded pudding, with fluky dark spots here and there through its dense layers, and small scoops missing. Sometimes I see it as an eviscerated old TV console, wires all disconnected and misconnected, tubes blown, dust in the crevices.

Some of this personal, low-tech evidence is apparent in basic functions like walking, or accurately sitting in the chair I'm approaching, or breathing if I am tired. It is apparent in activities requiring the processing of certain fundamental information. For example, no matter how many times I have been shown how to do it, I cannot assemble our poultry shears or the attachments for our hand-cranked pasta maker. At my writing desk, I finish a note and place the pen in my half-full mug of tea rather than in its holder, which quite obviously teems with other pens. I struggle to figure out how a pillow goes into a pillowcase. I cannot properly adjust Beverly's stereo receiver to access the radio; it has been and remains useful to me only in its present setting as a CD player. These are all public, easily discernible malfunctions.

However, it is in the utterly private sphere that I most acutely experience how changed I am. Ramachandran compares this to harboring a zombie, playing host to a completely nonconscious being somewhere inside yourself. For me, being brain damaged also has a physical, conscious component. Alone with my ideas and dreams and feelings, turned inward by the isolation and timelessness of chronic illness, I face a kind of ongoing mental vertigo in which thoughts teeter and topple into those fissures of cognition I mentioned earlier. I lose my way. I spend a lot of time staring into space, probably with my jaw drooping, as concentration disintegrates and focus dissolves. Thought itself has become a gray area, a matter of blurred edges and lost distinctions, with little that is sharp about it. This is not the way I used to be.

In their fascinating study *Brain Repair*, an international trio of neuroscientists—Donald G. Stein from America, Simón Brailowsky from Mexico, and Bruno Will from France—reports that after injury "both cortical and subcortical structures undergo dramatic changes in the pattern of blood flow and neural activity, even those structures that do not appear to be directly or primarily connected with the zone of injury." From this observation, they conclude that "the entire brain—not just the region around the area of damage—reorganizes in response to brain injury." The implications of this are staggering; my entire brain, the organ by which my very consciousness is controlled, was reorganized one day fourteen years ago. I went to sleep *here* and woke up *there;* the place looked the same but nothing in it worked the way it used to.

If Descartes was correct, and to think is to be, then what happens when I cannot think, or at least cannot think as I did, cannot think well enough to function in a job or in the world? Who am I?

You should hear me talk. I often come to a complete stop in midsentence, unable to find a word I need, and this silence is an apt reflection of the impulse blockage occurring in my brain. Sitting next to Beverly as she drives our pickup truck through Portland traffic at 6:00 P.M., I say, "We should have gone for pizza to avoid this blood . . ." and cannot go on. I hear myself; I know I was about to say "blood tower traffic" instead of "rush hour traffic." Or I manifest staggered speech patterns—which feels like speaking with a limp—as I attempt to locate an elusive word. "I went to the . . . HOSPITAL yesterday for some . . . TESTS because my head . . . HURT." Or I blunder on, consumed by a feeling that something is going wrong, as when I put fresh grounds into the empty carafe instead of the filter basket on my coffee maker, put eye drops in my nose, or spray the cleaning mist onto my face instead of the shower walls. So at the dinner table I might say "Pass the sawdust" instead of "Pass the rice," knowing even as it happens that I am saying something inappropriate. "Crown the soup" is, I think, a more lovely way to say "Garnish the soup" anyway. So too, a "kickback" is a more resonant name for a "relapse." *I'm having a kickback.* I might announce that "the shore is breaking" when I mean to say "the shower is leaking," or call a bookmark a placemat. There is nothing smooth or unified anymore about the process by which I communicate; it is dis-integrated and unpredictably awkward. My brain has suddenly become like an old man's. Neurologist David Goldblatt has developed a table that correlates cognitive decline in age-associated memory impairment and traumatic brain injury, and the parallels are remarkable. Not gradually, the way such changes occur naturally, but overnight, I was geezered.

It is not just about words. "Dyscalculic," I struggle with the math required to halve a recipe or to figure out how many more pages are left in a book I'm reading. If we are on E. Eighty-second and Third in Manhattan, staying with Larry Salander for the week, it is very difficult for me to compute how far away the Gotham Book Mart is over on W. Forty-seventh between Fifth and Sixth, though I spent much of my childhood in the city.

Because it is a place where I still try to operate normally, the kitchen is an ideal neurological observatory. After putting the left-over chicken in a plastic bag, I stick it back in the oven instead of the refrigerator. I put the freshly cleaned pan in the refrigerator, which is how I figure out that I must have put the chicken someplace else because it's missing. I pick up a chef's knife by its blade. I cut off an eighth of a giant white onion and then try to stuff the remainder into a recycled sixteen-ounce yogurt container that might just hold the small portion I set aside. I assemble ingredients for a vinaigrette dressing, pouring the oil into an old olive jar, adding balsamic vine-gar, mustard, a touch of fresh lemon juice, and spices. Then I place the lid on upside-down and shake vigorously, spewing the contents everywhere. I stack the newspaper in the woodstove for recycling. I walk the garbage up our two-hundred-yard-long driveway and try to put it in the mailbox instead of the trash container.

At home is one thing; when I perform these gaffes in public, the effect is often humiliating. I can be a spectacle. In a music store last fall, I was seeking an instruction book for Beverly, who wanted to relearn how to play her old recorder. She informed me that there were several kinds of recorders; it was important to buy exactly the right category of book since instructions for a soprano recorder would do her no good while learning on an alto. I made my way up to the counter and nodded when the saleswoman asked what I wanted. Nothing came out of my mouth, but I did manage to gesture over my right shoulder like an umpire signaling an out. I knew I was in trouble, but forged ahead anyway, saying, "Where are the books for sombrero reporters?" Last summer in Manhattan, I routinely exited the subway stations and led Beverly in the wrong direction, no matter which way we intended to go. She kept saying things like "I think west is *that* way, sweetie," while I confidently and mistakenly headed east, into the glare of the morning sun, or "Isn't that the river?" as I led her away from our riverside destination. Last week, in downtown Portland on a warm November morning, I stopped at the corner of Tenth and Burnside, one of the busiest crossings in the city, carefully checked the traffic light (red) and the traffic lanes (bus coming), and started to walk into the street. A muttering transient standing beside me on his way to Powell's City of Books, where he was going to trade in his overnight haul of tomes for cash, grabbed my shoulder just in time.

At home or not at home, it ultimately makes no difference. The sensation of "dysfunctional mentation" is like being caught in a spiral of lostness. Outside the house, I operate with sporadic success, often not knowing where I am or where I'm going or what I'm doing. Inside the house, the same feelings sometimes apply and I find myself standing on the top of the staircase wondering why I am going down. Even inside my head there is a feeling of being lost, thoughts that go nowhere, emptiness where I expect to find words or ideas, dreams I never remember.

Back in the fall, when it was Beverly's birthday, at least I did remember to go to the music store. More often, I forget what I am after within seconds of beginning the search. As she gets dressed for work, Beverly will tell me what she wants packed for lunch and I will forget her menu by the time I get up the fourteen stairs. Now I write her order down like a waiter. Sometimes I think I should carry a pen and paper at all times. In the midst of preparing a salad, I stop to walk the four paces over to the little desk where we keep our shopping list and forget "tomatoes" by the time I get there. So I should also have paper handy everywhere. Between looking up a phone number and dialing it, I forget the sequence. I need the whole phone book on my speed dial system.

Though they appear without warning, these snafus are no longer strange to me. I know where they come from. As Dr. Richard M. Restak notes in *The Modular Brain,* "A common error frequently resulting from brain damage involves producing a semantically related word instead of the correct response." But these paraphasias and neologisms, my "expressive aphasias," and my dyscalculas and my failures to process—the rapids of confusion through which I feel myself flailing—though common for me and others with brain damage, are more than symptoms to me. They are also more than what neurologists like to call "deficits," the word of choice when describing impairment or incapacity of neurological function, as Oliver Sacks explains in his introduction to *The Man Who Mistook His Wife for a Hat*. These "deficits" have been incorporated into my very being, my consciousness. They are now part of my repertoire. Deficits imply losses; I have to know how to see them as gains.

Practitioners of neuroscience call the damage caused by trauma, stroke, or disease "an insult to the brain." So pervasive is this language that the states of Georgia, Kentucky, and Minnesota, among others, incorporate the phrase "insult to the brain" in their statutory definitions of traumatic brain injury for disability determinations. Such "insults," according to the Brain Injury Association of Utah, "may produce a diminished or altered state of consciousness, which results in an impairment of cognitive abilities or physical functioning." The death of one Miles Dethmuffen, front man and founding member of the Boston rock band Dethmuffen, was attributed in news reports to "an alcoholic insult to the brain." The language used is so cool. There is this sentence from the Web site *NeuroAdvance.com*: "When there is an insult to the brain, some of the cells die." Yes.

"Insult" is an exquisitely zany word for the catastrophic neurological event it is meant to describe. In current usage, of course, insult generally refers to an offensive remark or action, an affront, a violation of mannerly conduct. To insult is to treat with gross insensitivity, insolence, or contemptuous rudeness. The medical meaning, however, as with so many other medical words and phrases, is different, older, linked to a sense of the word that is some two or three centuries out of date. Insult comes from the Latin compound verb *insultare*, which means "to jump on" and is also the root word for "assault" and "assail." It's a word that connotes aggressive physical abuse, an attack. Originally, it suggested leaping upon the prostrate body of a foe, which may be how its link to contemptuous action was forged.

Though "an insult to the brain" (a blow to the head, a metal shard through the skull, a stroke, a viral attack) is a kind of assault, I am curious about the way "contempt" has found its way into the matter. Contempt was always part of the meaning of insult and now it is primary to the meaning. Certainly a virus is not acting contemptuously when it targets the brain; neither is the pavement nor steering wheel, nor falling wrench, nor clot of blood, nor most other agents of insult. But I think society at large—medical scientists, insurers, legislators, and the person-on-the-street—does feel a kind of contempt for the brain damaged with their comical way of walking, their odd patterns of speech or ways in which neurological damage is expressed, their apparent stupidity, their abnormality. The damage done to a brain seems to evoke disdain in those who observe it and shame or disgrace in those who experience it. I know I referred to a feeling of humiliation when I expose my aberrant behaviors in public.

Poet Peter Davison has noticed the resonant irony of the phrase "an insult to the brain" and made use of it in his poem "The Obituary Writer." Thinking about the suicide of John Berryman, the heavily addicted poet whose long-expected death in 1972 followed years of public behavior symptomatic of brain damage, Davison writes that "his hullabaloos / of falling-down drunkenness were an insult to the brain." In this poem, toying with the meaning of the phrase, Davison suggests that Berryman's drinking may have been an insult to his brain, technically speaking, but that watching him was, for a friend, another kind of brain insult. He has grasped the fatuousness of the phrase as a medical term, its inherent judgment of contempt, and made use of it for its poetic ambiguity.

But I have become enamored of the idea that my brain has been insulted by a virus. I use it as motivation. There is a long tradition of avenging insults through duels or counterinsults, through litigation, through the public humiliation of the original insult. So I write. I avenge myself on an insult that was meant, it feels, to silence me by compromising my word-finding capacity, my ability to concentrate and remember, to spell or conceptualize, to express myself, to think.

The duel is fought over and over. I have developed certain habits that enable me to work—a team of seconds, to elaborate this metaphor of a duel. I must be willing to write slowly, to leave blank spaces where I cannot find words that I seek, compose in fragments and without an overall ordering principle or imposed form. I explore and make discoveries in my writing now, never quite sure where I am going but willing to let things ride and discover later how they all fit together. Every time I finish an essay or poem or piece of fiction, it feels as though I have faced down the insult.

In his book *Creating Mind,* Harvard neurobiologist John E. Dowling says, "The cerebral cortex of the human brain, the seat of higher neural function—perception, memory, language, and intelligence—is far more developed than is the cerebral cortex of any other vertebrate." Our gray matter is what makes us human. Dowling goes on to say that "because of the added neural cells and cortical development in the human brain, new facets of mind emerge." Like the fractured facet of a gemstone or crystal, like a crack in the facet of a bone, a chipped facet of mind corrupts the whole, and this is what an insult to the brain does.

Though people long believed, with Aristotle, that the mind was located within the heart, the link between brain and mind is by now a basic fact of cognitive science. Like countless others, I am living proof of it. Indeed, it is by studying the behavior of brain-damaged patients like me that medical science first learned, for example, that the brain is modular, with specific areas responsible for specific functions, or that functions on one side of the body are controlled by areas on the opposite side of the brain. "The odd behavior of these patients," says Ramachandran, speaking of the brain damaged, "can help us solve the mystery of how various parts of the brain create a useful representation of the external world and generate the illusion of 'self' that endures in space and time." Unfortunately, there is ample opportunity to observe this in action since, according to the Brain Injury Association, more than two million Americans suffer traumatic brain injury every year, a total that does not include damage by disease.

No one has yet explained the way a brain produces what we think of as consciousness. How does the firing of electrical impulse across a synapse produce love, math, nightmare, theology, appetite? Stated more traditionally, how do brain and mind interact? Bookstore shelves are now filled with books, like Steven Pinker's brilliant 1997 study *How the Mind Works,* which attempt to explain how a 3 ½-pound organ that is the consistency of Jell-O makes us see, think, feel, choose, and act. "The mind is not the brain," Pinker says, "but what the brain does."

And what the brain does, according to Pinker, "is information processing, or computation." We think we think with our brain. But in doing its job of creating consciousness, the brain actually relies on a vast network of systems and is connected to everything—eyes, ears, skin, limbs, nerves. The key word is "processing." We actually think with our whole body. The brain, however, takes what is shipped to it, crunches the data, and sends back instructions. It converts, it generates results. Or, when damaged, does not. There is nothing wrong with my sensory receptors, for instance. I see quite well. I can hear and smell, my speech mechanisms (tongue, lips, nerves) are intact. My skin remains sensitive. But it's in putting things together that I fail. Messages get garbled, blocked, missed. There is, it sometimes seems, a lot of static when I try to think, and this is the gray area where nothing is clear any longer.

Neurons, the brain's nerve cells, are designed to process information. They "receive, integrate and transmit," as Dowling says, receiving input from dendrites and transmitting output along axons, sending messages to one another across chemical passages called synapses. When there are lesions like the ones that riddle my gray matter, processing is compromised. Not only that, certain cells have simply died and with them the receiving, integrating, and transmitting functions they performed.

My mind does not make connections because, in essence, some of my brain's connectors have been broken or frayed. I simply have less to work with and it is no surprise that my IQ dropped measurably in the aftermath of my illness. Failing to make connections, on both the physical and metaphysical levels, is distressing. It is very difficult for me to "free-associate"; my stream of consciousness does not absorb runoff or feeder streams well, but rushes headlong instead. Mental activity that should follow a distinct pattern does not, and I experience my thought process as subject to random misfirings. I do not feel in control of my intelligence. Saying "Pass me the tracks" when I intended to say "Pass me the gravy" is a nifty example. Was it because gravy sounds like grooves, which led to tracks, or because my tendency to spill gravy leaves tracks on my clothes? A misfire, a glitch in the gray area that thought has become for me, and as a result my ability to express myself is compromised. My very nature seems to have altered.

I am also easily overloaded. I cannot read the menu in a crowded, noisy restaurant. I get exhausted at Portland Trailblazers basketball games, with all the visual and aural imagery, all the manufactured commotion, so I stopped going thirteen years ago. My hands are scarred from burns and cuts that occurred when I tried to cook and converse at the same time. I cannot drive in traffic, especially in our standard transmission pickup truck. I cannot talk about, say, the fiction of Thomas Hardy while I drive; I need to be given directions in small doses rather than all at once, and need those directions to be given precisely at the time I must make the required turn. This is, as Richard Restak explains, because driving and talking about Hardy, or driving and processing information about where to turn, are handled by different parts of the brain, and my brain's parts have trouble working together.

I used to write accompanied by soft jazz, but now the least pattern of noises distracts me and shatters concentration. My entire writing process, in fact, has been transformed as I learned to work with my newly configured brain and its strange snags. I have become an avid note taker, a jotter of random thoughts that might or might not find their way together or amount to anything, a writer of bursts instead of steady work. A slight interruption—the movement of a squirrel across my window view, the call of a hawk, a spell of coughing—will not just make me lose my train of thought, it will leave me at the station for the rest of the day.

I have just finished reading a book about Muhammad Ali, *King of the World,* written by David Remnick. I anticipated identifying a bit with Ali, now suffering from Parkinson's disease, who shows so strikingly what brain damage can do, stripped as he is of so many of the functions—speech, movement, spontaneity—that once characterized him. But it was reading about Floyd Patterson that got me.

Patterson was a childhood hero of mine. Not only did we share a rare first name, we lived in neighboring towns—he was in Rockville Center, on Long Island, while I was five minutes away in Long Beach, just across the bridge. I was nine when he beat Archie Moore to take the heavyweight championship belt, almost twelve when he lost it to Ingemar Johannson, and almost thirteen when he so memorably won it back. The image of Johannson's left leg quivering as he lay unconscious on the mat is one of those vivid memories that endures (because, apparently, it is stored in a different part of the brain than other, less momentous memories). That Floyd, like me, was small of stature in his world, was shy and vulnerable, and I was powerfully drawn to him.

During his sixty-four professional fights, his long amateur career, his many rounds of sparring to prepare for fights, Patterson absorbed a tremendous amount of damage to his brain. Now that he is in his sixties, his ability to think is devastated. Testifying in court earlier this year in his capacity as head of the New York State Athletic Commission, Patterson "generally seemed lost." He could not remember the names of his fellow commissioners, his phone number or secretary's name or lawyer's name. He could not remember the year of his greatest fight, against Archie Moore, or "the most basic rules of boxing (the size of the ring, the number of rounds in a championship fight)." He kept responding to questions by saying, "It's hard to think when I'm tired."

Finally, admitting "I'm lost," he said, "Sometimes I can't even remember my wife's name, and I've been married thirty-two, thirty-three years." He added again that it was hard for him to think when he was tired. "Sometimes, I can't even remember my own name."

People often ask if I will ever "get better." In part, I think what they wonder about is whether the brain can heal itself. Will I be able, either suddenly or gradually, to think as I once did? Will I toss aside the cane, be free of symptoms, have all the functions governed by my brain restored to smooth service, rejoin the world of work and long-distance running? The question tends to catch me by surprise because I believe I have stopped asking it myself.

The conventional wisdom has long been that brains do not repair themselves. Other body tissue, other kinds of cells, are replaced after damage, but we have as many brain cells at age one as we will ever have. This has been a fundamental tenet of neuroscience, yet it has also long been clear that people do recover—fully or in part—from brain injury. Some stroke victims relearn how to walk and talk, feeling returns in once-numb limbs. Children, especially children, recover and show no lasting ill effects from catastrophic injuries or coma-inducing bouts of meningitis.

So brain cells do not get replaced or repaired, but brain-damaged people occasionally do regain function. In a sense, then, the brain heals, but its cells do not.

There are in general five theories about the way people might recover function lost to brain damage. One suggests that we do not need all our brain because we only use a small part of it to function. Another is that some brain tissue can be made to take over functions lost to damage elsewhere. Connected to this is the idea that the brain has a backup mechanism in place allowing cells to take over like understudies. Rehabilitation can teach people new ways to perform some old tasks, bypassing the damaged area altogether. And finally, there is the theory that in time, and after the chemical shock of the original injury, things return to normal and we just get better.

It is probably true that, for me, a few of these healing phenomena have taken place. I have, for instance, gotten more adept at tying my shoes, taking a shower, driving for short periods. With careful preparation, I can appear in public to read from my work or attend a party. I have developed techniques to slow my interactions with people or to incorporate my mistakes into a longer-term process of communications or composition. I may not be very good in spontaneous situations, but given time to craft my responses I can sometimes do well. But I still can't think.

A recent development promises to up the ante in the game of recovery from brain damage. The *New York Times* reported in October of 1998 that "adult humans can generate new brain cells." A team at the Salk Institute for Biological Studies in La Jolla, California, observed new growth in cells of the hippocampus, which controls learning and memory in the brain. The team's leader, Dr. Fred Gage, expressed the usual cautions; more time is needed to "learn whether new cell creation can be put to work" and under what conditions. But the findings were deemed both "interesting" and "important."

There is only one sensible response to news like this. It has no personal meaning to me. Clinical use of the finding lies so far in the future as to be useless, even if regenerating cells could restore my lost functions. Best not to think about this sort of thing.

Because, in fact, the question of whether I will ever get better is meaningless. To continue looking outside for a cure, a "magic bullet," some combination of therapies and treatments and chemicals to restore what I have lost, is to miss the point altogether. Certainly if a safe, effective way existed to resurrect dead cells, or to generate replacements, and if this somehow guaranteed that I would flash back or flash forward to "be the person I was," it would be tempting to try.

But how would that be? Would the memories that have vanished reappear? Not likely. Would I be like the man, blind for decades, who had sight restored and could not handle the experience of vision, could not make sense of a world he could see? I am, in fact, who I am now. I have changed. I have learned to live and live richly as I am now. Slowed down, softer, more heedful of all that I see and hear and feel, more removed from the hubbub, more internal. I have made certain decisions, such as moving from the city to a remote rural hilltop in the middle of twenty acres of forest, that have turned out to be good for my health and even my soul. I have gained the love of a woman who knew me before I got sick and likes me much better now. Certainly I want to be well. I miss being able to think clearly and sharply, to function in the world, to move with grace. I miss the feeling of coherence or integrity that comes with a functional brain. I feel old before my time.

But in many important respects, I have already gotten better. I continue to learn new ways of living with a damaged brain. I continue to make progress, to avenge the insult, to see my way around the gray area. But no, I am not going to be the man I was. In this, I am hardly alone.

2

Wild in the Woods:
Confessions of a Demented Man

I am demented. I have been clinically demented for over a decade. I display dementia's classic "multiple cognitive deficits that include memory impairment but not impairment of consciousness," and am totally disabled. You might never know, just looking at me.

There are, however, a few tips to the naked eye. My brain damage manifests itself in specific motor malfunctions. So I walk like the character named Phillip Dean in James Salter's classic 1967 novel *A Sport and a Pastime,* who in a bad moment "feels awkward, as if the process of movement had suddenly asserted all its complexity and everything had to be commanded." This is an accurate description of how I feel when I walk. I have to think about every step or else the whole process of walking breaks down. Like Dean, I walk "as if made of wood," only I do it that way all the time. If I bend to pick up a dropped coin, I will probably fall over. There are squiggles of ink on everything I wear. Watch me struggle to affix the plastic blade attachment guide to my beard trimmer. See me open the pantry and stare into it with no recollection of what I was after an instant before or start a bath by rubbing soap over my still-dry body. Play cards with me and see how I discard an ace just after you've picked an ace up off the pile, or how I suddenly follow the rules of poker while we're playing casino. If the cat moves across my field of vision, hear my conversation stop as I forget what I am telling you. If we drive together and I tell you to turn left, be sure to turn right.

Dementia is a loaded word. To health professionals, it refers to a precipitous decline in mental function from a previous state and it has clear diagnostic criteria. But to almost everyone else, it refers to doddering senility. Either that, or craziness; the dictionary offers "madness" and "insanity" as synonyms. Dementia is the Halloween of illnesses, a horror mask, a nightmare affliction, its victims akin to Freddy Krueger or Michael "the Shape" Myers. It is so fearsome because it is so transformative. The demented are seen as out of control or out of touch, as beings given over to primal impulses. Plug "demented" into a search engine on the World Wide Web and you get referred to sites like "The Demented Pinhead Figurine," "Lunatic Lounge, the Home of Stupid Human Noises," or "The Doctor Demento Halloween Show."

We decry what we fear. We shroud it in myth, heap abuse upon it, use language and gesture to banish it from sight or render it comic. By shrinking its monstrousness, we tame it. So a new disease such as AIDS is known first as the gay cancer, or chronic fatigue syndrome is known first as the yuppie flu, officially trivialized, shunted aside. And there is little we fear so much as losing our minds. Synonyms for "demented" are "daft," "deranged," "maniacal," "psycho," "unbalanced." Or, more colloquially, "bananas," "flipped out," "nutty as a fruitcake," "out of one's tree." The demented are like monkeys, it would seem.

I became demented overnight. Sudden onset is one factor that distinguishes my form of dementia from the more common form associated with Alzheimer's disease. For the Alzheimer's patient, who is usually over sixty, dementia develops slowly, inexorably. People have the chance to see these conditions progressing, to adjust in stages, grieve in advance. Mine developed without prelude and without time to prepare, momentously, the way it does in people suffering strokes or tumors, a bullet to the brain, or exposure to toxic substances like carbon monoxide. For me, it was how I imagine the day some sixty-five million years ago when a huge meteorite stuck the earth, turning summer to winter in an instant.

Have you ever been delirious? Gripped by high fever or certain brain infections, diseases, or injuries; after too much to drink, sniff, or snort; after too many pharmaceuticals or too long a run; people can lapse into delirium. It is a short-term mental state characterized by confusion and disorientation. There is a loss of recent memory, an inability to think logically or calculate; there may be hallucinations and strange preoccupations. Most people have been there. Dementia resembles delirium in the same way an ultramarathon resembles a dash across the street. Same basic components, vastly different scale. If you've run delirium's course once or twice in your life, try to imagine a version that never ends.

In May 1989, six months after becoming ill, when I was examined by Dr. Muriel Lezak, associate professor of neurology and psychiatry at Oregon Health Sciences University and author of a 1983 Oxford University Press textbook, *Neuropsychological Assessment*, she conducted exhaustive tests with empathy and a tenderness of expression that moved me to tears. She found extensive problems in my ability to learn and remember, a tendency toward slowed processing, fragmented visual recall, and an overall "difficulty in keeping track of ongoing mental activity."

To her, I was lost within the thickets of my own thought processes. My responses struck her as "very fragmented into bits," and these bits "were scattered rather helter-skelter as he had seemingly lost sight of the original overall plan," all suggestive of a "significant visual learning deficit." I could not put things together, could not make sense of what I saw. Further, I had not "carried through in any logical manner." She summed up our session by saying, "Mr. Skloot no longer is automatically accurate in handling basic arithmetic or writing tasks, as one might suspect he normally would be."

You never dream of hearing such things said about you. But dementia is a biological catastrophe whose essence is intellectual diminishment, and I had diminished all right. Big time. My IQ was down about 15 percent. Unable to exercise, metabolism gone haywire, my body weight was up almost as much. I was, in many ways, so unrecognizable to myself that I dreaded looking in the mirror, confusing what was happening inside my head with what might show itself outside. People kept saying I looked good. The hard edge from rigorous training for marathon running and long-distance racing was gone; I looked softer, which apparently was not a bad thing. I *was* softer. I was also slower. I felt denser, tamped down, compacted. I lived with greater stillness; I had time, had an emptiness where there had always been fullness—of mind, of ideas, of agenda. I had so few defenses against the world—not only because my immune system was scrambled, but because I found myself more emotionally open—that I felt utterly exposed.

A process had begun by which I needed to redefine myself, to construct a new sense of who I was and how I dealt with the world as an intellectual shadow of my former self. It would be years before I could make much headway. Fortunately, my dementia does not appear to be progressive, at least not over the last decade, and is classified as static. I got where I was going fast and have stayed there, as though beamed down. Now I had an opportunity to reconfigure myself. At least that was one way to look at this. Becoming ill afforded me the chance to discover my emotional state and align it with my new biological state.

The word *dementia* has its root in the Latin *dementare,* meaning "senseless." Yet I have found my senses heightened following the loss of intellectual force. My responsiveness to odor is so strong that sometimes I think I've become a beagle. Intense spices—Indian, Thai, Mexican—feel exaggerated in their richness; I can become exhausted and confused by eating these foods. My skin often tingles, sometimes for no discernible reason, sometimes in response to the slightest stimulus. The same process that stripped me of significant intellectual capacity and numbed my mind seems to have triggered an almost corresponding heightening of sensory and emotional awareness. Sometimes this can be a maelstrom, sometimes a baptismal immersion. So when "demented" breaks down into "de" for "out of" and "ment" for "mind"—literally "out of mind,"—I interpret the verbal construction as having positive connotations. Not loony, but liberated. Forced out of the mind, forced away from my customary cerebral mode of encounter, I have found myself dwelling more in the wilder realms of sense and emotion. Out of mind and into body, into heart. An altered state.

This is actually biology at work. Dementia is, after all, a symptom of organic brain damage. It is a condition, a disorder of the central nervous system brought about, in my case, by viral assault on brain tissue. When the assault wiped out certain intellectual processes, it also affected emotional processes. I am not talking about compensatory or reactive emotional conditions; I mean the same assault zapped certain emotion-controlling neural tissue, transforming the way I felt and responded, loosening my controls.

It has not been customary to recognize the neurology of emotion. For the nearly four centuries since Descartes's *Discourse on Method* (1637), scientists have tended to focus their attentions on the mental processes of memory, thinking, or language production. Measurable, readily testable, objective material. Emotions, primitive vestiges of our evolutionary history, were thought of primarily as distractions to mental activity. And were difficult to assess objectively, either from within or without.

But in the last two decades, neuroscientists have made clear that, as Dowling says, "Feelings and emotions—fear, sadness, anger, anxiety, pleasure, hostility, and calmness—localize to certain brain regions." Dowling notes that "lesions in these areas can lead to profound changes in a person's emotional behavior and personality, as well as in the ability to manage one's life." This is what has happened to me.

Intelligence is only part of the story of human consciousness. The longer I dwell in this new, demented state, the more I think intelligence may not even be the most critical part. I have become aware of the way changes in my emotional experience interact with changes in my intellectual experience to demand and create a fresh experience of being in the world, an encounter that feels spiritual in nature. I have been rewoven.

This concept of emotion turns Descartes upside down. It also gives a clue about where to head within the wilderness of dementia. After all, when one way through the wilderness is blocked, survival dictates finding an alternative way. For me, as the softening of intellectual powers coincided with an intensification of emotional response, the way through this wilderness seemed obvious.

I noticed almost immediately after my illness began that my emotional condition was as altered as my intellectual condition. It was apparent in small, everyday experiences that had never touched me deeply before, such as being moved to tears by seeing an outfielder make a diving catch, hearing the opening melody of Max Bruch's "Kol Nidre," feeling the first spring breezes on my skin as I stood on the porch, my dog's yawn, or finding in the refrigerator a grapefruit neatly sectioned by my wife and wrapped in plastic for my breakfast. I could also erupt in tears over the least frustration — trying without success to decipher a menu, to replenish the lead in a pencil. It was apparent as well in the emotional upheaval that accompanies chronic illness, with its attendant loss of companionship and livelihood, freedom and diversion. I would look out my window, see joggers clomp by and, unable to run myself as I used to every day, be filled with a despair I would once have suppressed. Although I had nothing but time on my hands, the least delay in a bank or doctor's office would irritate me beyond all rationality. The gift of a portable phone from my former colleagues, with a note saying they hoped it would let them talk with me more often, shattered me with joy. Sometimes the emotional upwelling was embarrassing, as when the overture to *The King and I* sent me into a torrent of ecstatic tears. The arrival of two acceptances of my poems from literary magazines also broke me up. I was turning into a sentimental slob.

This was not merely a matter of being victimized by emotional storms. There was also disinhibition, a new freedom to express the emotions I was feeling. At first I felt swamped with ungovernable emotions, but I soon learned to swim within them, even to surf upon them. I was learning how to handle this new phenomenon. My relationship with my daughter deepened. Love and passion entered my life for the first time in decades. My brother's advancing terminal illness was something I could face openly with him after years of estrangement, spending time in his presence, crying together, finally finding the possibility of sharing the warmth we felt for each other.

Losses in my intellectual capacities are clear and measurable, the kind of losses that can be evaluated and scored. Changes in my emotional life seem every bit as great. But, perhaps in part because my form of dementia is not as grave as in Alzheimer's disease, these changes offer a counterbalance to my mental losses. I feel differently but in many ways feel more fully, more richly. It is as though I have been given an area of psychological life in which to compensate for what is missing. I have been resouled. I sense myself moving toward a more feeling-centered way of being in the world, largely because feelings are now more dominant, less concealed, and less suppressed.

In the spring of 1993, I married Beverly and moved to the woods. This is something I could never have imagined myself doing. In fact, it is the opposite of what I thought was needed after getting sick. Logic dictated that I stay in the center of things, close to friends, doctors, services, and entertainment. I should live where anything I might need was within walking distance. To do otherwise, I reasoned, would be to further isolate myself, and illness had isolated me enough already. It never occurred to me that city life could have a deleterious effect on chronic illness, or that it represented a clinging to old ways, or that the time had come to consider a new way of living since brain damage had changed so much about me.

I believed in the importance of staying connected to the city even though my intuition was urging me elsewhere. For instance, the first act of independence I had performed, about eight months after getting sick, was to spend a week alone at the Oregon coast in a small room overlooking the sea. The motel was called the Ocean Locomotion, of all things, though stillness was its primary attraction. I could walk the hundred yards from my room to a colossal piece of driftwood shaped like a davenport plunked just beyond the tide line and watch the breakers, the zany behavior of gulls, or sunset. Occasionally a ship would drift across the horizon. At the time, I could not have rationally explained why it felt vital for me to leave the city and be alone "in nature." But I was drawn there and knew that being away from the city was good for me. Back in Portland, I lived for a year in an urban townhouse close to the Willamette River and spent several hours every day sitting or walking on its bank, pulled there, trying always to find more and more deserted sites. Still, I remained in the city till 1993.

By then Beverly had entered my life. I knew that in 1989 she had purchased twenty acres of hilly forestland in rural western Oregon, had built a small, round house in the middle of the site, and had been living there by herself ever since. In time, she took me to see it.

The place, located two miles outside a small town of 1,100, and fifty miles from the nearest urban center, is so isolated that there are no neighbors within a quarter mile, and that neighbor is a vintner who does not even live on the winery property. The land is officially a tree farm, its rocky and irregular acreage filled with Douglas fir, oak, maple, the occasional wild cherry. Beverly left it rough and harvests nothing. The landscape is laced with blackberry vines, wild rose, hazel, and poison oak, and what has been cleared for gardens is under continual assault from what remains wild. A winter creek cuts through the middle, and during its months of loud life there is also a lovely view south into the Eola Valley through naked trees. Some mornings mist rises from the valley floor, climbs the hillside, blankets the house for a while, and then leaves a blazing sky behind, the whole show like a short drama entitled *Hope*. Some mornings cattle and horses call from the small farms at the base of the hill; once a llama that had gotten loose found its way up to the house, trailed by a massive billy goat with one broken, off-center horn.

I learned that nothing here obeys the rules imposed on it. The ground is hard, basaltic, unforgiving. Beverly dug out a small pond, working her pick and shovel like a convict, lined the hole with plastic, and filled it with water plants that the deer ate almost before she could get back inside the house and clean off. They stepped through the plastic liner in their zeal, so she replaced it with a smaller, preformed pond liner, and the deer now use it as their personal drinking fountain. She allowed a friend from work to keep bees in a small grove for a season or two, but the hive failed and now there are only wild bees on the premises. This is a place that does not tame, that fights back at efforts to diminish it.

When we discussed the possibility of my joining her, the idea of living in the country was appealing to me for several wrong reasons. I spent much of my life in cities. Not just in cities, but in apartments. At the time Beverly and I began to be together, I was living in a new apartment building downtown, right in the middle of Portland's hubbub, walking distance from the bookstores, theater, concert hall, artsy cinema, restaurants, the Safeway. For nature, I still had the Willamette two blocks to the east, so polluted that the Environmental Protection Agency keeps threatening to add it to the Superfund cleanup list.

I still equated the city with self-sufficiency. But after spending a few weekends at Beverly's place in the woods, I began to consider escaping the frenzy, fleeing the noise and energy and congestion. It would always be difficult for me to think clearly, but being surrounded by urban commotion made it worse. I felt scattered. I had come to see that it was impossible to slow down in the city. It was impossible to find harmony between my surroundings and my newly diminished self, reined in, slowed down, isolated from the worlds of work, running, and community that I had always lived in. There was too much stimulation, too much outer life for a person in my situation. I had nothing but time on my hands but was living where time seemed accelerated. I needed an emptier place, I thought, pared down, humbler; a place that I could embrace as fitting my circumstances.

But of course, rural life is hardly empty. The isolated, quiet, dull, out-of-the-way place where I have lived the last decade is actually teeming with life. Life in its immediacy, to be experienced without the mediation of thought or explanation, as well as life that offers contemplative lessons. You don't need to be quick, just open and responsive, to get what this hill is about. Dwindling well water, the delicate system by which electricity is delivered to us, the boundaries established for herbs or flowers or vegetables—the human imprint is fragile and contingent. Yesterday as I was writing this very paragraph, the power went out in a gust of wind and took along my thoughts. It takes rigor and flexibility to hold on, a dedication of soul, but the rewards are worth it. I had seen myself as dulled and emptied too, so it has been instructive to be reminded of how much life goes on beneath surfaces that appear quiet.

One spring night shortly before we got married, Beverly and I dragged her mattress outside and hauled it onto a platform made from a couple of chaise longues. We protected ourselves with an altar of citronella candles and a down comforter and prepared to spend a night under the stars. This was a first for me. Nice and peaceful, arm around my sweetheart, gazing up at the constellations, impressed by how much I could see. Then the action began. Bats swooped to catch the bugs. Owls started calling. Frogs in the pond. I could hear deer moving through the woods just to the east of us. A skunk sashayed underneath our chaises and headed toward the compost pile. My first response was fear, a city boy stalked, then laughter, and soon a joy so vast that I felt caressed by it.

There are some days, when Beverly is at work and I am here alone, that I do not speak aloud at all during the daylight hours. Yet I am not restless or bored, yearning for the city, and this is not an exile. Till I got here, till I gave up my city home and began learning how to be in these woods, I did not really understand how much I needed to live like this. Functioning now at a more appropriate tempo, looking closely at the world I live in because there is not much else to do, I sense and begin to understand more about what has happened to me.

When the coastal wind blows hard through the trees and I see them swaying, I lose my balance, even in bed, because the damage to my brain has affected the system by which I hold myself in place. For me to retain balance requires work and a focus on what holds still; it requires a recognition of limits and place. I need to stop thinking altogether to do it right. Seeing those trees every morning also reminds me that this is a land of second growth. Much of our hill was harvested many years ago and I live within the density of what grew back. It is a good place for me to live, a workshop in survival, in coming back from damage.

A person doesn't escape to a place like this. It's not exile, it's home.

I am not getting any better. But I am also not getting any worse. At fifty-four, after thirteen years of living with static dementia, I have discovered just where that leaves me. Since I cannot presume that I will remember anything, I must live fully in the present. Since I cannot presume that I will understand anything, I must feel and experience my life in the moment and not always press to formulate ideas about it. Since I cannot escape my body and the limits it has imposed on me, I must learn to be at home in it. Since I can do so little, it is good to live in a place where there is so little to do. And since I cannot presume that I will master anything I do, I must relinquish mastery as a goal and seek harmony instead.

The short, grizzled guy living atop the Amity Hills looks like me and for the most part seems like me. He goes out in a storm to bring in a few logs for the wood stove; he uses the homemade privy balanced between a pair of oak when the power is out, which means the well cannot pump, which means the toilet cannot be used; he has learned to catch live mice in his gloved hands in his bedroom in the middle of the night and release them unharmed in the woods; he sits in an Adirondack chair reading while bees work the rosemary and hyssop nearby. He is my twin, all right, my demented self, wild in the woods, someone I did not know I had inside me.

3

In the Shadow of Memory

"Every day hundreds of human brains are injured," writes Howard Gardner in *The Shattered Mind*. Through accidents, strokes, tumors, or disease, people's brains, and in turn their minds and their way of experiencing the world, are altered in an instant. Nothing prepares us for this. Nothing equips us to cope with it except the very thing that has been damaged: the brain and its peculiar mesh of signals and switches that comprise our individual selves.

"The brain-damaged patient," Gardner goes on to say, "is a unique experiment in nature," allowing researchers to understand how the brain works by observing what happens when it does not. People with damaged brains offer neuroscience a deeper grasp of such human functions as language, perception, memory, mathematical or abstract reasoning, the ability to play a concerto, the ability to hit a curve ball. They expose the groundwork of "our sense of self, of the essence of our human consciousness" by revealing what happens when things "go awry."

Things have gone awry in me. Though I might have sought designation for uniqueness in some other way, at least I know now that my experience can be of use.

A nationwide research study, in which I was included as a subject, found that the brains of people with conditions like mine were riddled with "anatomical holes" that show up as "bright lesions on magnetic resonance imaging scans of the subcortical region." As reported to the American Society for Microbiology and in *JAMA: The Journal of the American Medical Association,* researchers "do not know whether the holes will heal." Mine have not yet. A spray of holes prickles my brain and nearly everything about me has changed.

Among the functions that have been damaged, the one I am most troubled by is the corruption of memory. After more than a dozen years, I am still not used to it. My memory, in all its aspects, has been destabilized. My personal past, what is referred to as episodic memory, is not totally gone, but large pieces of it are. My recollection of the world I have lived in, my semantic memory, is also unreliable. Gaps exist in the historical record. Surrounding myself with reference books helps to fill them, and so does reading, but I am apt to forget what I have learned that way. Shockingly, even my ability to recall things that I have just thought or experienced, to remember faces or names or conversations or inspiration or sensation is unpredictable. I can still type without having to look at the keyboard (except for numbers) and I have managed to ride a bicycle, so my memory for tasks, my procedural memory, seems fairly intact. Though I tend to turn a screwdriver the wrong way or to pour liquids into inverted bowls, I can perform relatively well on most activities I once performed flawlessly. But learning new tasks is monumentally difficult. From mastering the controls on our new bread-making machine to understanding how to play "Go," I am a hard study. This is not the way I used to be. Before 1988, I did not realize how much of my way of being in the world was predicated on a stable, functioning memory system.

In his book *The Making of Memory,* the British neuroscientist Steven Rose says, "Memory defines who we are and shapes the way we act more closely than any other single aspect of our personhood." He adds that "we know who we are, and who other people are, in terms of memory. Lose your memory and you, as *you*, cease to exist." Well, it is not quite that bad for me, fortunately. I am not like some of those patients reported by Oliver Sacks, Harold Klawans, Daniel L. Schacter, Philip J. Hilts, and other students of neuroscience, patients who are fully amnesiac, lost in time, or utter strangers to themselves and their families. But I am deeply altered, truly other, and this forces me to question the very integrity of my being. Now that I cannot reliably recall what happens to me, what I have set out to do or have actually done, or who the gentleman insisting that he is my dear childhood friend might be, who is this person?

In his *Confessions*, Augustine likened memory to a great harbor receiving "in her numberless secret, and inexpressible windings" all manner of sensory information, each bit entering by its own gate and laying up there for later retrieval. This notion of memory as a harbor also intrigued the great Irish painter Jack Yeats, younger brother of the poet. "Memory Harbour, 1900" is an early masterpiece collecting images that Jack Yeats would draw upon throughout his artistic career, as though the harbor itself, with its metalman on a pedestal, its captain's car, and its old pilot house were a repository of one life's meaning. At a glance, the whole thing resonates for Yeats and for the viewer as well, because Yeats packs both order and emotional fullness into this cluster of remembered images from his past. "No one creates," he once said, "the artist assembles memories." This is exactly what I cannot reliably do. The harbor has been bombed. It is littered with scraps that no longer fit together.

We are on our way out to the car when I remember that I have forgotten my book bag. How am I supposed to keep a doctor's appointment without my book bag? Experience suggests that I will stay in the waiting room at least long enough to finish the novel I have been reading and begin the treatise on the nature of memory.

So I tell Beverly I forgot something, reach into my pocket for the keys while walking back toward the house, open the door, say hello to the cats, and look around the upstairs as if I had never been there before. TV is off. Lights off. Answering machine is on. Stove is cool.

The house always astonishes me. It looks like a double-decker wine cask made of cedar, capped with a roof that tapers to a five-foot circular skylight. A permanent wooden yurt in the middle of a second-growth forest in wine country, the house is technically twenty-four sided but, especially from the inside, the experience is of roundness. No sharp edges or corners, a great sense of openness and spaciousness despite its being so small. I stand in the middle of the living room looking out the south-facing wall of windows and, for the life of me, cannot recall what I am doing here. But it sure is a nice place to be. I am certain that Beverly is outside, but am I inside because I was supposed to get something? As usual, I try to reason out what is going on since I cannot recall. Already wearing my jacket, so that's not it. I check my pockets and find the vitamin holder, chock full of its many pills. Not that. Not hungry, so I wasn't after food. Must eat to keep up my health. Doctor! We are going to see the doctor. I check in my wallet to be sure I have the little red registration card that Oregon Health Science University issued to me and expects to see before I can be examined. Everything seems to be in order.

I walk back out to the car and get in. Beverly looks over at me but does not start the engine.

"What?" I ask. The goofy, what-did-I-do-now feeling is beginning to spread down my neck like a blush.

"Where's your book bag?"

"Downstairs in the writing room. Why?"

"I thought that's what you went inside to get."

"Right." I have been through this sort of thing countless times already. So I open the car door, get the keys out while I walk, repeating over and over "book bag, book bag."

Of course, it is not just that I was distracted from remembering my book bag because we were hurrying to leave the house. We left in leisure, as we often do, anticipating a glitch. Nor was I prevented from remembering it once I had returned to the house because my mind was elsewhere; it was, in some senses, nowhere, or perhaps everywhere, but not truly elsewhere. Nor is this an outtake from a John Cleese routine, maybe something called *The Ministry of Feeble Brains*. I have, in recent weeks, provided myself with many other sterling examples of a short-term memory in tatters.

For example, reading the recipe for chicken cacciatore, I realized that I needed to slice a half-pound of mushrooms. By the time I turned to get them from the refrigerator, I had completely forgotten what I was after. Nothing to distract me there; the memory just slipped away like soap in the shower. A few nights ago, I thought of a brilliant idea for the start of a new essay about the way my emotions have changed since the onset of illness, and forgot the point in the few seconds it took for me to grab my pen and a chartreuse Post-it note. Maybe I should have reached for the pink ones instead. At the reception in Portland after a recent lecture by John Updike, I shook hands with a good friend's new sweetheart, heard her name, told her I was pleased to meet her, and forgot her name before I reached the end of the sentence.

I know. It happens to everyone. But not as the norm, not predictably. If it were only a problem with short-term memory, I don't think I would mind it so much when people say, "Oh, I do that all the time." I would be able to stop myself from telling them, "Well, I didn't! Not until December 7, 1988." If it were only short-term memory that was my problem, I might not say, "Yeah, well, can you learn how to use a new camera or boom box? Can you compute change from a ten-dollar purchase? Do you lose the fifty dollars you had in your pocket while you're browsing through a bookstore? Do you forget phone numbers in the act of dialing them? Do you get lost in your own neighborhood? Do you call your cat by the name of the dog you had ten years ago?"

Numbers can be a terrible problem. I spent seventeen years (I checked; it *was* seventeen) working in the field of public finance and fiscal policy. At one point, I managed the budget of a four-hundred-million-dollar state construction agency. Numbers were second nature to me until I got sick. Now I cannot get my daughter's street address right, no matter how many letters I write to her. I either transpose the numbers (131 ½ instead of 311 ½) or flip-flop them altogether (113 ½ instead of 311 ½). I can no longer add or subtract numbers in my head if they're larger than two digits, or at all if I have to "carry" numbers. We just canceled our long-distance telephone credit card and ordered a new one; if I use it often enough, I may have its fourteen numbers memorized by the time I can forget it again because of age-related senility. With my agent's telephone number on a card before me, I added it to my speed dialing system incorrectly and ended up calling a New York City garbage collection company, which was perhaps more of a symbolic error than I would care to admit. I believe that I multiply and divide numbers the way a new Chinese immigrant speaks English, as if I'd never really seen the alphabet before, as if I couldn't quite form the sounds. So I think of my math as having an accent.

We do not tend to realize that learning new tasks is a function of memory. But it is—procedural memory, they call it, or skill memory. So not only is my memory for *naming* unreliable, my memory for *doing* is compromised as well. When I bought a more sophisticated computer last year, the process of learning how to use it nearly drove me nuts, and I still cannot use WordPerfect efficiently, especially since it keeps changing through updates intended to humiliate the brain damaged. Weeks of repetition were needed for me to learn how to use my new fax capabilities, though the process requires all of four simple steps. Same with Beverly's vcr, despite years of trying, since it operates differently from my own. Use it, hell, I am incapable of calling up the menu properly. I cannot light and manage the fire in our wood stove, though Beverly has repeatedly shown me how to do it, and though I once wrote the steps down on an index card, which I have lost. My failures to learn simple tasks frustrate me and make me feel as if I am letting her down, no matter how often she tells me otherwise.

I forget which people I have told what item of news, repeating myself shamelessly. I forget to do anything that I have not written down in my calendar book, on the Post-it notes that festoon my living spaces, in the notebooks I keep in the bedside table or on the living room credenza or on the washing machine in the bathroom or in the glove compartment of the car. For weeks, a friend was telling me about her forthcoming book tour to Seattle and Bellingham, yet when she hadn't sent me any e-mail for five straight days I became very concerned, completely forgetting that she was gone. I forget what day or month it is. I forget my dreams. Follow directions? Give me a break.

It is the summer of 1988, a warm July evening, and I have just turned forty-one years old. Within the last year, I have run my fastest marathon and my fastest ten-, eight-, and five-kilometer races ever, winning ribbons for my age group in the latter three categories. I am on a roll. Lining up with other "masters runners" on the track at Lincoln High School, I am about to run a one-mile race for the first time in my life. Uncertain how to do it, how to pace myself since I'm used to the longer distances, I decide to shoot for a conservative time of 5:20 and to run each mile at an identical pace of one minute twenty seconds per lap.

When the gun sounds, I take off and set my internal clock, falling into a stride that feels right for the goal. Halfway around the first lap, I glance at my watch: thirty-two seconds. In my head, I calculate quickly, slow down just a bit, and finish the lap exactly as the official calls out eighty seconds. Bingo. To keep myself occupied and distracted, I begin to calculate what my times would be if I could sustain a 5:20 pace for a five-kilometer race, converting miles to meters in my head, dividing accurately, multiplying accurately while I run and listen to the times being called and even hear distinctly the cheers from my friends who have come to support me. Holding steady, I finish the race in 5:19, take my pulse as I walk around the track, and calculate how long it should take to return to resting count.

Exactly six months later, to the day, I got sick in a hotel room in Washington DC. I was fine on the long flight from Portland, fine during the evening as I prepared for a conference on national energy policy. But I woke up transformed.

It was 6:00 A.M., and I knew I should go out for a brisk five-mile run around the mall, but I could not remember how to shut off the alarm on my wristwatch, beeping at me ominously from the bedside table. Too exhausted to fold back the covers, I tried to determine what time it was back home in Oregon, see if that explained why I felt so tired, but could not figure it out. Was 6:00 A.M. here, so it was . . . I could neither remember whether to add or subtract, nor how much, nor what the alternative sums or remainders might be. I finally got up, put on my running gear, and sat on the edge of the bed, trying to understand how to make my shoes stay on, since tying the laces was proving impossible. I tried to put my blue wristband over my head like a headband and could not understand how it had shrunk so much on the flight across country. I tried to open the room door by pressing on its hinges; I tried to get on the elevator before the doors parted.

At work the next week, I could barely perform simple tasks. Familiar phone numbers—for the lobbyists in seven states with whom I regularly consulted, the vice president of Government Affairs to whom I reported, my grown stepson in his new apartment—were forgotten. I erased a brief memo on my computer, a memo I could not finish anyway but wanted to save to develop later, when I felt better. I got lost walking the few blocks down toward the shop where I always went to have coffee. In a meeting to discuss proposed changes to federal regulations on electric power, I was unable to grasp the basic concepts being discussed—power pricing policy, power production, power sales—concepts with which I had been dealing for three years. At the snack bar on the mezzanine, I could not remember how to choose the bag of pretzels I'd come to buy, nor figure out how to begin operating the machine.

Within six weeks, I had performed so poorly on a neuropsychological exam that the administering doctor, Muriel Lezak, explained my results with real astonishment. It was, she felt, a strange assortment of "significant cognitive problems" and an abnormal "difficulty in keeping track of ongoing mental activity." What she called my "severe visual learning disability" and my "great difficulty in organizing and synthesizing visual material when the burden of making structure is on him," I experienced as virtually total alienation from the person I knew myself to be. Nothing made sense anymore. I was lost in time and space, it seemed; I felt myself, my mind, to be incoherent and my world to be in fragments.

"Remember," Dr. Lezak said, looking at me across her desk, her dark, tired eyes suddenly softening, "inefficiency in mental processing is not stupidity."

Always a person drawn to order and structure, a poet whose work often rhymed and had traditional formal organization, a novelist given to carefully arranged narratives, I would have to learn to yield to the fragmentation of my experience, viewing it as a kind of antiorder. Randomness, elusiveness, and impermanence announced themselves as essential truths; my quest would have to be for understanding, not order.

One of the strangest aspects of living with certain kinds of memory loss is knowing that the forgetting is happening. I know I am not going to remember things that I desperately want to remember and have only limited success in using private encoding techniques to hold on to what matters.

I find myself highlighting nearly the entire text of a book in yellow, repeating to myself each idea there, closing my eyes and saying it over and over. Yet an hour later, when I pick up the book again, I have little recall of what the point was. Something about patients who deny the existence of deficits, a woman lying in bed with a paralyzed left side but insisting that the only reason she could not move her left arm was that it was tired today. It all sounds semifamiliar and quite personal. I realize it is ironic to forget details of a chapter on amnesia, but at the time the humor escaped me.

In addition, I know I am making mistakes and cannot prevent them. This morning, I told Beverly that I would take out the baggage instead of the garbage, but by now she is so used to my malapropisms that she did not seem to notice. Last month, crossing a street at the designated area, leading with my cane, I assured her that the rapidly oncoming cars would stop for us since we were in the car wash. Of course I meant to say crosswalk; I heard myself goof and grimly corrected myself, but this sort of thing is now common with me. I have called a concerto a rintoletto, which sounds like a wonderful thing but does not even exist; and—a catastrophic mistake for me—I called the Brooklyn Dodgers the Boxers. When I announced that "the carbon came dewy," I meant to say that the barbecue had gotten moldy over the winter, while we had it stored in the shed. These gaffes especially concern me when I am speaking in front of an audience, or when I read from my own work. I feel only minimally in control of my word-finding capacities, or my ability to remember words and concepts. I am safe with them only when I am alone and writing, able to correct myself before anyone sees or hears the mistakes. In public, I sometimes find myself throwing together an odd gestural salad, my hand movements wrong for what I am saying, like an orchestra conductor performing a golf swing when he wants the woodwinds to join in.

The sum of my experiences, the store of knowledge I have accumulated, the training and discipline of thought that have shaped the kind of person or the kind of writer I became, all these require an access to memory that is no longer routine for me. You cannot think if you cannot remember; at best, you can react.

When Beverly and I watch movies, I am a textbook example of memory's malfunctions. Though a passionate student of film, I have trouble naming movies in which I've seen an actor whose work I admire and hardly ever can recall an individual director's previous work. This is a topic in which I was well versed before getting sick. I lose the thread of narrative; foreshadowing is wasted on me. Sometimes, Beverly will miss a scrap of dialogue and ask me what was said; I can repeat back flawlessly several sentences at a time, provided she asks me within about five seconds of hearing the speech. But I cannot remember a word of it, despite having already said the speech myself, about ten or twenty seconds later. We tried an experiment, once this occurred to me, and shut off the sound after I repeated a speech, so that there would be little distraction. Gone in twenty seconds. This is a fine example of an intact "working memory"—that storehouse of transient information in memory's busy harbor which is quickly raided for material that will be stored or encoded into the short-term or long-term memory banks—working with a damaged encoding system. These are functions controlled by different parts of the brain. So I can often retain material for a few seconds but fail to organize and categorize the information correctly and therefore lose it. If there are any distractions—music playing, other people talking nearby, movement outside the window, a gesture of the hand, a competing thought—I will almost certainly lose what I might otherwise remember.

This is no significant loss when all that is at stake is a few lines of dialogue from a movie. But the same thing happens when I read, for example, and have great difficulty retaining new information, losing the thread of plot or character, failing to absorb important data, key facts (the hippocampus is where?). It also happens when I converse with someone, when I get a flash of inspiration that should be retained, an idea for something I want to write, a line of poetry.

These are unnerving occurrences, regardless of their frequency. I know that I knew what I no longer know. It is there as a kind of shadow memory, something at the edges of awareness, elusive and troubling. Many of my memories seem to be like this, whether immediate or short term or long term; memory is often a vague, partly hidden, distorted realm for me. And threatening at times, because I never can be sure when it will function well. I have had to learn how to be in public again, how to shed the shame and anxiety that memory loss engenders and work with what I have available.

What all this suggests, and what I have learned intimately, is that human memory is not one thing but many things, a system, a layered or modular set of functions. We may experience memory as a fluid and continuous thing, a film or an album or a script, but it is in fact a delicately wired arrangement of separate operations. To experience it as such is terribly strange. As Daniel L. Schacter explains in his brilliant book *Searching for Memory,* "We have now come to believe that memory is not a single or unitary faculty, as was long assumed. Instead, it is composed of a variety of distinct and dissociable processes and systems. Each system depends on a particular constellation of networks in the brain that involve different neural structures, each of which plays a highly specialized role within the system." But that is not how it feels to most of us, until things go wrong, until there are things like holes in the brain that interrupt the flow.

For me, the damage seems to be almost everywhere, but not too deep. All sorts of system components seem slightly off, but no one component has broken down fully. I do not think it is always 1956 or fail to recognize faces while readily recognizing voices; I do not mistake my wife for a hat. But I have a little of all these people in me, as though my brain had been scattershot, messing up the connections but not utterly destroying anything.

You lose an old photograph of yourself at four, perched on a tricycle with your father, who would die in the next few years, crouched beside you and smiling at the camera. You break the gravy boat inherited from your grandmother, the maroon Myott/Staffordshire with gold trim in a bouquet pattern that you remember seeing drip on her linen tablecloth in the apartment on Central Park West. You lose the scent or feel of a lover's presence, an old friend's voice, the precise contours of your sister's face. When this happens, it feels as though you have lost a bit of yourself, so fragile is the material of memory.

In early 1990, I received a letter from the owner of a major Manhattan art gallery. He had seen three of my poems and an essay in recent issues of *The New Criterion* and wondered if I was the Floyd Skloot who grew up in Long Beach, New York. Because, if so, then I was his best friend. His name, Larry Salander, sounded vaguely familiar, but I could not remember anything more about him. I called my mother, who, at eighty, not only remembered Larry but remembered his father as well because Mr. Salander had bought all our furniture when we were forced to move after my father's death. She told me that I had played on a basketball team with Larry and sent along a newspaper clipping about our team that she had saved since 1964.

I wrote to Larry, saying that I was the Floyd Skloot from Long Beach (how could there be another person with such a name, after all?), but that I had no memory of him. Certainly, I could have written more tactfully, or more fully, but I was bedridden at the time. He says that he threw my letter in the wastebasket and was deeply offended, furious that I did not remember him. But he then calmed down and wrote back anyway to explain that he had been my neighbor, playmate, and teammate. He recalled being in my house with me the evening after my father died. He was filled with the memories I had lost and, when I explained my situation, was eager to share them. In the years that have followed, Larry not only helped me reclaim many of those memories, he resumed his place in my life as a friend so close that I cannot get through a week without talking to him. His own paintings have graced the covers of two of my books. In many ways, Larry is a symbol for me of all that can be lost, of the preciousness and tenuousness of memory, but also of hope, since he is back and so is some of what I had lost.

As I turned fifty, the world and my place in it looked much different than I had imagined they would. I have come to place tremendous value on the intensity and power of the moment, since I could never be sure a moment would last in memory. It must be savored, and to do that I have had to simplify my life, slow it down and reduce the number of things competing for attention. The more complex my life becomes, the more of it eludes me. I live in rural isolation with no neighbors closer than a quarter mile. My old calendar books, the kind with one week spread across each page to allow for all the entries, have been replaced by a thin monthly calendar book with tiny boxes for each day. Blank boxes far outnumber filled ones.

I try to resist the feeling that, in losing so many elements of memory's function, I have lost myself, that I am adrift. Without Beverly's abiding love and support, I am sure it would be much more difficult to feel anchored. But at times the sense of having a scrambled memory, of its unpredictable and unreliable performance, makes me feel eroded. Or perhaps the more accurate word is haunted.

Memory loss moves through everything else like a ghost; nothing can stop it. It insinuates itself into life moment by moment, invisible to others except in how it makes its host respond. Having lost the integrity of my mental process, my past and often my present, I sometimes sense images floating away like ghosts too, the familiar transformed in a flash to the strange. I am haunted by what I have missed, though it happened to me.

Oliver Sacks refers to a patient suffering from an extraordinary loss of recent memory as having lost "his moorings in time." He also says that "to be ourselves we must *have* ourselves—possess, if need be, repossess, our life—stories. We must 'recollect' ourselves, recollect the inner drama, the narrative, of ourselves." This is what we need to hold on to, by hook or by crook, if we are to keep whole. People with memories damaged by injury or illness usually tell their stories only to their physicians, loved ones, or friends. By telling it more widely, I am not only helping myself remember, I am bearing witness, and trying to reclaim my humanity, bringing it out of the shadows of lost memories and into the light of experience.

*"Balance control in man requires an accurate
integration of multiple sensory inputs
and a rapid yet appropriate motor response."*

The American Institute of Balance

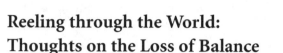

Reeling through the World:
Thoughts on the Loss of Balance

Beverly and I were discussing the difference between GARRULOUS
and LOQUACIOUS. This is not, I wish to mention, typical of our
firelight conversations. But Beverly was preparing for the Graduate
Record Exams after twenty years away from school, and I was supposed to be ERUDITE, so we had been sifting through her flashcards
and study guides. I got up intending to ASCERTAIN what *The Random House Dictionary of the English Language* had to say, crouched
to remove the twelve-pound TOME from the bookcase's lower shelf,
and keeled over onto my face like a HARLEQUIN.

Earlier this month, in a kind of trailer for this performance, I
had opened my refrigerator door, squatted to rummage through
the vegetable crisper, and toppled slowly onto my back. I lay there
for a moment like Gregor Samsa with his arms and legs waving
"helplessly before his eyes," then sat up, closed the door with my
foot, and decided I was no longer hungry for a carrot.

Variations happen to me all the time. In Powell's City of Books, a
vast Portland store crammed with shelves that are as high as basketball backboards, I was looking for a collection of poems by an author whose surname begins with *Sh*. Unfortunately his books, like
my own, are currently shelved at ankle height. Refusing to squat, I

hunched down carefully. But as soon as I began searching among the books I lost my balance, this time falling to the right, landing amidst titles by James Wright.

The problem goes beyond the act of lowering my body by bending my knees. I reach up for a pair of sweats stacked on the top shelf of my closet and flop face-forward into the pants and shirts dangling from their bar. In the shower, I close my eyes, tilt my face upward for a nice hot rinse, then suddenly lurch toward the edge of the tub and barely catch myself before falling out into the sink. I sneeze and, carried forward by the momentum, land on my knees. I don't think even Chaplin came up with that one. If I get distracted by a sound in the woods while walking up to get my mail, I'm likely to trip over the uneven gravel of the driveway at my feet. Forget walking on the rolling hillside that surrounds our home, even with the help of my cane. Forget escalators, which are particularly INSIDIOUS. Forget boats or banking airplanes, where the horizon shifts and my connection to the world's surface disappears. I have this ongoing sense of myself as reeling through the world, stumbling on breezes and stray thoughts, held upright by only the thinnest of tethers.

Until it goes haywire, we normally do not appreciate how elegant the system is that keeps us upright. Quiet, its workings do not typically produce poetic responses in the way that a gorgeous sunset, the cry of a peacock, or the touch of a lover does. As James P. Kelly says in *Principles of Neuroscience*, "Unlike taste, smell, hearing, vision and somesthesis (touch), the sense of balance is not prominent in our consciousness." However, he adds in a masterpiece of understatement, disruption of this relatively hidden sense causes "sensations that all too quickly impinge upon consciousness." In other words, we tumble out of the shower.

I am certainly not alone in the experience of balance loss. According to a report from the University of Washington Health Sciences University, "it is estimated that one in three people will have a balance disturbance of some kind" during their lives. That's more than seventy-five million people in this country alone. Most of these disturbances are short lived, due perhaps to a severe cold, an inner ear infection, a reaction to medication, a temporary problem with an eye. My own loss of balance, one among many neurological deficits resulting from damage to my brain, appears unlikely to go away.

Before December 1988, I was a well-coordinated man. I loved to race along wooded trails as I finished a ten-mile run, zigzagging at full speed to elude my beagle in our daily game of tag, hopping from rock to rock across Balch Creek, flying over roots in my path. But by the end of the year, I couldn't walk straight or avoid bumping into walls. My world in general listed to the left and, especially in the late afternoons, my gait resembled that of a pig trying to run on slick hardwood. Not a pretty sight.

I had always prided myself on a certain level of grace and balance in my movements. As a high-school football player, a ridiculously small running back, I was praised by the league's coaches for being difficult to knock off my feet. I competed in the long jump in track, turned the pivot at second for the baseball team. I loved jazz dancing and at age fifteen was cast as A-Rab in a summer production of *West Side Story*. The director made clear that it was because of my footwork and despite my erratic tenor.

As an actor in my early twenties, following a performance as Pompey the Bawd in Shakespeare's *Measure for Measure* that I was sure would catapult me to leading man status, I was asked to play the title role in Sean O'Casey's *Cock-a-Doodle Dandy*. A rooster. Because of my athletic ability, I was told, and not as a statement about the subtleties of my acting craft. After the first read-through of the play, when the director heard my dispirited gobble, he suggested that I wake up before dawn and drive to nearby farms to hear what cocks actually sounded like when they crowed. I was to be a representative of the life force, not a damn roasting hen. As rehearsals progressed and the set was constructed, we added occasional fancy twists to the cock's dances as he pranced down the steeply sloped walls and along the narrow ledges. Then came dress rehearsal. My costume included a pair of yellow tights with three toes; a pair of knickers heavily weighted with feathers and ending in a stiff, ten-pound tail; a bulky umpire's chest protector to give me the proper shape; a coat of feathers that weighed an additional dozen pounds and had wooden rods inside the sleeves so that I could make my "wings" flap realistically; and a full face mask with beak and crown. I was blind, slick footed, and carrying almost 20 percent more weight than normal. The first time I ran down the wall, momentum carried me right past my leap-off point. I landed in a heap on the stage with my tail sticking straight up and was unable to right myself. I can still remember the director running down the theater's aisle, yelling "Somebody straighten up my cock."

The point is, I had fine balance, notorious balance. By opening night, just forty-eight hours after that initial pratfall, I had metamorphosed into a graceful bird. But now, no amount of practice or adjustment will return me to normal balance. My world has become both literally and figuratively off kilter; I am no longer at home in it—can make my way through it only with great care. I have lost trust in my body.

I am not dizzy. Dizziness refers to lightheadedness, a sense of the body turning or spinning in place, or a feeling that a person is somehow outside the body. Nor do I experience vertigo, when the exterior world seems to be doing the spinning while the body remains in place.

My loss of balance never feels like something strange going on inside my head. It's just that I cannot automatically maintain my position in space. The falls come suddenly, like speeding cars rounding a blind corner. I feel bowled over rather than unsteady.

In *The Man Who Mistook His Wife for a Hat*, Oliver Sacks says that humans maintain balance through "complex integration of the three secret senses: the labyrinthine, the proprioceptive, and the visual." In the ongoing feedback loop between my body and the world outside, this is precisely where I run into trouble: integration. No single part of the system fails; rather, the separate pieces do not properly coalesce.

The labyrinthine sense is a function of the inner ear. A maze of winding passages locked beyond the fibrous seal of the eardrum, the inner ear hides among the skull's hard bones. It sits there like a wizard in the labyrinth's vestibule, which is why the communication between inner ear and brain is referred to as the vestibular system.

Vestibular balance is controlled by three semicircular canals set at right angles to each other. They work, as the American Institute of Balance explains in its on-line information center, "to stabilize the eyes (and hence the visual world) in space during rapid unpredictable head movements." Sheets of tiny hair cells float in these canals like seaweed, detecting position, sensing gravity or acceleration, sending the data on to the brain by way of nerve fibers. In addition, two saclike organs resembling alien wine gourds, the utricle and saccule, send similar information downward to the muscles of the spine and lower limbs.

The inner ear, in its delicate intricacy, is a marvel of evolution; think of the risks to our ancestral survival if we could not efficiently run, climb, leap, change direction in flight, or perch on a ledge. To borrow a metaphor from one of Oliver Sacks's patients, it is as though we carry around our own mobile spirit level. The workings of our inner ear clearly have evolved to allow us to execute the most complicated maneuvers without having to think about them.

In 1992, when I still lived in downtown Portland and was courting Beverly, we strolled from my apartment to the riverfront one evening during the city's great summer Rose Festival. Of course we thought it would be romantic to ride the Ferris wheel, a moderate one by any standard, but especially when compared with the Coney Island and Rockaway Playland of my youth. We thought we'd get a glimpse of the river and the festival from above, laughing as we shared the car with a teenaged couple. But we were floating backward and rocking and the lights were blinking. Nothing seemed to register properly. What overcame me was neither nausea nor queasiness nor fear of heights, but rather a deep sense of being totally cut off from my body. I was not outside it, floating unmoored—a hallmark of dizziness—but rather lost somewhere inside it. I felt as though I were caroming within the body's framework like a pinball. This was not a sensation I found the least romantic.

The body's second balance system, proprioception, is defined in Gordon M. Shepherd's standard text, *Neurobiology*, as "all sensory inputs from the musculoskeletal system." Proprioception includes sensation from muscles, tendons and joints, skin. Shepherd says that because we are always changing in relation to our environment, humans "require constant monitoring of those relations." We take in information "about different aspects of position and movement" from anyplace in the body that is capable of movement, a constant stream of feedback. Proprioception is most purely seen at work in the position of a ballerina performing an arabesque or in the gymnast doing a flip and then folding over herself on a balance beam. All sensory receptors are On; all systems are working in harmony without the benefit of conscious thought.

Sacks thinks of proprioception as "the eyes of the body, the way the body sees itself." It allows the body to sense where we are, to recognize itself and determine its place in the world. When proprioception fails, we flail, we fall. Sacks has harrowing stories of a woman in a "sensory darkness," trapped by a breakdown of this system and unable to stand, unable to hold anything, unable to feed herself because her hands wildly overshoot their target.

Our bodies are supposed to work. We're not supposed to have to think about how they work, or concentrate on most of their functions. Imagine having to focus all your energies on watching where you place your feet in order to avoid collapsing in a heap because you were distracted by a casual conversation or smelling the aroma wafting from that pizza parlor. Imagine yourself doing what I did last year in a restaurant—engaging in intense conversation with your spouse while chewing your sandwich, losing track of your tongue, and biting it so severely that you need four stitches to close the wound. I regularly reach for objects—a mug of coffee, a pen, my wife's face—and miss them by few fractions of an inch. As suave as that may make me sound, I have done even better. Imagine being balanced on elbows and knees above your lover, losing yourself in lovemaking, only to find yourself flopping off to the left of her body. Now that's what I call suave.

Vision is the third component of the balance system. Working together with the canals of the inner ear, the visual system is organized to stabilize the eyes and make the world we see cohere. While we move, we need to hold images stable before us. Baseball outfielders are adept at this, keeping fly balls steady in their sight while racing after them. Simply to walk, we need to hold moving targets in place and to measure the distance between two targets. Fans of *Star Trek: The Next Generation* remember the android, Data, whose head twitched in its effort to assess visual information. I identify with him in this. Even with acceptably corrected eyesight, I cannot rely on what I see to maintain my balance. I misinterpret, smacking my shoulder against doorjambs or my hip against tables, ducking down when I see locomotives on railroad overpasses seeming to float across the road, misstepping onto curbs.

My eyes are fine, as are my proprioceptors and my inner ear. Information gets where it is supposed to go in my brain. The problem is in the putting together. I get things wrong; my brain misperceives what my eyes see perfectly well, what I know to be right there, what I know to be a wall. It works in reverse as well: I will suddenly recoil from phantoms, like a person dodging a tree limb glimpsed on the edge of sight, my brain again misperceiving, misfiring. Of course, the niftiest number is when a sudden movement away from nothing knocks me off balance and I stagger into an obstacle that really is there.

Though doctors know *what* is happening in my brain, as of now they cannot say for sure *why* it happens. Either because of the lesions, a chemical disarray in the mix of neurotransmitters, cellular death, or some other factor, integrating balance data received from my vestibular system is faulty. Sometimes it works, sometimes not, like a vending machine that needs a good kick to dispense its treats. At least it doesn't malfunction all the time.

My brain has become disorganized in other ways too. Easily overloaded with stimuli, it cannot handle doing two things at once.

That normally is not a problem for most people, but it quickly blows my connections and my brain seems to short out, like an old house whose wiring is not quite up to code. Where I should be integrated, I am not. I sometimes experience my self as disintegrating and, not surprisingly, this causes me to fall.

It is common to hear the brain referred to as a machine, a computer-like storage and retrieval system. New research made possible by contemporary technology makes this comparison less convincing than it once sounded, but it still has a certain charm. So I can understand that, like an outmoded PC, my brain's processing capacity is very limited. I have to think consciously about many of the bodily actions that have always been unconscious, break them down into components like a dancer counting his steps during a waltz. The less I ask my brain to do simultaneously, the more effectively it operates.

William James said that "consciousness deserts all processes where it could no longer be of use." He was talking about general principles of psychology but might as well have been talking about the body's unconscious functions. If the ballerina were to think about the mechanics of her moves, if she were to call consciousness back to where it had deserted her because it was no longer of use, she would most likely stumble or at the very least move without grace or expressiveness.

For me to maintain balance, I must summon consciousness back to the fore in the process of movement. What this leads to is a manner of movement that I find humiliating, an unnatural caution and tentativeness that feel alien. Who is this man? I can no longer abandon myself to my body's operation, something that had been—as recently as fourteen years ago—among my chief pleasures as a runner, a chef, a lover. I had better think about staying on my feet when I squat or reach up or hear someone call my name on the street.

It is difficult to avoid seeing the loss of balance as an apt metaphor for chronic illness in our society. Removed from the customary worlds of calendar and clock time, the obligations of work, the fields of play, a chronically ill person seems to have stumbled, to be out of sync. Such people are often viewed as a counterweight, pulling the economy down with them, creating a burden on those who still work. The language of balance dominates colloquial usage; we say they have *fallen ill, come down with a disease,* or been *knocked off their feet.* They are *flat on their backs.* They have *dropped out of sight.* Recovery is associated with *righting* themselves.

From within the experience, the feeling of being off kilter or out of plumb is a primary part of adjusting to chronic illness. Body chemistry itself is often out of balance, of course, which contributes to this feeling. But it also has to do with seeing the world pass us by, inducing a sense of cosmic vertigo. Perhaps this is why when point of view is established for a sick or unstable person in films, it is often done with the camera tilted at odd angles.

The sense of misalignment also leads to a letting go of many things that were important before. Symbolically, you have to free your hands for other purposes, such as catching yourself when you fall. In other words, the priorities change. I gave my bicycle to my friend Annie Callan, who had no car and needed the bike to get around town. Newly mobile, she began to include in her rounds regular visits to my home, so I had the lovely benefit of her company in return. I started going to baseball games again, even though I could no longer fool myself into thinking I could have made the same leaping catch that Ken Griffey Jr. just made. Returning to the ballpark not only gave me deep pleasure, it opened up a new activity for Beverly and me to enjoy together. After the first couple of times that watching our trees dance in the wind caused me to fall over, I learned to savor the vivid sound of wind heard with my eyes averted.

In addition to physical equilibrium, of course, balance refers to qualities of symmetry, poise, equanimity, or composure. In these senses, disturbed balance implies a deeper kind of loss, something to do with a way of being rather than posture or movement. Chronic illness clearly upsets this sort of balance too, but I am concerned here with the physical dimension of balance.

More than any of the body's other senses, the loss of balance carries with it a figurative meaning consonant with the missing sense. We would not say that a blind person lacks "vision," only sight, or that someone with a damaged sense of taste was "tasteless." But in the case of the loss of balance, the literal and metaphoric meanings seem to converge. I think this is because balance is among that rare category of experience in which, to paraphrase the British scientist Nicholas Humphrey's *A History of the Mind,* sensation and perception come together. Normally, Humphrey observes, "Subjective feelings and physical phenomena are alternative and essentially nonoverlapping ways of interpreting the meaning of an environmental stimulus arriving at the body." When we smell a rose, he says, it is sensation that explains what is happening to us and perception that explains what is happening out there. But I believe that our sense of balance is meant to bring inner and outer worlds together seamlessly, to harmonize the two, and when it fails both sensation and perception are distorted.

Moving slowly and with awkward gait, breaking movements into their component parts, relying on a cane, people with balance problems are highly visible. It is one of those shameful symptoms, like drool, that calls attention to infirmity. I have, if you'll pardon the pun, stumbled on numerous techniques for managing the problem unobtrusively. For example, when Beverly and I walk together, she holds my left hand, which stabilizes me. The few times she walked on my right, she kicked my cane out from under me, which did not help as much. Within weeks of moving away from the bombardment of urban stimuli, I was not only sleeping better, but walking better too. I go barefoot indoors and wear soft shoes outdoors to maintain the closest possible feeling of contact with the walking surface. I try very hard to do one thing at a time.

Usually cloaked or managed adequately with a cane and concentration, my balance disorder tends to show itself when I am caught off guard or most relaxed; it sometimes seems that the vigilance required to manage it is more debilitating than the symptom itself. Indeed, my problems with concentration and memory, fatigue, and muscle and joint pain are often more debilitating to me than my balance disturbance. But they are invisible. So even my public presentation of illness is out of balance.

While trying to heed Susan Sontag's admonition against seeing illness as metaphor, I cannot help but experience the loss of balance as having deep personal meaning. However, for me the "meaning" is less connected with my relationship to the world than with my relationship to my body.

Because the management and assembly of data seem to be my underlying neurological problems, I feel slow. I know I miss things that normally I would notice and respond to; I can see the mistakes, the falls as they happen but cannot stop them. The means I use to compensate for my lack of integration separate me further from the "natural man"; I no longer feel safe being instinctive in my responses. This is new to me, but not exclusively negative. I'm calmer, more deliberate than I was; I take fewer physical chances, as a man in his fifties probably should. What all this means, I believe, is that I am seeking to deal with my brain's inability to unify and control balance-related activity, its failure to integrate, by attempting to integrate that failure into my life.

I dream of moving with grace. In some of these dreams, I am flying. The problem is that I'm flying upside down, with my face toward the sky, and to see anything other than clouds or stars I must bend myself backward like a bow. This proves aerodynamically inefficient and I begin to slow down. To avoid crashing, I have to straighten myself out again, but then I cannot see the mountains and trees, the beautiful lights, the world down there. Also, I cannot get my arms to stretch out like wings. Instead, they're clenched tight to my sides with my hands extended outward, moving rapidly like flippers to control speed and direction. I race ahead, I swoop, but I don't soar. Nevertheless, I wake happy, feeling cleansed.

To me, this is a dream about accepting limits. Wonder is available, both in the flying itself and in those sights I am able to see— cloud patterns, stars, the sky itself flashing past. But I must learn to relish looking at them and to let go of the urge to look down except for a few moments at a time. I can steer, can guide myself, just not in the approved manner and not with the grace I desire. Yet when I consider it, eventually I can see that there is a certain loveliness, even grace, in the kind of upside-down, flipper flying that I can do.

In another series of dreams, I am playing on the steel girders of an apartment building under construction on the island where I grew up. I am running along the narrow beams, leaping from one to another in a high wind, laughing along with my best friend, Jay, who runs behind me. This, I know, is a variation on memory rather than a dream of pure imagining. Jay and I did climb on the girders of a building that, strangely enough, soon became my home after my father died. There was always a strong wind off the ocean. But we were never as high as in my dream, because once construction advanced beyond the second story, we quit. Because summer had ended and football practice had begun, not because we were cautious.

Among other, obvious meanings, I think this is a dream about knowing and loving what supports you. The joy of movement in this dream is akin to flying but somehow connected to the idea of home. I am exploring the structure that will in time support the place I live. If I can feel free and confident in it, then maybe I can live well. Someone I trust is accompanying me, sharing both the danger and the discovery. In the dream, the beams seem to give as I pass over them, to be unsteady, but they hold. The parallels with my body's structure seem obvious. As a child, I played this body hard and without care, injuring myself many times but always feeling confident in it. So now, when things suddenly don't work right, I must remember that it is the same old body I always knew and relied on. I must come to trust it again, even though it sometimes fails me, even on the island of illness, even in the high winds that challenge my balance.

"Achill was home, birds coming low at dusk
over chill acres, strewn out

like words on a darkening page"

John F. Deane, "Cycle"

5

Living Memory

I didn't keep a journal of our time on Achill Island. I figured I'd surely remember everything that mattered during the month we were there. For a person with my memory problems, this was akin to stalking butterflies with a hula hoop.

Though I didn't mind walking with a cane, I found myself unable to adapt to writing a journal. In 1990, when I was a subject in the clinical field trial of a new drug that was supposed to cure my illness, I bought a hardback notebook and took a pen with me to the hospital. But all I ended up recording was my daily blood pressure and temperature, the weather, and the precise duration of each intravenous infusion. No thoughts or feelings, no descriptions of the setting or view, nothing about the staff or patients. Those topics came later, glanced in random shards of memory, vague and unreliable; I used them in my poetry or fiction. When I tried writing an essay—the truth as unvarnished as I could make it—I needed to talk with my fellow subjects in the trial, those who had kept journals. But still I didn't use a journal four years later in Ireland.

Much of what I recall has been kept alive in memory the way Beverly and I have learned to nurture what matters most to us. We talk about it. We talk as things happen and we talk later, intricately, deeply. At the dinner table, in bed as we move toward sleep or awaken, we allow ourselves the extravagance of intimate conversation, filling in details, making sense of what we have seen and done and felt. Over the years we've been together, this has always been our way. Without fuss, Beverly mastered the art of helping me to consolidate memories of our life together.

We came home from Ireland with fewer than three dozen photographs to prompt our recollections, but with hours of commentary behind us. Then, over the next few years, Beverly painted a number of moody, sensuous landscapes, pictures that emerged from her memory of Ireland and of earlier times spent in similar scenery. I wrote a few poems, often about the same subject as Beverly's art. Our memories flowered together under repeated waterings, my own next to hers, with the whole becoming ours.

We turned a sharp corner, saw a cluster of small, slate-roofed houses off to our left, a post office teetering at the edge of a cliff to our right, and had cleared Dugort proper before we could locate the village on our map. We passed between its so-called golden strand, windswept and empty in the early evening gloom, and a vacant caravan park. Then the bus struggled up out of the village and came to a stop with its nose pointed toward heaven. It rolled backward a few feet until the hand brake held.

Outside, about a dozen sheep clustered as though waiting to board the bus. Beyond them we could make out the red gate to a low building built into a fold of land. The driver glanced up at us in his mirror.

"The Böll Cottage, then. Here you go."

Beverly and I looked at each other and shrugged. It took us a good two minutes to collect everything from the seats around us, balance our loads, scuttle up the aisle. I accidentally placed the tip of my cane on top of an old man's foot. He nodded, obviously expecting nothing less from a Yank.

We would be spending the next month here at the Heinrich Böll Cottage on Ireland's Achill Island. Böll, the German Nobel Prize-winning novelist, had used it as his family's beloved retreat and a place to write from 1954 till his death thirty-one years later. The cottage has remained in his family, operated for half a year as a residency for visiting artists and occupied the other half year by Böll's son, the painter Rene. Though the residencies are primarily for German or Irish authors, my long friendship with Irish poet Thomas Kinsella, and his with the Achill-born poet and novelist John F. Deane, who was then helping to administer the Böll Foundation, had led us here.

Earlier in the year, John had written to tell us that Achill Island was "a wild place, beautiful in its wildness." He'd said it was "like a wolf. Untamed. Threatening. Attractive." Each adjective separated into its own island. We'd studied John's tightly condensed letter, then read a couple of guidebooks and declined his initial offer of a month's stay in November, when freezing winds might have blown us clear back home. Instead, we opted to wait another seven months and hoped for a balmy June-July. Instead of the famous gray of a harsh Achill winter, we dreamed of seeing what Yeats called "the purple hush" of the heather in bloom, though we got there a bit early.

Stuck into the Atlantic in County Mayo, off Ireland's northwest coast, the island is fourteen miles long and twelve wide, the country's largest but still only fifty-seven square miles, connected for the last century to the mainland by a revolving bridge. Sparsely populated, Achill is able to sustain only a small fishing and crafts presence. Most of its young people are gone. Its famed basking sharks are gone, killed off for their oil. As the map and guide we had purchased in Westport explained, "Emigration continues to be the biggest problem."

Achill is famous for its scenery, the staggering views from its cliffs, the lakes, its bare and somber mountain named Slievemore, and storm beaches that have a very short tourist season. Catholics swarm there from the north during the summer's Protestant holidays. It was a sometime home to the infamous Captain Boycott and to numerous writers whose work I always loved—Graham Greene;

Louis MacNeice, who wrote about "white Tintoretto clouds beneath my naked feet" while standing on an Achill hilltop; and of course Heinrich Böll—as well as painters such as Paul Henry and Camille Souter.

There would be no television in the cottage, no radio or computer, not even a typewriter. John had written, "Bring pens." I was going to write the old-fashioned way, longhand in notebooks, and Beverly was going to paint landscapes. Renting a car and paying for petrol were too expensive; we would stay put, isolated with each other exactly the way we loved to spend our time, even at home. We would learn the land and its history, read, and work through the long northern summer days.

Now we stood beside the road and watched the bus struggle the rest of the way uphill. It shifted at the crest as though catching its breath, squared-off body wobbling like a punchy boxer, and slowly dropped from sight. In moments, the motor's sound was swallowed by wind.

There were no signs of life. We were opposite the last house at the edge of Dugort, just shy of a crossroads where two routes looped to the same place about five miles west, Keel Strand. Though we were alone we felt surrounded, which might explain why we didn't move despite the rain. Maybe it was just the sudden wind, so cold for the end of June, and the engulfing drizzle. Or the smell of burning peat. Or the stark shadow of Slievemore, its cliffs looming behind us as though in solidarity with the low clouds. Or maybe it was the month's worth of groceries and towers of toilet paper, and our backpacks stuffed with clothes, books, and art supplies we had just dragged across the entire width of Ireland.

At 7:30 in the evening, we were only two and a half hours later than predicted. But that would be no problem because John had told the caretaker, Michael Carr, we would be there. Michael had left a key under the welcome mat.

Except, of course, he hadn't. Not in the flowerpot and not on the window ledge either. We piled our stuff behind the cottage and walked back through the gate. Across the road, just a few hundred yards east, almost buried by its shrubs, was another cottage with peat smoke coming from its chimney. We knocked several times before an elderly woman, shielding herself behind the door, glowered at us.

"What do you want?"

"Well, we've come to stay at the Böll Cottage. But the key . . ."

She smiled and nodded, inviting us in before I could finish, waving her hand, saying, "All right, all right, I thought you were a couple more Germans yourselves. The place is running wild with them. Will I call Michael for you?"

Our residency on Achill was going to be a kind of homecoming for Beverly. She saw it as returning to a deep part of herself, the part that had led her to study geology in college two decades earlier and, more recently, to paint landscapes in thick oils. She loved to immerse herself in a harsh northern countryside, reveling in its bogs and ancient stone circles, its lean light, all so different from the lush land where she had grown up in Oregon.

When she was in her thirties, Beverly had lived for four years in northern Scotland as a member of the spiritual community of Findhorn. She'd spent so much time on the islands up there—on Erraid or Iona, where she helped crofters plant potatoes and gathered seaweed for Findhorn's legendary gardens, or on Skye and Mull and the other small islands of the Inner Hebrides—that these places had taken hold of her, or perhaps reclaimed her soul. She climbed their mountains and hiked the wilds, spending as much time alone and away from the group setting as she could. While our month in Ireland was for me a first exposure to the country whose poetry had influenced me since I began writing in 1969, for Beverly it was a spiritual pilgrimage back to the latitudes in which she had discovered her true self.

So she didn't need Michael Carr to show us how to light a peat fire, though he did just that after riding over from the pub on his motorbike to let us into the cottage. It had a kitchen and living room, a bath with the deepest tub I'd ever seen, four bedrooms—

one of which contained a deflated three-speed bicycle—and the feel of a building in constant evolution. It had been expanded away from the road, inching back toward the small mountain, Krinnuck, where cattle grazed. The cottage's *U* shape enclosed a small courtyard and two entrance doors. Clearly, the rear bedroom was the artist's studio, filled with light even now; my writing room, where I liked to imagine Böll composing the novel that I was reading, *Group Portrait with Lady,* had a view down to the sea a quarter mile away. Or it would have, if the fuchsia weren't blocking the way.

After we unpacked and as the sun went down, I found an old pair of scissors in the desk drawer. I went out to trim the fuchsia, walking back indoors and sitting at the window to gauge my progress. Böll had written in his book *Irish Journal* of "the blue tongue of the sea thrusting into the island in bays" and I was determined to keep trimming till I loosened that tongue.

Beverly, setting up her studio, was singing Bonnie Raitt songs in her racy alto. We were far too tired to sleep, and anyway, daylight lingered till about 11:00 P.M.

By noon the next day, I remembered how humiliating it is for me to write in longhand. The effects of brain damage are immediately apparent on the page, my letters jumbled, words missing, sentences colliding, spelling contorted. The handwriting looks like a poor forgery of my former script. My paper becomes a jungle of dense linguistic growth, cross outs and arrows and looping lines connecting disparate thoughts, the whole thing too dense for the least sense to shine through.

I ripped page after page off my pads, crumpled and tossed them into the wastebasket. This wasn't the normal process of revision, it was a parody of composition; I was as lost as a rat in a maze. My own confusion made visible on the page brought all thought to a standstill.

At home, writing at my computer, I maintain a sense of order and progress by moving words around, "cutting and pasting." My software signals when a word is misspelled and mistakes can disappear rather than mass on the page like glacial debris. Now the wastebasket was filled and, in delicate counterpoint to my melody of frustration, I could hear Beverly's brushes knocking against the lip of an empty tomato soup can back there in her studio.

All morning, I had written only one line that I could both decipher and might be able to keep. Sitting on an island at the western edge of Europe gazing at its Atlantic shore, and having grown up on an island at the eastern edge of America gazing at the opposite Atlantic shore, I scrawled, "This is where the sea of my childhood ends." Then I ran out of paper.

Beverly decided to take a break with me. She wore her hooded sweatshirt and sweatpants, dressed for an Oregon winter as we walked the half mile downhill to "The Necessary Shop" attached to the caravan park, dotted here and there with tourist vehicles. Maybe the shop would have writing paper in stock, and we could assess the available supply of groceries.

For the three months before our trip, I had been walking for up to thirty minutes a day through the woods around our home, hoping to build myself up for island life. But the exercise only exacerbated my other symptoms, and I was listing badly to the left as we passed the locked Protestant church, a remnant of the Achill Mission from the 1830s. Beverly nudged me gently back toward the shoulder. I wanted to walk as much as possible, to see as much of Achill as I could, but it would be best to stay off the center of the roads.

When we reached the shop, the door was locked. The owner had left a note saying that customers should use the pay phone around back and call him. He was somewhere in the caravan park and would hear the ringing, would answer if he could, and would open the shop in due course.

He showed up an hour later, let us in, looked us over carefully, and said to the wall something like "cantbestayinherewhentheres-nohelpoveryonder." No one on earth mumbled more rapidly, a voice with the rhythm of a breaking wave. On a bottom shelf behind an assortment of biscuits, I found the only paper he had in stock. The short blue stack of school exercise booklets was covered in dust, their pages ideal for me with their widely spaced lines and nonexistent margins. I grabbed a half dozen. They would have to do, though I knew that if I began ripping pages out the whole thing would fly apart on me.

I walked over to Beverly near the shop window, where she stared at a bin of wilted greens and two gnarled tomatoes. She held a small jar of jam in one hand and looked bereft. The pickings for fresh produce were worse than for paper; she was going to starve.

Beverly was in the bathtub and I was sitting in the living room naked, waiting my turn, reading Böll, when the German photographer walked into the cottage. Two cameras dangled from his neck. He had long blond hair swept back in a ponytail, a neat blond beard, and an oblivious smile.

"Ist das das Haus von Heinrich Böll?" he asked, crossing the threshold between kitchen and living room. He stuck out his hand.

Beverly shrieked and slammed the bathroom door. I put the open book face-down on my lap and declined to stand up.

There was no sign on the gate, no sign on the door, and we'd been besieged daily by German tourists. Long before it had been turned into an artist's residence, the cottage had been written up in a German guidebook that was, obviously, still in print. A group of tourists had peered into the windows where Beverly was painting, their faces pressed to the glass, hands cupped beside their eyes. A young couple had left the gate open, permitting the sheep to follow them, and had split up to circle the house in opposite directions and meet in front of my window like burglars casing a joint. People knocked at all hours of the day. We'd been told by both John and Michael not to let tourists in; this was a private residence, not a museum, we were to say, and currently being used by us as a place of retreat.

I explained this to the photographer as calmly as I could under the circumstances. He smiled and nodded but didn't leave, so I tried some German leftover from college studies a quarter century earlier. Maybe my vocabulary was a bit rusty, because his response was to take a camera off his neck and begin looking around.

I waved my arms and stood, forgetting about the book, and said "Nein, nein, gehen Sie outside, pal. Now." Which seemed to get through. He closed his eyes, which was decent of him, frowned, and put the camera back. When he walked out, he left the door open.

It was not going to be easy being a vegetarian in Ireland. Especially on an island whose soil hadn't supported crop farming for a century or more. We'd brought oatmeal from home, rice, boxes of pasta, lentils and split peas, canned soups. We'd purchased potatoes and a few carrots in Westport the day we first traveled to Achill. But if Beverly was going to eat right, we would need to resupply ourselves with fresh fruits and greens.

Somehow, we had to get ourselves over to Keel. With one lame bicycle between us, we set out directly into the morning wind to find a grocery and to rent ourselves a second bicycle in Keel.

I didn't know if I could still ride a bicycle. When people say that it's one of those things you never forget how to do, they're not taking brain damage into account. Given the state of my memory and balance, I could imagine myself trying to use my cane while cycling, or maybe coasting in elaborate circles, or more likely falling into the peat bog.

We started off by walking the road past McDowell's Hotel, the same route our bus had taken when it disappeared that first night. We'd brought a backpack for groceries and several layers of shirts to protect ourselves from the wind, figuring we could remove a few for the return trip, when the wind would be at our backs.

The first hill was all right. But by the time we'd pushed the bicycle up the next hill on its flat tire, the time had come for improvisation. We rested just below the Deserted Village, a collection of seventy-nine collapsed oval, stone houses on Slievemore's flank, remains of a "booley" where people would live while their animals pastured in summer. This one was abandoned in the wake of Ireland's Great Hunger of the late 1840s and was now inhabited solely by sheep with the fleece on their flanks dyed red.

My suggestion, perhaps a remnant of teenage bravado, was to

pedal the bicycle myself while Beverly sat on the handlebars. It would work; I'd done it many times, albeit forty years ago and with an intact brain. She looked at me like I'd gone nuts, overcome by the shadow of the booley. Her suggestion was for me sit on the bicycle while she walked beside it and helped maintain balance. That would get me used to the thing and at the same time spare me some of the labor of walking. We still had four and a half miles remaining. To save my dignity, I proposed that we walk together up the hills, following her plan, and coast down on it together, perched like living sculpture, following mine.

It took us two hours, but we made it to O'Malley's Island Sports and Grocery giddy with accomplishment. I hadn't fallen and there was enough left of the bicycle's wheels to permit the young attendant to repair both tires. Inside the store, Beverly was instantly ecstatic: glistening fruits and vegetables, everything she needed, plus freshly baked soda bread filling the place with its scent, the same brand of bikkies she ate for dessert all those years in Scotland, and for me salmon caught that morning in the waters of Keem Bay. The lamb looked excellent, but we'd both noticed the young lambs playing in a field behind the store and I let the meat stay in its case. We rented a second bike, filled the backpack and four plastic bags with food, had inexpensive and delicious sandwiches for lunch, then walked across the street to the Keel Strand and a view of Inishgalloon. We planned to take the other road home instead of repeating our journey, which would give us a long view of the sandy grassland banks between Lough Keel and the strand.

But Beverly was somber. "Do you feel that?"

"Oh, yes," I said. "It's an overwhelming view. I feel touched by . . ."

"I didn't mean the view. Did you feel the wind?"

"The wind?"

"It's coming from the east. In our faces again."

Beverly was painting the same scene I could see from my window. When I walked back to the studio to visit with her, I knew she was working on the same scene because the shapes she'd painted matched the shapes I had been seeing off to my right, eyes glazed by the scramble of letters in my exercise book. But otherwise, what she saw was nothing like what I saw.

To Beverly the mountain's crest was cobalt green, as though all this rain had spread joy instead of gloom. Personally, I was with Böll, who wrote about "the mountains dark brown like mahogany." If they'd even been *that* bright. All I saw was murk, a surreal invasion of bog seeping into every form of life and staining it the way it stained the creeks. The fuchsia offered the only color I noticed, an obscene red amidst all the raw umber and gray. Beverly was seeing the foothills grin purple, with scattered folds of alizarin crimson, and she spotted dozens of zinc-white sheep and bog cotton bursting with light.

Back in my room, seated again at the desk by the window, I looked beyond the elderflower and hawthorn and now found calm seas flashing in ultramarine where a moment before all I could find was fog. Just over the top of the sheared fuchsia I noticed a movement that must be wheatear. Then there was a sudden lemon-yellow cascade of sunlight, maybe the first I'd seen since we arrived.

Without a word, she was helping me to see what was right before my eyes, lifting me out of the bog of self-absorption that illness so easily becomes. I am often turned inward by the very nature of the damage to my brain, checking systems, working at remembering, thinking about where I walk, looking hard at the obstacles in my path so they will register and be avoided, reminding myself to breathe. When I listen to people speak, I have to alert myself to block out competing stimuli—here on Achill the raucous call of a corncrake or cattle lowing on Krinnuck, rain against the windows, the movement of hedge or heather in wind. Each slight peculiarity of sensation, however normal, raises an alarm for someone who is chronically ill. Was that slight twinge in my gut something sinister? Why is my right eyelid fluttering? We become obsessed with the inner world.

So it is good to be brought out of symptom mania, to be brought back to outer life. I realized how much richer Beverly's experience of this place was, how much richer her experience generally was, how open she was. Sometimes I felt as though I held her captive on the island of my illness, however willingly she stayed with me, but her spirit was one of engagement with the world. It was wonderful to see her here, in an element where she was so comfortable. I realized how much I might be missing. Here, and at home.

There is, according to John F. Deane, a way of living "an island life." In his poem by that name, Deane wrote, "God, on our island, insinuated himself, / like the thousand varieties of rain, / everywhere." Rain is rain unless you attend to it. That's what I needed to do, attend to things, though I wouldn't mind if it stopped raining.

Achill is an island of living memory. All folded and faulted quartzites and schists, Achill is about six hundred million years old and looks it, weathered and spare, enduring. By its very nature, the landscape shelters the past, capturing and preserving whatever is buried in bottomless bogs. The cut turf presents us with raw opened ground, to borrow Seamus Heaney's phrase, a vista that draws the eye into the very center of the ancient land. Curraghs, traditional tar-coated fishing crafts used in this part of Ireland, decompose upside down where they were left near the shore or in fields. The rock faces are etched by centuries of ocean wind and surf. It is as though I can look at Achill and see that the past is never lost, even if my memory is splintered, the body like this land recording its history even if I am not aware of it.

The island sustains the distant past of human habitation as well, undisturbed in stone circles or ruined dwellings, their forms simply incorporated into daily life. Sheep shit on stone platforms there since the Bronze Age. Achill holds on to ancient quarrels between Catholics and Protestants so that even the layout of a small village like Dugort reflects the discord, this part Protestant and that part Catholic, grievances visible and audible in fences or local palaver. Natives build memorials to tragedies inherent in island life or in the peculiar life of this land—lost sailors and fishermen, émigrés drowned in Clew Bay, sheep farmers perished on Slievemore. At the edge of Dugort's golden strand, situated on a cliff, there is a children's graveyard where the unbaptized were buried in the past. We found it by accident, walking up the steep, grassy slope east of the beach. Looking down into the swirling water was like staring into the mouth of limbo.

When the rain finally let up for a few days, we could not bear to be in the cottage past midmorning. Packing lunch and warm clothes, just in case, we rode a couple of miles south across the island's haunch to find the sand and shingle beach at Dookinella. Like escorts, a pack of Jack Russell terriers, each looking like the mongrel cousin of every other in the group, followed us yapping and leaping along the road. We had to stop and let a flock of sheep cross to fresh pasture. Beverly pointed out the dome-shaped stacks of hay, so unlike the neat boxes on the farmland at home. Soon we passed a tiny lake, Sruhillbeg Loch; a monument to Father Manus Sweeney, a local priest executed in 1798 for speaking to French troops over in Newport; then another graveyard for unbaptized children before reaching Dookinella itself, a town whose sharp hills were too much for me.

Growing up on the south shore of Long Island, living now close to the Pacific shore in Oregon, I had never seen a beach quite like the one at Dookinella. We rode along hard sand until reaching a vast stretch of stone, which was the actual beach, cupped between enormous formations of windswept rock. A seal popped its head up in the shallows to watch us clatter to a place of rest. The dark Minuan cliffs seemed to release a skyful of birds. Above us, high in Waterfall Valley, there was a dried-out holy well, St. Fionan's, whose memory was now captured in the secular trickle of the Sruihill River making its way down toward the sea.

We were freezing despite the sun, but happy and somehow reassured to be here in the living presence of the past. We'd forgotten the camera, as usual, and Beverly hadn't brought her sketch pad because this was a day off for both of us. She lay back and seemed lost in daydream; I skimmed a few stones in honor of the little boy harbored in the shaky marina of my body.

The next day, which was the Day the Sign Was Put Up, we walked the half mile west to the Deserted Village. As we left the cottage behind, we looked back to see a group of tourists examine the new sign on the gate, which told them this was Böll's cottage but private property and off limits to tourists, confer for a moment, then lift the latch and walk through.

Having locked the doors, we decided to continue our journey. We climbed up the hillside so we could enter the Deserted Village's stone huts. The feeling here is of a lived life, noisy with families during summer when tending the sheep was their excuse for living above the familiar earth. The harsh edge of stone and hunger and ever-present wind prevent the fantasy from getting too romantic, but the old booley settlement is not altogether sad. We survive what comes over us, what finds us out of nowhere, by a mixture of adaptability and patience and community and luck, or we perish. We pay attention and remember together, part of the process of endurance.

Beverly sat on a wide, flat stone that had been laid across its circle of stone supports eons ago. Using her knees to support the sketch pad, sitting well away from a pile of sheep shit, she quickly lost herself in the view south. This could have been where MacNeice saw the clouds racing below him over Lough Keel, but today it is color and form rather than cloud that dominates. I watched her pencil move, watched her beautiful face express joy at being where she felt at home and doing what she was called to do. Her eyes shielded by a visor, missing nothing, she took a chunk of cheese from my hand without glancing away from the view as she captured a moment we have savored ever since.

2

The Family Story

6

The Painstaking Historian

I don't *think* my mother really believed she was Anastasia. For one thing, to admit she was Anastasia was to admit she was born in 1901 and she already had enough trouble admitting to 1910. My mother kept her year of birth as secret as the location of the crown jewels, though she did imply that a few of those might be found in her safety deposit box.

Also, there was the problem of explaining how she'd escaped from that closed killing-room in Ekaterinburg back in July 1918, when her father, Nicholas the Tsar of All the Russias; her mother, the Tsarina; her brother and her sisters were all assassinated by a savage team of revolutionary guards. Though she had nothing but scorn for pretenders who surfaced over the years, my mother wisely kept her secret to herself. It was difficult, but she never outright said that she was Anastasia Romanov.

However, the title of Grand Duchess was certainly a decent fit. Lillian, Grand Duchess of All The New Yorks. That had quite a lovely sound to my mother's ears.

So what if Nicholas and Alexandra never meant anything but harm to our people? To my mother's way of thinking, pogroms were nothing personal. Besides, they mostly affected my father's ancestors, those Jewish peasants in eastern Russia and western Poland, not her own ancestors. Well, maybe her father's family had some trouble there in Cracow from time to time, but not my mother's mother in Galicia. Well, not as often. And anyway, those days were over, the Communists were in charge of Russia now, there was no point in being obsessed about Cossacks anymore, and on their own the Tsar and Tsarina were very classy individuals. Look at how handsome he was, how elegant she was. These people understood style; they understood the value of privilege and the exclusive life, even if what they excluded sometimes were the Jews. It could easily have gone the other way, right? Jews on the throne, Russians on the outs. What a couple, that Nicholas and Alexandra, true lovers till the end. But for a few quirks of fate, my mother very well might have been one of them. And then she was.

For someone whose background was in the theater (as a painter of costume mannequins, sure, but she'd always planned to move up), filling out the royal role wasn't much of a problem. First, there was the accent. My mother, Bronx born and Manhattan raised, spoke with an intermittent eastern European accent that was part Hungarian, part Russian, a little Polish, and some accidental Yiddish, as though Zsa Zsa Gabor were imitating Akim Tamiroff doing Molly Goldberg. Then there was her carriage, erect despite the tug of gravity from her great torso, chin raised at all times, hand in the air when she sat and smoked her Chesterfields. There was the slow closing and opening of the eyes, a shade shy of boredom but far from interest. There were the props. She wore stoles and coats made by her furrier father who, she hinted, may have done a stint as the Tsar's own haberdasher at the Winter Palace. She wore jewels fabricated by her cousin who, it turned out, seemed to have been the Tsarina's jeweler for a brief time when she came to the Crimea, despite the fact that my mother's cousin never traveled outside Manhattan. There was a Fabergé egg with the "Fabergé" somehow erased, a polished samovar and Russian tea service, and sterling silver from Moscow purposely stored in a box with a misleading domestic label. There were silks, dolls within dolls, a balalaika disguised temporarily as a ukulele, and winter hats for everyone direct from St. Petersburg via my grandfather's shop in Manhattan.

On the one shelf in our living room that housed books, my mother kept a set of red, cloth-covered hardbacks. They were un-opened because, she implied, some were gifts from the authors themselves, old friends of the family like Dostoyevski and Tolstoy and Turgenev, and therefore priceless as well as extremely valuable to her personally. Inside the piano bench she kept sheet music by Rachmaninoff and Tchaikovski though she only played Tin Pan Alley and Broadway hits. This refusal to play her beloved Russians, I was given to know, was to keep her heart from breaking, since her ties to the old country were so deep.

The air of closet drama about her past was intoxicating. We weren't to tell people about her real background—only my mother, on occasion, would let something slip—because there were still savages in power and it was important not to reveal her where-abouts. Actions, however, would speak volumes. True aristocracy, she felt, revealed itself in every gesture, every deed, even if she did happen to be married to a kosher-chicken butcher with a multi-broken nose and one glass eye, even if she did live in a small East Flatbush apartment, even if her power was now limited to those living directly in her small domain.

I will never forget my mother's shock when, at a fancy Brooklyn restaurant where we had gone for luncheon (not lunch), I ordered beef stew. There was an audible gasp and a widening of the eyes as she waved her hand in the air, unable to utter words but signal-ing to the waitress that my wishes were erased. Then she leaned over and hissed at me, "Only peasants eat stew!" She was morti-fied. She never told anyone what I had done, though eight years earlier, when my brother had ordered a shit sandwich at Schraft's, his performance had provided her with a frequently recounted tale, charming in a way that my own grave error of class etiquette appar-ently was not.

In the apartment building, we couldn't actually have servants and Hussar guards, but we did have a maid. Though my father struggled for decades without success to make his Union Street poultry market profitable, we had a maid. Though the apartment was small enough to be cleaned by a good sneeze and though my mother was physically healthy, did no work, belonged to no clubs, engaged in no civic or cultural activities, and had few friends, we had a maid. It drove my father nuts.

"Just tell me one thing, all right? What is it you do all day that you need a maid?"

"Don't you start with me!"

Lassie was the name of the maid during most of my childhood years. Lassie Lee Price. She loved to tell the story of her first day working for my mother. She rang the doorbell at 9:07 A.M. and I—age four—opened it, looked up at her, and said, "You're late." After fifty-one years, it still brings me no end of shame. Lassie essentially raised me, this little Tsarevich-in-waiting disguised as a dirt-covered shortstop outside the apartment and, inside, crawling on the carpet under her feet playing penny-baseball with my vast collection of trading cards. Thanks in large part to Lassie, to feeling her tenderness and love, to witnessing the way she handled and humored my mother, to her daytime protection, I had some balance in my young life. I knew I was all right as long as I didn't touch anything after Lassie left. Hands to myself. Stay in my room at the far end of the palace.

I behaved well, wore the proper uniform, and spoke properly. Living within my mother's empire (New York was, after all, named the Empire State for a reason), the privileges and responsibilities I bore were made clear to me, as were the consequences of failure. I might masquerade as a pint-sized Brooklyn Jewish schoolyard athlete, but she was determined that I never forget I was the son of Lillian, Grand Duchess of All the New Yorks. Surely, I figured, the Dodgers wouldn't object to a Tsarevich at shortstop, provided he could hit to the opposite field.

I believe it was in the exercise of power within her domain that my mother's true nature manifested itself. As I got older, I had a recurring dream in which she had actually ascended to the throne in some distant land and, like a stroke victim, could only say one thing over and over: "Off with his head."

Indeed, my mother was a born tyrant, ruthless, suspicious, given to tantrums and unpredictable violence. She yearned for adulation and obedience, was driven to shape the world to her wishes, brooked no contradiction, and I have come to believe it was the privilege of absolute power and control rather than the privilege of absolute wealth and possessions that fed her delusions.

When it became clear that my father would not, in fact, treat her the way she wished to be treated, would neither return her to her throne nor eradicate the uprisings all around her; that her two sons were tainted by associations with peasants, by strange appetites for Velveeta or football, by profanity and rock 'n' roll; and that time and the world were passing her by (it was already the 1950s!) without granting proper recognition; my mother's frustrations grew unmanageable. Her eccentricities and flamboyance turned into open hostility and she became dangerous.

The elevator is too slow so I always use the stairs after one of my mother's beatings. Except when she locks me in my toy chest and I can't get away until she calms down.

I sprint down the first twelve steps of each flight, then leap the second twelve to reach the landing on a run. I can cover all four floors in less than a minute and be outside before her screams stop echoing in the stairwell.

It is right after one of these beatings, in the fall of 1954, that I race from the building and am run over by a Packard Clipper Super Hard-Top. The sound of the car's horn is exactly like my mother's frenzied voice in my ears.

The driver is an off-duty cop who sits on his bumper and cries. He says I came out of nowhere like a deer. A friggin' fawn, he says. I am underneath a parked car where no one can quite reach me.

My eyes are still black from when my mother threw me against the sink in my grandmother's bathroom. My back, bruised from being kicked while she held me trapped behind the open bedroom door a few days before our visit to my grandmother, is in the pastel stages of healing. Doctors at King County Hospital, across the street from our apartment, do not differentiate among the various discolorations when they work on me after I was run over. Maybe they think the Packard did it all. Maybe they are like my teachers and don't see the bruises at all. Or maybe they are more worried about what has happened inside my head.

The bright light in the room is very cold. They joke that my mother is in worse shape than I am. She screams as they examine me, saying over and over, "See what these kids do to me?"

In its "Diagnostic and Treatment Guidelines on Mental Health Effects of Family Violence," the American Medical Association discusses the chemical process through which the brain is essentially rewired by childhood abuse. "Multiple exposures to trauma, so common in family violence, cause repeated mobilizations of autonomic and endocrine hyper-arousal ('flight or fight' response). With time there may be alterations of adrenergic, serotonergic, endogenous peptide, and hypothalmic-pituitary-adrenal responsiveness, causing a generalized loss of neuromodulation and affect regulation." In other words, a pattern of chemically based fear response becomes embedded in the brain's structure, rendering a person incapable of anything but a chemical hyperresponse to the least perceived danger. Stress hormones repeatedly released under pressure of abusive situations damage tissues as well as establishing a response pathway that becomes habitual.

It is not simply that the mind remembers traumatic or violent experience; the body remembers too, down to the molecular level, and is altered because of it. There are permanent neurohormonal effects of trauma, which involve changes in levels of chemicals essential to the brain's normal synaptic functioning. There are also neuroanatomical effects such as decreased volume of the hippocampus, the brain's horseshoe-shaped guardian of event memories.

According to a Yale University study in 1995, the hippocampal damage "is wrought by hormones flooding the brain during and after a stressful episode." A kind of cellular static is set up, which inhibits the flow of electrical impulses and indicates a shift in normal processing of information. There is also chronic activation of the amygdala, the brain's center of emotional memory and automatic fear response, and decreased activation of Broca's area of the brain, which is responsible for the production of language as a person is stunned into silence by the unforgettable and terrifying eruption of intimate violence.

"The brain," Debra Niehof says in her book *The Biology of Violence,* "is a painstaking historian." We not only keep score, we establish a permanent record and even put it out on the wires, forever broadcasting in one way or another the story of our traumatic past. Niehof likens the brain to "an ardent correspondent" making careful documentation of experience "in the language of neurochemistry."

Memory is a chemical process. There are several kinds of processes at work to produce the set of cellular associations we commonly refer to as memory. These processes, enacted in the synaptic medium of neurotransmitters, are governed by a combination of genetic makeup and personal experience. Nature and nurture (or, in certain cases, antinurture) combine to configure the brain's circuitry. So when we say we are shaped by our memories, we're speaking with neuroscientific accuracy, at the level of synapse and dendrite and axon. In particular, vivid and dramatic memories such as those formed under traumatic stress tend to shape us most indelibly. When our attention is riveted, when we have released the cascade of chemicals associated with the body's automatic fear and attention responses, we have also set up the mechanism by which the most tenacious of our memories are formed.

"Repeated exposure to danger," Niehof says, "prompts a clandestine overhaul of the noradrenergic alarm system." Repetitions of the dangerous events, as commonly occur in situations of child abuse, establish a pattern of response in the brain. In effect, trauma "disrupts function throughout the brain's alarm system." The result is that we respond to even the mildest of stressful events as though they were catastrophic, as though they were a reenactment of abuse.

Painstaking historians never forget. They have become programmed for faulty perceptions and responses to danger because memories of childhood trauma don't just get stored in a prominent spot for easy recall, they become part of the brain's layout. In Niehof's words, "Trauma effects are especially important early in development because they encourage adaptation and early adaptation resets physiological systems in ways that leave them very different from normal."

Patricia McKinsey Crittendon, in *Violence against Children in the Family and Community*, elaborates the way brain chemistry mirrors behavior. Child abuse, she says, "affects the way information is mentally processed and used to organize behavior." In essence, "the defensive response is said to be primed. The more intense and frequent the danger that is experienced early and throughout life, the more rapid, protective, affect laden, and preconscious will be the response."

Though we have known this from behavioral observation or from psychological examination for at least a century, now we know it neurologically as well: brains are branded by trauma. This explains why some abused children grow up with symptoms of depression or social withdrawal, for example, or to be violent themselves, or to manifest post-traumatic stress disorder. A sensory record of sudden, vivid experience literally gets seared into the tissues, altering pathways, reconfiguring the combination of proteins. It is a literal transformation; there is nothing metaphoric about how people register childhood trauma.

My mother never broke my bones or fractured my skull. She never tried to poison me or scald me or cut me open. I know that in some senses I got off easy, compared with the violence loosed upon other children in the world. She stalked me and beat me, locked me in closets and toy chests and bathrooms, humiliated me in public and private, was sweet and crooning one minute and savage the next, staged phone calls committing me to mental hospitals or to juvenile prisons, convinced me I had nothing to say or offer the world. But it truly could have been much worse. When the ones we love and trust turn on us, when there is no certainty of love, when the safety of our family life collapses, it takes with it our system for responding properly to the world.

Freud, the neurologist turned psychiatrist, imagined that we all have a kind of "protective shield" in the psyche; in *Beyond the Pleasure Principle,* he wrote that "any excitations from outside which are powerful enough to break through the protective shield" become deeply wounding ("trauma" comes from the Greek word for "wound"). In assessing the conditions he labeled traumatic neuroses, and which later became known as post-traumatic stress disorder, Freud wrote, "The chief weight in their causation seems to rest upon the factor of surprise, of fright." I think that the surprise, the unpredictability, the astonishing recognition that I was never safe, never able to trust my own mother or the moment I was living in, and the fright caused by the intimacy of her violence, were more damaging to my brain than any physical blows or abusive treatment she meted out.

My brother and I were both drawn to violence and danger. As though trying to diminish the surprise around our mother, to neutralize or perhaps feed the fear, we went after physical punishment elsewhere with a genuine fury.

He was eight years my senior and by far the largest person in our family, half a foot taller than our father by age fourteen and, for most of his adult life, weighing what both of our parents weighed combined. My brother loved to hit. He never raised his voice or threatened, and his temper was the more frightening because it erupted from silence, from stillness. As a high school sophomore, he threw a fellow student out of a classroom window to settle an argument. Fortunately it was a ground-floor classroom. He got in neighborhood fights, once whacking his best friend over the head with a hammer while playing in the apartment's courtyard, two blows that crisscrossed the head. He played tackle football on

Brooklyn's concrete streets and on his high school team until getting thrown off for school behavior violations. As soon as he could drive, he drove fast and had an escalating series of traffic accidents until nearly being killed at the age of twenty-one by running his tiny Plymouth Valiant into the wall of a delicatessen in the middle of the night.

One of my earliest clear memories of my brother takes place in our Brooklyn apartment, in our parents' bedroom. He has yanked me down off one of their twin beds to trap me on the floor between the two and is methodically punching me all over the arms and legs. He turns me over to get the front side too. It is as though our parents' behavior toward us has somehow stained our own behavior toward one another.

At other times, silently in the sanctity of our shared bedroom, he would punch me high on the shoulder or thigh muscles to enforce a maze of rules for our cohabitation. He had perfected the placement of his blows so that they did no skeletal damage but left eloquent bruises that I had to cover up with long-sleeved shirts and jeans or risk additional punishment. It was done as a kind of game, actually, played with a certain level of humor, even enjoyment, laughter, and I was never tempted to talk about it with anyone. Though he often protected me, he would sometimes turn on me as well, a pattern that would continue to evolve as long as he lived.

I fought back. After he tore up one of my most precious baseball cards (Ferris Fain! A two-time batting champ!), I ran into the kitchen, seized a butter knife, ran back to our bedroom, and threw it at him where he sat at his desk doing homework. I missed. I was seven at the time. Our parents wouldn't believe him, even when he retrieved the knife from where it had landed behind the radiator. As I grew older, I would wrestle with him despite the vast difference in size, using my greater speed and agility, willing to trade five minutes of pain for the chance to land one decent blow.

In the early fall of 1961, when I was fourteen, I had the "growth spurt" that brought me most of the way to five feet, four inches and 140 pounds and abandoned me there. So, of course, I played high school football. A running back and safety on the freshman team, I wore my brother's number 35 with the bottom of the numbers disappearing into my pants.

When our bus pulls into the parking lot at a school in Malvern, we all pile off in our snazzy blue uniforms, cleats clacking on the pavement, and begin trotting toward the back of the building. No cars are in the lot yet, but it's still early. Then the coach begins blowing his whistle and yelling. I can't hear him because I'm running ahead of everyone and singing our fight song like the rest of my teammates and wind is whistling through the ear holes of my helmet. *Marines, da de ya de ya de ya, Marines.* Someone grabs my arm and turns me around. We have to get back on the bus. This is the wrong field.

It is also the last thing I remember until the next night. Apparently, after tackling their huge fullback on four straight plays in the second half of the game, I was knocked unconscious on the fifth play and began convulsing on the twenty-two yard line. My brother was at the game, pacing the sidelines as usual and shouting instructions at me, often in contradiction to the coach. Everyone knew who he was and tolerated his shenanigans as a kind of mascot. Seeing me down, he vaulted the fence and rushed onto the field to cover my body with his before anyone else realized I'd been hurt.

I remember waking up in my room on Sunday evening and asking him what happened. He looked over at me from his bed and said, "If you ask me that one more time, I'm gonna knock you right out again."

The next year, I was back on the team, playing the season's first two games with a hand broken during our final preseason scrimmage. I ignored the injury and told no one my hand was broken until the pain forced me to drop the football whenever it touched my hand. A serious impediment for a running back. When I had healed enough to return for the season's final game, I was again knocked out, though only for a few minutes, by an elbow to the head while moving in for a tackle. The year after that, I was back on the team again, playing another two games before having my ribs broken. When they healed, my brother and I decided to test their strength by playing a game of tackle football in our backyard. When I dove for a loose ball, he landed on top of me and we found out that the ribs were not as strong as they needed to be.

My brother and I never responded to danger the way most people did. On the one hand, we placed ourselves in situations that seemed certain to injure us. On the other hand, we were crazed by vigilance, alert to the least sign of threat. Of course, this had the effect of helping to create the very crises we were desperate to avoid, endless fights and accidents, adolescent social isolation, incompatible first marriages, lifelong chronic illnesses, and finally total disability for both of us.

A year before my brother died, we spent an afternoon together with our wives in San Francisco. As my sister-in-law pushed his wheelchair along Fisherman's Wharf and I wobbled with my cane beside him, trying to keep pace, I thought about hanging signs around our necks saying "The Crown Princes of All the New Yorks."

Does an injured brain, like a broken bone or wounded skin, become more susceptible to further injury? Does it attract pathogens the way a weakened member of the flock attracts predators?

It is well known that stress affects the immune system, compromising its response to infection. The loop connecting stress-related chemicals and immune-system chemicals is a tight one. When trauma occurs in the body, it activates certain immune-system responses in the brain. "Trauma in peripheral tissues," according to Stephen J. Hopkins and Nancy J. Rothwell in their 1995 article for the journal *Trends in Neuroscience,* "induces cytokine-mediated events in the central nervous system, via either the circulation or secondary induction within the brain." It is as though the body understands trauma as a kind of pathogenic invader, like a virus or bacterium, to be attacked and destroyed from within. But these same cytokines are toxic to the body's neurological tissue. Thus the response to repeated trauma—production of cytokines—poisons the brain itself. All this is the flip side of the issue of the brain's branding by trauma. Not only is the brain rewired to lock the hyperresponse to stress in place, it is also eaten away by the consequences of this response.

By the age of twenty-one, I not only had a brain wired for overresponse to stress, I had a brain damaged by its steady exposure to the neurochemicals associated with that response. I had a damaged immune system (by 1968, I had had three episodes of mononucleosis). And I'd had at least three significant head traumas from being run over by a car and being knocked unconscious while playing football.

As made clear by William J. Winslade in his book *Confronting Traumatic Brain Injury*, "A blow to one part of the brain can trigger a massive release of normally well-controlled brain chemicals which, in turn, can damage sections of the brain not involved in the initial injury." Winslade explains that "free radicals, amino acids, and perhaps even nitric oxide play a role in this secondary damage," which he refers to as a "cascade of biochemical events." These cascades occurred on top of the frequent cascading of stress-related chemicals in my brain released during the episodes of domestic violence. "The healing brain," Winslade says, "is incredibly fragile," and even minor injuries to an already compromised brain can reverse healing.

It is little wonder to me that when I contracted the virus that attacked my brain, my body and my brain were in no condition to defend themselves. Whether the lesions on my brain have been produced by the virus or by my body's programmed hyperresponse to the virus, those lesions are there and my neurological function has been seriously damaged.

One of my favorite childhood games was mirror boxing. I could spend hours dancing half-naked with my image in the glass, throwing jabs and hooks, setting myself up for the right cross, the deadly uppercut. No matter how I feinted and dodged, the image would follow me, its punches matching my punches. The fighter in the mirror tired when I tired, rallied when I rallied, and its eyes returned my own shifting moods. There was no winning or losing, no gaining an edge on this guy, so that the whole purpose of mirror boxing became movement itself, movement and punching for the sake of the punch.

The full-length mirror located inside my closet door was also where I pretended to be a singer, strumming at my black and white baseball bat while lip-syncing to a stack of forty-fives. I could be anybody. My range was astonishing—from Elvis to Chuck Berry to the crazy falsetto of Lou Christie and even all five voices of the Dell Vikings at once.

This was where I practiced my batting stance too, and perfected my swing. Converting guitar to bat, I taught myself to switch-hit, working endlessly in front of the mirror to level out the stroke both left and right. I was Willie Mays right handed and I was Duke Snider left handed, and in a grand finale I was Mickey Mantle going both ways.

If the door was swung open to its fullest, I could play solo war games as well. Hiding behind the bed, I would spring up and point the knob-end of my bat, now a rifle, at the image pointing its rifle back at me from across the room. We tended to miss each other entirely or kill each other simultaneously, and I could watch myself killed twice.

In my brother's last long toxic nights our mother came to him. It was really all he had ever wanted. As his mind clouded with renal poisons and the mysterious metallic aftermath of dialysis, he kept hoping that she would come to see him, that she would acknowledge the gravity of his condition and say she loved him, that she would care for him as his failed kidneys and heart ended his life at fifty-seven.

Even the Tsarina herself, Alexandra Romanov, former Princess of Hesse-Darmstadt and favorite granddaughter of Queen Victoria, had room to care for her sick son. She nursed him through the agonies of hemophiliac crises, tormented by his sufferings, and was rendered nearly helpless with concern over her young boy's health. One line of reasoning holds that the success of the Russian Revolution in 1917 was largely attributable to Alexandra's obsession with her son's worsening health. Alexis's sufferings, the uncanny way in which the "mad monk" Rasputin seemed able to help him, Alexandra's growing belief that no one and nothing but he might save her son, and her resulting willingness to do whatever Rasputin wished in matters of state as the country sank more deeply into World War I all fed the frenzy of revolution while the Tsar was off at the front. Such was her devotion to a suffering son.

Surely our mother would want to see her own suffering son before he died. And so she was there. Not in person, of course, from all the way at the other end of the continent, but in his hallucinations.

When she came, she was filled with punishment. He was a *trombenik*, good for nothing, a parasite, a glutton. He waved his arms as though defending himself against her blows, head jerking back and forth on the pillow of his recliner.

For his entire adult life, my brother kept himself as far from our mother as he could. Not only physically, by living in California, and not only logistically, periodically refusing to visit or speak with her by phone for years at a time, but emotionally as well. On the wall of his apartment, he had our father's plastic cigar holder enshrined in a plastic holder, a rare photograph of our father with his glasses gripped in one hand and smiling gently, a copy of the Skloot family tree. There was nothing about our mother, but all his conversation—especially in the last two years of his life—veered back toward her.

"Do you think Ma knows how sick I am?" he asked me. "Do you think she understands?"

I have always believed we must know and understand our history in order to escape it. The only way to break the cycle of abuse, I felt, was to acknowledge to myself what had happened when I was a child, to hold it consciously aloft and name it. My brother, on the other hand, felt that he had to forget about history in order to escape it. Refusing to discuss what had happened when he was a child, burying it as far down as he could, he hoped to banish it from his life. He felt that his body, no matter the ultimate consequences, deserved its pleasures, smoking four packs of Kents a day, eating until his weight approached four hundred pounds. Certain forces loosed by his childhood experience, he seemed to feel, were inevitable presences and would do with him whatever they wanted, so he might as well enjoy himself while he could.

Neither of us, it turned out, had the right answer. For all my fastidiousness about health and openness, I could not protect myself from the virus that targeted my brain in 1988. I did not get sick because my mother abused me as a child. But no matter how directly I faced the truths of my childhood, my body was not equipped to ward off the pathogenic assault on its regulatory center. Nor was my brother's body equipped to deal with the pressure he imposed on it for ignoring the truths of his childhood.

My mother, nearing ninety and in superb physical health for her age, lived by ignoring the truths of her childhood altogether. Not caring for the historical record at all, she imagined and soon accepted an entirely false one, living within the framework of a dream. At its core, I see, she has embraced everything represented by the enemy, assuming their qualities, turning herself into a replica of all that would have heedlessly destroyed her. Her strategy was to lose herself entirely in the process of modeling the oppressor's ways; she became her own and her children's worst enemy. Ignoring whatever displeased her about her own life, choosing instead to hold Russia's imperial family as her ideal and emulate those who would have thought nothing about killing her, she has fashioned a sordid truth that let her live a long and reasonably contented life.

It is an intriguing lesson. As I move through the second decade of a life changed utterly by brain damage, I see that, in many ways, it was changed by brain damage from the start. Viral lesions are only the next stage, encountered at forty-one, of what began when I was a child at the hands of my mother. The task is to incorporate the new programming, the ongoing history, into a coherent life. The painstaking historian, documenting its own history in the language of neurochemistry, is working on this new chapter slowly, recording the way learning happens after the damage has been done.

7

Zip

The flower song ends and there is distracting movement on stage. Men arrange tables and chairs, a singer slips off his jacket, half-naked women sashay across the nightclub set. It is the first scene in act two of *Pal Joey*. I can hardly sit still as Melba Snyder and seedy nightclub singer Joey Evans meet stage right to conduct their haphazard interview. The waiter brings them fake Scotch and water. After telling a few casual lies, Joey leaves and the lights start to change: we are finally ready for Melba's song, the racy showstopper.

But the woman now spotlit on stage looks more like a fullback than a stripper. Short and squat, arms encased in white gloves that reach nearly to her neck, she begins a bump and grind that suggests shedding tacklers rather than inhibitions. The music blares for an instant and she breathes deeply. In her snug gown, lime green and black with great poufs at the shoulders, she seems to be wearing a uniform, not evening wear.

The audience, which has filled the auditorium of the synagogue, is not reacting properly. Some chuckle, some laugh, others shift around in their seats. A few people mumble the way I have heard old men mumbling in this place before, lost in their prayers. The couple sitting beside me looks worried. We had expected cheers, maybe even a few whistles or hoots of encouragement as the song progressed, and had rehearsed how she would pause between lines to let the laughter die down. But we never expected confusion.

In the glare of the light, I see now there is a look of rapture on my mother's round face. She reaches toward the heavens. She rotates her palms. Her long-lashed eyes are closed and a smile has just begun to stretch her mouth as the muted trumpet growls to signal her next lines. *Zip! I was reading Schopenhauer last night.* Each *Zip!* is accompanied by a rim shot as she slides another zipper down somewhere on her costume, or slips the glove off another finger. *Zip! And I think that Schopenhauer was right.*

I am eight years old and I know this routine cold, having helped my mother rehearse it every night for the last two months. Schopenhauer, she said to me, was a Swiss poet. Zorina and Corbina, whose names would occur in the next two lines, were Hungarian dancers, married but not talking to each other. She had explained that the line *I have read the great Cabala* referred to an Arabian novelist whose book had been made into a movie starring Humphrey Bogart before I was born. For a few days, she had practiced running her hands down her sides and over her belly, asking me if I thought that worked. I shrugged, which she took to mean No. How about this: she bent forward and tried to make her tightly corseted breasts swing in unison, but lost her balance and decided not to risk it in the performance. She turned around and wriggled the way I had seen her wriggle to get into her girdle, but with her rear end stuck farther out. She tried curtseying. She crossed her hands over her lower abdomen like Eve after eating the apple.

"You're no help," she said.

Sitting in the synagogue in my aisle seat, leaning way over to the left so I can see past the people in front of me, I am singing the lyrics along with her but trying to keep my voice down so as not to disturb anyone. *Zip! I'm a heterosexual.*

She is coming to the most difficult part, the final two lines of the refrain, which require that her voice surge into the limits of its upper range. She also has to be finished removing her gloves so she can fling them into the audience, first the left when she sang *Zip! It took intellect to master my art,* then the right when she sang *Zip! Who the hell is Margie Hart?* Even from where I sat, even if I looked somewhere else on stage, I could see the strange, inward-turning expression of joy in my mother's eyes.

Though there was no Hungarian blood anywhere in her lineage, my mother sometimes saw herself as the lost Gabor sister. There was Magda, Eva, Zsa Zsa, and, it turns out, Lil. After all, there were two lost Marx Brothers (Gummo and Zeppo) and a fourth, vanished Stooge (Shemp), and who ever remembered Diana Barrymore? Such things happened all the time. Perhaps this explains her fascination for stories of switched identity: the only book other than *Babar* that I can recall my mother reading to me was Twain's *The Prince and the Pauper*, over and over again.

Her father, Max, was from Cracow, which he left at age fourteen to become what he called "a man from the world." He had traversed Europe during the first years of the new century, living in Paris for a while, learning a trade before coming to New York. A furrier, he met Rose Landorf when he offered himself as an apprentice in her father's upper-west-side shop and demonstrated an especially good hand at sewing chinchilla. The Landorfs, late of Tarnow, only forty-five miles east of Cracow, had several daughters working in the family business. The ones Max was most interested in—Eda and Eva—were younger than Rose; if he wanted to marry a Landorf, it had to be Rose, one year his senior. He took what he could get. They were together for the next seventy-two years.

My mother was born in 1910 and grew up in the small fur shops her parents operated. As business improved, they moved gradually downtown from the Bronx, finally landing in the same Manhattan neighborhood as the Landorfs. Alert to the implications of neighborhood boundaries, my mother considered the Upper West Side her native land. Max worked in the back of the shop on pelts, Rose waited on customers, and my mother watched everything. It was a busy world her parents moved in, too busy to spare much time for a little girl. But she loved to see the wealthy women parading around in front of the shop's mirrors, admiring themselves as they caressed a sable coat, fox stole, or mink jacket, spinning in an air suffused with exotic perfumes. Men hovered in the background saying flattering things and taking out their money. This was the way to live! Elegance, hauteur, privilege. She enjoyed hearing them speak, especially the extravagantly wealthy immigrant women who seemed to return annually for a new garment, always trailed by a new man, always polite but distant to the shopkeepers and ignoring the child. Lil hardly cared about that; she studied these women. She would be treated this way, treat men this way, treat shopkeepers and workers and herself this way.

From the start, she was a good mimic. Recasting herself, reinventing herself, she assembled a vision of true grandeur. She called people "dahlink." Sometimes she stopped speaking in midsentence, pretending to struggle for a word in English that she knew perfectly well in the Hungarian she didn't speak, mumbling and narrowing her eyes as she translated to herself. She had a painting, purchased from a street vendor in Florence Venice Rome Paris Berlin; she believed it to have been painted by Toulouse-Lautrec's bastard son. All piano music was either written or directly influenced by Chopin, a distantly removed possible cousin.

My mother experimented with various dyes to keep her hair, whose natural color I have never seen, properly blonde. She favored lavishly layered dresses, droopy hats wider than her shoulders, shawls or capes in all weather, everything in attention-grabbing colors. She seemed taller when she sat than when she stood, posing with her back arched, neck stiff, ring-laden fingers splayed across her hip, perched rather than settled on a chair or sofa. Her brown eyes, protuberant by nature, were kept wider by a look of perpetual surprise, a look whose meaning I came to understand not as wonder at the world's miracles but as astonishment at one's audacity in addressing her without permission.

Glamour was inherent in certain people, she felt. Regardless of their circumstances, some people were just naturally aristocratic.

Despite being butchers. Butchers who lacked culture and breeding. Despite living in six-story Flatbush buildings across the street from the county hospital where no one in their right mind would allow themselves to give birth and where the criminally insane were locked up.

While some things could not be taught, other things could never be forgotten. Taste, for example, or panache, nobility of heart. The elect, the geniuses of the soul, always knew one another.

The haut monde myth must have been very difficult for her to sustain. For my mother, it was not enough to be looked at and admired, even envied; she had to reign. My father, spending more and more time at his failing chicken market, was not a willing subject. So the next best thing to reigning, I imagine, was being adored, worshiped, which perhaps explains her theatrical aspirations, where she could rule the stage, the world of illusion.

Starring as a performer had been her lifelong ambition. She dropped out of public school after the seventh grade, in the mid-1920s, took art classes, and got a job painting mannequins for a theatrical costume designer. She sang pop songs, accompanying herself on the piano, and briefly had a five-minute radio show on WBNX in the Bronx, produced by a family friend named Barney Barnett. She was scheduled opposite Rudy Valee, which explained her small audience. The show turned out to be the climax rather than the start of her career, however, and the decade between her radio work and her marriage to my father has always been blurred by an absence of detail.

"I had so many suitors, dahlink," she would say, as though being courted were her full-time occupation. Though the facts and sequence may not have supported it, still she always claimed to have given up her burgeoning life as a star to marry my father and raise her two children, spaced eight years apart.

In 1950, a song from the ten-year-old Rodgers and Hart musical *Pal Joey* was suddenly rediscovered and became one of the most popular songs in America. For sixteen weeks, "Bewitched, Bothered and

Bewildered" was featured on *Your Hit Parade* and occupied the top spot on five different occasions. All in all, seven competing versions made the Top Forty, including renditions by Doris Day, Mel Torme, the Harmonicats, and, biggest of all, by pianist Bill Snyder and His Orchestra.

Interest in the old show, which had opened on Christmas night of 1940 and run for eleven months before fading from view, was revived. Back in 1940, audiences were not ready for a story about a two-bit crooner scheming and hustling his way into women's beds and ownership of a nightclub of his own. But the songs were grand. After the success of "Bewitched, Bothered and Bewildered" in late 1950, Columbia Records decided to produce a cast album in the studio, assembling a mix of new and original stars. By 1952 *Pal Joey* was again running on Broadway and this time was a genuine hit, running for nearly two years before going on a twelve-city tour. There was talk of a movie version to star the original Joey, Gene Kelly, then talk of a version with Marlon Brando, but the film would have to wait for five more years and Frank Sinatra before being made. Meanwhile, *Pal Joey* began to work its way into local community theater productions, which is where it caught up with my mother in 1955.

By late fall of 1955, season of Sputnik I and polio vaccines and the Brooklyn Dodgers finally winning a World Series, life in Brooklyn was undergoing dazzling changes. The Dodgers' victory suggested a great shift in the loser, wait-till-next-year identity that had long haunted the borough. But that was misleading. The team announced a plan to play eight games the next year in Jersey City, which my father said was the beginning of the end of Brooklyn baseball. Not only were the Dodgers disappearing, but the ubiquitous trolley cars that Brooklyn pedestrians always had to dodge (hence the name Dodgers) were disappearing as well. By 1956, they would all be gone. So was the delightful newspaper, the *Brooklyn Eagle.* Houses were being knocked down everywhere; supermarkets were appearing to threaten my father's livelihood. The vacant lot where I played across the street from our apartment building was being developed and would soon house the Downstate Medical Center. There was a rumor that our apartment building would be purchased for conversion to dormitory space and the two hundred families occupying it would have to relocate. The city was changing, the world was changing, and my parents could not count on anything anymore.

As I look back on this time in our lives, I think of it as the breaking point for my mother. For the last two decades, she had been struggling in the quicksand of mundanity—not only did she fail to marry a count, she had married a one-eyed Brooklyn slaughterer of poultry who never heard of Gustave Flaubert or what's-his-name Korsakov. She had never traveled outside the state of New York as an adult, so it was difficult to keep her tales of European experience sounding fresh. Her husband left home at 3:30 A.M. and returned at 6:30 P.M. ready for dinner and sleep. She herself maintained a shadow schedule, going to sleep at 3:00 A.M. and rising shortly after noon so that, with the exception of Sundays when they visited relatives in Brooklyn or Manhattan, my parents seldom encountered one another. Nobody played music but her, nobody thought about culture but her, nobody *yearned* for anything except maybe a good meal, a few laughs, some peace and quiet, or the 1955 Topps baseball card of unknown Dodgers outfielder Bert Hamric to complete a useless collection. My mother's only hobby was making table centerpieces out of the cardboard cores of toilet paper rolls and stacks of handmade greeting cards out of buttons and scraps of fabric that she loved too much to sell or send. There wasn't much social life.

It was, I believe, no coincidence that my mother was notoriously difficult to wake from sleep. She did not want to leave her dreams or face the day.

Nightly during 1955 it seemed that my parents always talked about what to do in the face of all those changes on the horizon. He would sell his chicken market. He would open a business of his own, we would move out of the city. The children would get rooms of their own. There would have to be new jobs, new friends, new everything.

This kind of talk went right through me. Living with them, I had already learned that in our family change erupted without warning. Fights—verbal and physical—altered the very texture of every evening. Talk and plans were just the background music to dinner. Nevertheless, they often spoke about changing their lives, sending out signals of dissatisfaction with the way things were going. "I gotta have chicken fricassee every goddamn Wednesday?" my father would say. "We never go anywhere," my mother would say. Then talk flared into actions that distracted them from what they were talking about.

My mother constantly redecorated the apartment's four small rooms, moving furniture around, switching paintings from room to room, getting new towels or drapes or appliances. She had the place repainted and repapered whenever the lease would allow it. She talked on the phone with her friends about whether to get a nose job, discussed it with my father, swore to us that she would, then changed her mind, asking me whether or not I thought her nose was beautiful the way it was. No one sat still; there was a restlessness everywhere we were.

After months of discussion, my mother decided to try out for a play at the temple over on Eastern Parkway. The theater, a word she pronounced with three syllables, was after all her natural calling. Even strangers who met her for the first time told her so. It had been a mistake ever to give it up. Also, I think theatrical performance seemed to her a legitimate, sanctioned way to enact her secret desires. She could be someone else, someone she was supposed to be, and she could be in the spotlight. They were going to do *Pal Joey*, she said, and began to sing "Bewitched, Bothered and Bewildered" while my father ate his flanken.

The role of Melba Snyder is a fascinating cameo in the musical version of *Pal Joey*. She appears in only one scene, has two dozen short speeches to deliver, sings one song, and disappears. But she is memorable.

The actress playing Melba routinely gets costar billing. Shrewd and sassy, the character transforms from buttoned-down professional woman to sizzling sexpot in a matter of moments. She is an authentic female shape-shifter, impossible to predict or know. Everything about her is illusion. It was, I believe, a part my mother felt born to play.

Melba works for a Chicago newspaper, the *Herald*, where she writes a column about the city's nightlife that she signs "M.S." She arrives at Chez Joey, the club financed by Joey's wealthy lover, Vera, to interview the hot singer and figurehead, who does not know the famous M.S. is a woman. Once he is set straight, Joey, ever on the make, weaves a shoddy fabric of lies about a past in high society, lost fortunes, and Ivy League education, trying to snow Melba with his false savoir-faire. She sees right through him; she makes Joey look ridiculous in his obvious fabrications and dismisses him, complaining that she must "get some pictures of this tripe. God knows why."

At this point, the nightclub manager steps in and tries to smooth things over, telling Melba, "You mustn't mind him." Worldly-wise, she segues into her song by saying, "Him? After the people I've interviewed? It's pretty late in the day for me to start getting bothered by the funny ones I talk to."

Her song, "Zip," is a parody of the best interview Melba ever had. Though she has interviewed Pablo Picasso and Igor Stravinsky, her "greatest achievement" was an interview with Gypsy Rose Lee, the burlesque queen, mystery novelist, playwright, and actress. Lee had explained to Melba (and showed her) that whenever she stripped, her mind was actually focused on matters of cultural and artistic depth. *Zip! I consider Dali's painting passé. Zip! Can they make the Metropolitan pay?* The ecdysiast as closet critic.

So despite what she looks like and what she does, Miss Lee inside was the exact opposite. *Zip! It took intellect to master my art.* This pleases Melba Snyder, who is also unlike what she seems, and I think it pleased my mother, who believed herself entirely separate from her surface image. Indeed, my mother may have lost touch entirely with her surface image, seeing in the mirror and insisting that others see a precise reflection of her fantasies. The most dangerous question my mother ever asked was "Do you like the way I look?"

In John O'Hara's novel *Pal Joey*, from which some of the musical's characters emerged, Melba is even more unpredictable than she is on stage. When she first appears in print, wearing a man's suit that Joey considers too masculine even for himself and sporting a crew cut and eyeglasses, he dismisses her as a "lesbo." Then, after interviewing him, Melba changes clothes and reappears in panties and bra to pose for photographs with Joey. Suddenly, she is so gorgeous that he "forgot about Lana Turner." Joey says he would do "anything to get my hands on her." Indeed, Melba is a figure of immediate transformative power, able to change herself utterly and to turn Joey's perceptions of her inside out. She is irresistible.

The layering in this situation is complex but also evocative of my mother's way in the world. On stage, an actress plays a reporter of uncertain identity—known only by her initials—who exposes a man posing as more accomplished and sophisticated than he really is. She then sings a song in which she imitates a strip-tease artist proclaiming that despite impressions to the contrary she is an intellectual. And here was my mother, of all people, portraying savvy, sexy, no-nonsense Melba strutting her stuff. Surprising everyone out of complacent and mistaken attitudes toward her. Being irresistible. In the synagogue.

Physically, my mother, who was four feet, ten inches and continually struggling with her weight, did not look the part. Actresses like tall, slender Eileen Heckart (1959), or the lithe former dancer Bebe Neuwirth (1995), or the one-time cabaret singer and cocktail waitress Kay Medford (1961) typically played the role of Melba on stage. In the 1957 movie starring Sinatra, the role of Melba was cut entirely, but the song "Zip" was delivered by Rita Hayworth (and dubbed by a sultry Jo Ann Greer) in the role of the wealthy heiress who finances Joey's club. Rita Hayworth! I think that even in her fantasies, my mother never went that far. Still, the theater has a long history of successful performances by actors cast against type, and there was a peculiar resonance for her in portraying, in essence, two women at once pretending to be something they are not, insisting on their higher-class inner lives, proclaiming their intellectual natures, hiding a torrid but disdainful sexuality, making a life out of being listened to or looked at and admired.

It was all very difficult for a boy to figure out. My mother's particular blend of disconnectedness and flamboyance was at its peak in this situation. So were her confused notions of being a woman in a man's world, pampered and feared. The way her self-loathing and self-adoration blended made a volatile compound; though I was too young to appreciate that, I do know that I was afraid she might come apart onstage before my eyes. I remember worrying about whether she would make it through her number without tumbling over her spiked heels. Also, despite the director's having shortened her song by one chorus, she had had trouble remembering the lyrics near the finale and I worried throughout the song about her fumbling at the end.

I could not tell if people were laughing at her or with her, if she was perceived as ridiculous or brilliant, if there was shame or admiration directed at her. What I felt was relief when "Zip" ended, since that meant I would not have to help rehearse it anymore.

Over nearly sixty years, the material constituting *Pal Joey* has gone through steady transformation until it became the opposite of what it was at the start. Its honest sense of human behavior was abandoned for a fantasy projection of decency, a victory of charm and illusion over fact. It glimpsed the sordidness of actual life and asserted an alternative reality.

Beginning in 1938, John O'Hara began publishing a series of twelve short stories about Joey Evans in *The New Yorker*. These stories were in the form of letters from the second-rate lounge singer and master of ceremonies to his more successful friend, a bandleader named Ned. The letters, signed with regards from your Pal Joey, recounted manipulative antics in which Joey took advantage of one or more young women, sought to con money from people (including Ned), and was forced to move from town to town as his victims got too familiar with Joey's ways. He is last seen saying goodbye to the one woman, Linda, who might truly be able to love and save him, in order to pick up another woman strolling past the site of their farewell. Taken together, these stories paint the dark portrait of an immoral charmer, a louse on the loose among the innocent women and audiences of the Midwest.

O'Hara, who had already written his classic novel *Appointment in Samarra* and the grim roman à clef *Butterfield 8,* as well as two widely praised collections of short stories, quickly tired of Joey Evans. In 1940, he added two more stories and published the group of fourteen as a short novel. Ironically, it went on to make him the sort of fortune that eluded his scheming protagonist.

O'Hara's biographer, Matthew J. Bruccoli, has said that "although the Joey stories and their spin-offs brought John O'Hara his first great popularity, they are not important in themselves." Derivative of Ring Lardner's epistolary novel *Alibi Ike,* and borrowing mood and language from the stories of Damon Runyon, O'Hara's pieces lack firepower or originality. They are slick and readable, an unhappy man's portrait of his world, but it is difficult to have sympathy for Joey or his troubles and we are never brought inside his disguises to glimpse his inner life. Clearly, O'Hara's heart is not in the writing, which is only a cut above the sort of hackwork that Joey himself did. According to Bruccoli the stories "delayed O'Hara's development as a novelist, for their earnings relieved him of the pressure to write."

That sidetrack happened because, in October 1939, O'Hara sent a letter to the composer Richard Rodgers. O'Hara said, "I got the idea that the pieces, or at least the character and the life in general, could be made into a book show, and I wonder if you and Larry (Lorenz Hart) would be interested in working on it with me." Rodgers was then in Boston and had been worried about what to do next.

In his autobiography, *Musical Stages,* Rodgers recalls that "the letter was a total surprise, and a welcome one." What attracted

Rodgers and Hart to the idea of working with O'Hara on a musical about Joey Evans was the uniqueness of a character like Joey as the focus of an American musical. "The 'hero' was a conniver and braggart who would do anything and sleep anywhere to get ahead," Rodgers wrote. "The idea of doing a musical without a conventional clean-cut juvenile in the romantic lead opened enormous possibilities for a more realistic view of life than theatregoers were accustomed to."

Hart was attracted to the material for different, almost complementary reasons. It spoke to his soul. In Frederick Nolan's biography, *Lorenz Hart*, the point is made that "writing the kind of cynical, callous, suggestive lyrics needed for characters like Joey and his older benefactress was a paid vacation for Larry Hart." According to Nolan, the singer Mabel Mercer described Hart as "the saddest man I ever knew."

Their reply to O'Hara was swift and positive; correspondence about adapting the material followed. But O'Hara wanted to write something new altogether, using only bits of his existing Joey material and developing a fresh story with characters invented for the stage. It took him longer than any of the participants had anticipated. In fact, Rodgers finally nudged O'Hara with a telegram saying "SPEAK TO ME JOHN SPEAK TO ME." One wonders whether O'Hara took so long in part because he felt the material, slight as it was, slipping away from him, if he was having second thoughts about what was happening. *Pal Joey* was getting spruced up.

The finished book for their musical had mutated into a story of blackmail and intrigue, but its edges were rounded. Rodgers and Hart wrote at least two love songs for it that have entered the canon of popular music, "I Could Write a Book" and "Bewitched." Moderately successful, the show opened to generally favorable reviews. There were only a few dissenters such as Brooks Atkinson, who admired its expertise but wondered, "Can you draw sweet water from a foul well?" After all, *Pal Joey* was a story in which, as Rodgers noted, "there wasn't one decent character in the entire play except the girl who briefly fell for Joey—her problem was simply that she was stupid." Yet despite its lack of sunny conventionality, the musical tried to reveal a softer heart, which was the key to its success as entertainment.

It was still a story about people trying to disguise their true natures and motives via deception and self-delusion as they conned each other out of money. It was still a relatively unsentimental look at the seedy truth of male-female relations, at casual manipulation and betrayal, but the musical was easier on Joey than O'Hara's stories had been. It was also simpler and less subtle. Joey manages greater success and intimacy before his fall, which comes because Joey is a victim, betrayed by others rather than doing the betraying. He shows more talent and moxie than in the novel. He does not have his old bandleader friend Ned to manipulate, which focuses the action more fully upon his relations with women, which are culturally more normal for the times. Rodgers and Hart viewed the story of Joey as being about someone with "too much imagination to behave himself," someone who "was a little weak." A far cry from the predator O'Hara first imagined, who was neither imaginative nor weak but calculating and hard. As a result, the musical forgave Joey in ways that neither the author's original tales nor Joey himself ever could. It became possible to say, as critic Denny Martin Flinn does in his history of American musical theater *(Musical: A Grand Tour)*, that "the gigolo character was irresistibly charming." Much of the cynicism behind O'Hara's stories had lightened. Why, the musical starred the sweet Gene Kelly.

An even greater transformation occurred during adaptation for the screen version, which Pauline Kael has called a "blighted Hollywoodization of the musical." The score, as Kael puts it, has been "purified along with Joey's character." Some changes were superficial—the story takes place in San Francisco, for example. But major changes entirely alter the meaning of the material—Joey falls in love with Linda and does the right thing at the end, abandoning his scheming and potential riches to marry. He has a moral center; he is a decent fellow.

The material was turned virtually inside out so its sheen could impress. It pandered even more than the stage version by taking the heel beyond lovable to loving. The film is a stunning act of wish fulfillment and audience manipulation, taking the words of two famously miserable men and shaking them free of despair. Less believable in each incarnation, *Pal Joey* on screen has been distilled into a curmudgeonly story that inadvertently praises the triumph of inauthenticity.

In a technical sense, inauthenticity certainly rules: except for Frank Sinatra as Joey, none of the lead actors actually sings her songs, with Kim Novak's voice being dubbed by Trudy Erwin and Rita Hayworth's by Jo Ann Greer. Songs that have nothing to do with the story are imported in order for Sinatra to perform an anthology of Rodgers and Hart hits guaranteed to please audiences and sell recordings. These are, of course, customary Hollywood maneuvers. What is more compelling is how deception and flim-flammery have gone from being the problem to being the solution.

No character in the film is authentic, no one is what he or she seems. They seek happiness by making the world accept their act, or by modifying their act until it sells, rather than by being true to themselves. Even Linda, a model of integrity through previous incarnations of the story, succeeds only by pretending to be what she is not—first an exotic dancer willing to strip, then a woman not in love with Joey. We see that Joey is really a man of honor, though he seems a cad; his original lies about himself (that he is honest, that he cares) turn out to be the truth, though he does not know it; the wealthy widow who falls for him and buys him his nightclub is in fact an exotic dancer herself; and when people say *No* they mean *Yes*, and when they lose everything they win.

I believe that this vision of the world is precisely the one my mother used to write her operating manual. Sham, artifice, fantasy became for her the reality they were enlisted to replace. Looking back to her involvement with *Pal Joey*, I can recognize how slippery the truth always was in her mind. What is authentic and what is counterfeit for her were entwined in ways that made them inseparable. Perhaps no longer vital.

My mother elevated wishful transformation to an art form. Life disappointed her, so she replaced it. The trick was that she always insisted her audience—particularly my father, my brother, and me—see it her way. That the performance seldom worked never stopped her from taking the stage again.

Surely the flip side of my mother's pretensions and fantasies was a deep feeling of inauthenticity about her life. Her return to the theater not only let her temporarily escape the mundane lower-middle-class trap she was in, it let her be who she felt she should have been. Portraying Melba, despite what would seem to be her limitations in the role, was a start. After we moved to Long Island, she performed in *Mame, The King and I, Fiddler on the Roof,* and many other musicals, always playing a person who was not at all what she seemed.

Dating Slapsie

By the summer of 1937, when he found my mother's name and phone number on a matchbook in his jacket pocket, Slapsie Maxie Rosenbloom was no longer Light Heavyweight Champion of the World. He did not recognize her name, but the handwriting was his.

Just shy of thirty-three, Slapsie Maxie was closing down a busy, almost manic fifteen-year-fight career that already included nearly three hundred fights. Between 1930 and 1934, his reign as champ, he'd fought 106 times, which averages out to almost one bout every two weeks.

After losing his title to Bob Olin, he maintained the old pace as long as he could still find opponents. He fought the same boxer, John Henry Lewis, five times in three years. He fought some of the era's greats, Jim Braddock and Harry Greb and Mickey Walker, as well as the Millionaire Murphys and Big Boy Brays. But by the summer of 1937, with age and too many shots to the head slowing him down, the schedule had thinned. He had only ten more bouts left as a boxer and he had time on his hands. This could not have been an easy period for him.

By the summer of 1937, my mother was no longer a painter. She was also no longer a theatrical costume designer or a torch singer.

She was almost twenty-seven, terrified of being a spinster, and worried that her performance as New York's Most Eligible Young Lady was about to be canceled for lack of interest.

Max Rosenbloom had the smashed nose, cauliflower ears, and muttered speech of a classic palooka. He was marked physically, and this was highlighted by his nickname, "Slapsie," which suggested both a lifetime of punches taken and a faintly swish fighting style. But he'd earned the moniker nobly, having been christened Slapsie Maxie by the writer Damon Runyan, of *Guys and Dolls* fame, who admired the way Rosenbloom cuffed opponents with open gloves while dodging their blows. A notoriously difficult man to hit, he was a defensive stylist with flashy footwork and was long winded enough to outlast the sluggers. But he was feather fisted: in all those three hundred fights, he managed only nineteen knockouts.

Rosenbloom was effective in the ring because he was wary in the ring. Despite his image as a punch-drunk lug, despite the quasi-demeaning nickname, he was canny and sharp, a streetwise pugilist whom Joe Louis refused to fight, despite knowing he could win, because he also knew the challenger would make him look bad. Rosenbloom may have preferred gambling and parties to heavy training, but he was a solid professional and has been elected to both the Ring Boxing Hall of Fame and the International Boxing Hall of Fame.

For all his intelligence and accomplishment, however, he was stuck playing Slapsie Maxie. The role of a lifetime. At age twelve, the young Max Rosenbloom had been steered toward boxing by actor George Raft, who discovered him fighting on the Lower East Side streets. The kid had just gotten out of the Hawthorne Reform Home for Jewish Boys, where he'd been sent after hitting a teacher and knocking out two of her teeth. So from the start there was to be a hint of the underworld about his life: Damon Runyan, George Raft, reform school and the mean streets of the city, and of course boxing. This wasn't a romantic character discovered by Spenser Tracy or named by F. Scott Fitzgerald.

A fighter who disguised real substance behind pizzazz and a misleadingly dense persona, and who seemed to be a favorite with movie and theater types, Rosenbloom, not surprisingly, in the twilight of his ring career found his way to Hollywood. By the summer of 1937, he'd begun his career as a small-time actor and already been cast in nine films. He started out portraying boxers and sometimes, to keep things simple, played a character named Slapsie Maxie Rosenbloom. He played slap-happy prizefighters like the Champ in *Two Wise Maids*.

It was a small stretch from those roles to playing trainers, cons, and hoods. He was already parodying himself, nobody's fool despite the image. This was a man who made a career out of protecting himself in the ring, though fully willing to be in harm's way. He was ever alert, in the ring or out, and had his eyes on the next move. He knew how to bob and weave at whatever life threw his way.

Just then, mid-July of '37, Slapsie Maxie was in a state of transition. Looking around for what came next, even if it came from the flap of a forgotten matchbook. It had been a long time, maybe a full year, since he'd last worn the jacket in which he found my mother's name. *Lillian Alfus? Who the hell was that?*

So he did the only thing a man like Slapsie Maxie would do. He called her. It was a Sunday morning and he had tickets for the Yankees game. That season, the Bronx Bombers were invincible once again, the team of Lou Gehrig and Bill Dickey and a young Joe DiMaggio. They had two twenty-game winners on the mound and they were coasting back to the World Series. This was a team to see, and Slapsie Maxie had two box seats.

As my mother told it, her plan was always to snag a Prince. A Jewish Prince, of course, and preferably a Celebrity Prince rather than just a prince Prince.

The list of men whose proposals she had turned down was so

long, she implied, that it was impossible to remember them all. There were doctors—a renowned heart man, a pioneering surgeon, a skin man who catered to royalty—and there was a dentist who did the teeth of Vivien Leigh, a professor of Portuguese literature at the Sorbonne, an actor whose name she was not at liberty to divulge, a financier, and the man who invented milk. There was an exiled Baron from either Liechtenstein or Lithuania, depending on when she thought to mention him. There was an unnamed composer who, if you listened carefully to her description, might have been George Gershwin. With my own eyes, I have seen a box filled with photographs of men she could have married. The Lawyer. The Influential Agent. The Chemist. She could have lived in Vienna, in Paree, Roma. I might have been a little Dane in Copenhagen, which she pronounced "Coop-in-howen" with her eyes half closed.

Slapsie Maxie was no Prince. But he was Jewish, a genuine celebrity, someone destined for Hollywood glory. He was a performer. And he *had* worn a crown, sort of, as a boxing champion. He was a catch, at least in theory, at a time when her catchings had thinned.

They had met at a party thrown by Sam Landorf, her mother's older brother. Uncle Sam owned a successful business that produced dresses for fashionable young girls, and was well connected. He knew people. His seasonal party was something he put together every year at a fancy hotel on the Upper West Side. It was, my mother said, a place to be seen.

Precise details were always a bit vague, but she was invited at the last minute, after Uncle Sam had been sufficiently badgered by his sister. My mother had nothing to wear. She had to get her hair done. She needed new shoes, matching gloves. She had to take a taxi at the last minute.

My mother says everyone who was anyone in New York was at Uncle Sam's party that night. She danced the last dance of the night with Mr. Rosenbloom, who was very light on his feet for such a big man, and who was so taken with her that he asked for her phone number and promised to call. She watched him write the number on a matchbook, which he slipped into a pocket of his jacket. Then the former Light Heavyweight Champion of the World bowed like a gentleman was supposed to bow before sashaying out the door.

My mother says she was asleep when he called. A year had passed; she had forgotten all about Slapsie Maxie as a suitor. It was hardly the first time a promise to call had been broken.

Her habit was to sleep late on Sunday mornings. Actually, her habit was to sleep late every morning, since she liked to stay up till 3:00 A.M. But on this particular Sunday morning in the summer of 1937, she says, she was more asleep than usual.

Her brother Albie took the call. He would have doubted that the man on the phone asking to talk to Lillian was really Rosenbloom, but he remembered the story of Uncle Sam's party. My mother says that Albie shook her awake.

"Lil, get up, Slapsie Maxie's on the phone."

"Right," she says she said, "and I'm Shirley Temple."

"It's him. Hurry up."

She says she picked up the phone, heard him tell her to be ready in an hour, hung up, and went back to sleep. Albie waited a few minutes, then, knowing how long it took her to get ready in the morning, kept waking her till she got out of bed.

When Rosenbloom arrived at the apartment, my mother was not ready. Albie offered him coffee and they went into the living room. She could hear pacing, the staccato of male voices talking in very short sentences, and she got herself dressed in double time. According to her brother, Slapsie Maxie kept threatening to leave if she did not appear immediately. They were double parked downstairs.

My mother says that the doorman was awestruck to see her leave the building beside the Champ and climb into the back seat of his car while the chauffeur held the door open. She was only a little alarmed when Slapsie Maxie sat in front with the chauffeur instead of in back with her.

"Where are we going?" she asked.

He turned around and, my mother says, looked at her for longer than he needed to. "Ball game," he said, then turned back and did not look at her again.

My mother was no baseball fan. Though Albie had had a tryout with the New York Giants as a catcher, she thought the game was for silly people and was proud of him for spurning the Giants' meager minor league offer. Still, it was something she felt she ought to mention.

"My brother played for the Giants."

"I like the Yankees," was all Slapsie Maxie had to say about that.

As they drove up to the Bronx, she tried to make conversation. It was a lovely summer morning, wasn't it? Did he think he might play a role in the movie of "Gone with the Wind?" She had read that it was going to be filmed soon. Had he driven over that new bridge in San Francisco on one of his trips to Hollywood? She did not like the way he looked over at the chauffeur. Wasn't it awful about the *Hindenberg* burning up over in New Jersey a couple months ago? All those people lost.

As they approached Yankee Stadium, he turned around at last and smiled at her. Then he said that he had only two tickets to the game, his chauffeur would be going in to watch it with him, and she could use the car if she liked.

That was it. My mother says she thought about taking a train home but hailed a cab instead. Rather than going back into the apartment to face her brother, she went around the corner to a luncheonette and had a tuna fish sandwich for lunch.

Slapsie Maxie was not the marrying kind anyway. His one fling at wedded bliss lasted six years, from 1939 to 1946, and after divorcing Muriel Falder he remained a bachelor till his death thirty years later.

He was, my mother came to realize, at best a blue-collar Prince. Once established in Hollywood, Rosenbloom acted as he had fought: nearly a hundred films, taking on anything. He was mostly a comedian, getting laughs by being stupid. He did war movies and westerns and *Abbott and Costello Meet the Keystone Kops*, for heaven's sake. He came back east to perform on stage at Westbury Music Fair as—what else?—a gangster in *Guys and Dolls*. He turned up on television as Joe Palooka's sidekick Clyde the Trainer, played "the Strongest Man in the World" on *I Dream of Jeannie*, and even appeared in *The Munsters*. That would never do; it was good that things had not worked out between them.

Yet despite her yearning for gentility, and hopes for a life of high society or high culture, my mother was obviously drawn to bruisers. She went for the men most likely to dislike her style. From the women she admired—besides Zsa Zsa Gabor, there was Yma Sumac and Carmen Miranda—I understand that she valued glamour and contempt, the allure of exotic superciliousness, invincibility. These were women who took up vast amounts of psychic space, performers who overwhelmed: Gabor with her litany of lovers, Sumac with her four-octave range as a singer, Miranda with her wild I-yi-yi-yi-yi-yi and her tutti-frutti hat. There was something mysterious and controversial about them that my mother admired. They'd made themselves up. People thought Yma Sumac the Aztec Princess was really Amy Camus from the inner city, and the lacquered Spaniard Carmen Miranda was just a little kid from Portugal who, like Zsa Zsa, made it big by being outrageous. They were too hot to handle, which is just what my mother wanted to become. One look, and men would know they should keep away, but would be unable to resist. To tamper with her was to risk doom. It was a difficult act to pull off.

My mother seems to have wanted exactly the life she was least equipped to live, one of independent enchantment in which the private life merged with the public life, and she gravitated toward men she could disdain for denying her its pleasures. At heart, it seems, she wanted either to vanquish or surrender but not to live in harmony or balance.

Perhaps she knew that the men she dreamt of marrying would expect her to appreciate more than just the names of classic authors and European composers. She would have to know their works as well, the substance. These were things she wanted to like more than she actually did like. She talked of the symphony but went instead to the nightclubs and theaters she really loved. She owned the classics but read only magazines. She pretended that her opinions of *Droll Stories* or *Anna Karenina* were beyond the capacity of her listeners to understand and therefore kept silent about them.

Perhaps she knew that the men she felt most called to marry would refuse to let her live out her dreams. I believe my mother was deeply unhappy with herself for liking what she liked, for being who she was. She disapproved of the kind of woman who would want so desperately to be with Slapsie Maxie Rosenbloom.

Nonetheless, she loved to tell the story of her date with him. It vied for popularity with the story of her listener-free radio show. Time and again, my mother gladly made herself the target of her own self-mocking disclosures. There was also the story of the time she tried on clothes at a famous Manhattan store and left without buying anything, only to be stopped on the street by a woman who informed her that she was dressed in a slip. There was the story of my brother calling to her in the shower, screaming as though horribly hurt, then stopping when my mother arrived naked before his door and asking her to please turn around so he could see the back. I used to think these only showed her hunger for the spotlight — any spotlight — but now I see other possibilities. Her tales may be another form of self-punishment, making her appear both sexy and foolish at once. A performer caught in front of the wrong audience, which is the story of her life. Or they may reveal a sense of shame, a way of throwing rotten tomatoes at herself for failing to live up to her own expectations.

In the fall of 1938, my mother married a man she says she would never have imagined knowing. Her parents were shocked; her brother was shocked. She herself was and remained shocked. Now she cannot remember anything about him except that he owned a kosher, live poultry market. With his flattened nose and lumpy hands, his big ears and square jaw, my father bore a striking resemblance to Slapsie Maxie. In miniature. His best friend was an enormous former heavyweight boxer who had taken a dive against

Primo Carnera. My father looked and talked tough, though he was a sentimental man who liked to take care of people, to visit his mother and five siblings every week and his father's grave monthly. His poultry market was located in Brooklyn's Red Hook district, and he got along with the Mob and the unions, a man's man in a bloody world. He had little interest in culture.

It seemed as though my mother never forgave him for marrying her. They were miserable together, the violence of their feelings barely contained, spilling over into language, erupting against their two children. My mother's demeanor shrieked of despair as she slept far into the afternoon and remained awake far into the night. She deserved another life, different in every way, where day and night could be reversed, and she held responsible those of us who failed to provide it.

Time was not kind to Slapsie Maxie Rosenbloom. Like my mother, only at a much younger age and in a much seedier version, he ended up in a residential hotel. But he was alone there, out of the public eye, and sinking into the dementia that plagues many retired boxers. In his midsixties, he was mugged outside the hotel, bashed on the head with a pipe. He was soon committed to a sanitarium in Pasadena.

In a 1983 article for *Sports Illustrated,* Jeff Wheelwright reports of a reunion between Rosenbloom and a boxer he'd fought twice during World War II, when they performed for soldiers in the Pacific. When Slapsie Maxie did not recognize him, his old foe said, "You remember New Caledonia, don't you?" To which Rosenbloom replied, "I don't even remember old Caledonia."

Though sportswriter Red Smith believed that the superbly defensive Slapsie Maxie had not gotten hit enough times to sustain brain damage, his image was that of the punchy buffoon. But his story, sad in its way, is one of triumph. He invented himself and played the part well enough to succeed in two competitive careers; though he is mostly forgotten as an actor now, he is rightly regarded as one of the century's great boxers.

He may not have remembered who my mother was—not when he found her name in his pocket, not when he saw her in her apartment, and not after he dumped her outside Yankee Stadium—but his role in my mother's life story was never forgotten. He helped shape her image of herself, for better or worse.

Time has in many ways been very kind to my mother. After my father's death in 1961, she married a sweet-spirited, forgiving man who never criticized her performances. He played straight man to her outlandish shenanigans, endured public tongue lashings, lost more games of Scrabble than he won. When she decided that his lifelong career as a postal service employee would be demeaning to her, he retired and—at age sixty—learned the women's fashion business, even moving to Rome—Roma, at last—for a year to manage Albie's dress shop. When the oxygen he needed to help his failing respiration kept her awake, he tried to soldier on without it. When diuretics caused him to leave the bed at night, waking her up, he stopped taking them. When he revived after fainting from lack of oxygen and too much retention of liquid, he lay there and didn't complain that his son had to drive across Long Island to assist. She had a quarter century with this gentle man whose name she no longer remembers.

At ninety, she says she is the envy of all the other girls in the retirement hotel. She still has beaux. Her current boyfriend is so constantly by her side that the hotel's owner calls them "Romeo and Juliet." This delights her: a Shakespearean label! She makes grand entrances into the dining room for her meals. She sings "Younger Than Springtime" and "Bewitched, Bothered and Bewildered" in the choir whenever they can find enough residents capable of participating. I have never seen her so happy.

Though it would be better if I were more famous. My mother called recently to discuss a matter of importance to her. First of all, it was true, wasn't it, that I had won the Pulitzer Prize for my second best-selling novel, the one in which she figures as a major character? No? Well, but it was reviewed on the front page of the New York Times Book Review, was it not? In the middle of the thing, briefly noted? Okay, better than nothing, and they raved about it, right? Well, see, the Times liked your book. And that was the one about a father and his teenaged daughter, not about her? Goodbye.

Later the same night, she called again. I could tell she was not alone in her room and was anxious to get right to the point.

She cleared her throat, paused, and said, "You went to high school with somebody famous, didn't you, darling?"

I know who she means, of course. For years, she has been introducing me to waiters, shop clerks, hair stylists, and her fellow residents as someone who went to school with Billy Crystal. "Well, I did, and he went to school with me."

It was a silly distinction, I know. But an automatic one as well; I had been down this road with her enough times already.

"What was his name again?" When I told her, she repeated it and said, "I remember he was such a lovely and talented boy. And he was at your Bar Mitzvah, right?"

"No, actually we weren't that close. But our family and his family were at my friend David's Bar Mitzvah."

She covered the mouthpiece and said, "I told you!" Then, to me, said, "We saw him in a movie tonight. They show films in the bingo room, but the screen is too small, so we left. As soon as I saw him, I knew who it was! Didn't he make a movie out of one of your books?"

The Family Story

The only time I ever saw my father run was in the summer of 1954. I was seven, a budding speed demon myself, and he was visiting me for the weekend at camp in the Poconos. The shock of seeing him sprint made me laugh out loud. I remember people pointing at him in astonishment as he raced toward first base, saying, "Look at that little guy go!"

He was as fast as I'd imagined, but that wasn't what did it. My father ran like a horse. His gait was full gallop with a skip that sent him airborne between steps. No one ran like he did. A wild horse with a fat Havana cigar in its mouth.

The family story was that my father had competed in the 1928 Olympic trials. He was a high school hundred-yard-dash whiz from Brooklyn hoping to go to Amsterdam and trounce the great Percy Williams of Canada. But he was tripped in the finals by the runner beside him. Having lost his right eye as a child, my father ran blind on that side; he never even saw the guy, who must have strayed from the next lane and gotten away with it. After that, my father went to work in the family business, the wholesale Kosher slaughter of poultry.

The story doesn't quite hold together. He would have been twenty at the time of the trials, a year out of high school and committed to the family business. He got up at 3:30 six mornings a week, drove down to Red Hook, and worked till 6:00 at night. No time out to train or race, no coaches, no special diets or energy or room for anything outside the trade. His market, which he always referred to as The Place, demanded exactly the kind of devotion that Olympic training required. In the two photographs I have of him from the late 1920s, my father looks nothing like a world-class sprinter. He is round, frowning, aproned, and armed with a knife at the gaping door of The Place.

The Olympic trials story came from the same source, my mother, who began identifying me to all her acquaintances as an internationally acclaimed author the day my first novel was published by a small press in an edition of two thousand. This is the same woman who, before agreeing to marry my father, visited her doctor to ask whether a man with a glass eye might produce children with vision problems. Truth is, I think my father may have placed third in some interscholastic track meet as a teenager. That would explain his tarnished medal, which I kept in an old cigar box in my toy chest, a bronze coin imprinted with the thumb-smoothed form of a runner's body caught in midstride.

He certainly never reminisced to me about a racing career. But he was fast; I saw that with my own eyes. And he ran just like Whirlaway.

Second son of Polish-Russian immigrants, my father was born in the year Henry Ford introduced the Model T. He was born near the end of the Innocent Oughts, when Theodore Roosevelt was president and there were forty-five states in the union. Nickelodeons and fountain pens were hot new fads. The first subway from Manhattan to Brooklyn began to operate in 1908, and elevated trains began crossing the Williamsburg Bridge, opening his Brooklyn up to the rest of the city. The year he was born there were more lynchings in America than fatal car accidents. This was the last of the slow eras, with no radios or televisions, only a few phones. My father was from another world.

The cornerstones upon which his early life rested were family, neighborhood, work, and synagogue. He came from a close-knit, closed-off nook on Keap Street in Williamsburg that shaped his sense of home. When this came apart, when the world fragmented and accelerated and he learned from a stone thrown into his eye that life could sneak up on a person, that the worst threats were unseen threats, I think it shattered something vital in him. The boundaries of neighborhood and family did not keep him safe or whole; thinking that they did left him half-blind to further dangers.

The family story is that losing his eye devastated him. His sisters say he was never the same. The jubilant, playful little boy became withdrawn, moody, his kindness now laced with rage. He was eight years old when it happened. A footrace that he won, an angry neighborhood slowpoke, a small stone flung as revenge. They tried to cheer him up during the long convalescence, but his famous smile was gone. After a while, his parents bought him a violin, thinking that perhaps this would help him focus on something new and give him hope. I try to imagine him tucking it under his squared-off chin, holding a bow in his hand, straining his precious eye to read music, practicing in that crowded apartment among his five siblings and two exhausted parents. Everyone who remembers my father and his violin admits it was only another early failure. But I think it may have been good for him anyway, a clarifying experience, something that drove him back outdoors and stepped up his pace. He ran and won again. He had plenty to catch up with after missing a year of school and was proud that he graduated. Then he took up the cleaver instead of the bow and filled his days with hard work. He was tough and looked tough, an Edward G. Robinson figure with his nose and hands smashed, lumpy, and scarred; his right eye frozen in space; his thin mouth always working around that cigar so that words or the occasional chuckle seemed to ooze from its corner. He was quick to raise voice and fist. But he was accident prone and remained essentially vulnerable, living at home till he married at thirty, working with his family, cherishing routine.

In that Brooklyn childhood, hope was having a business of your own. The neighborhood teemed with fellow Jews who'd fled the Tsar, settled in tenements, then slowly moved off to better neighborhoods. Families were used to living three or five to a room. People from places like Vasilishok or Kuzhi or Bransk were now jammed together in apartments that held more people than the villages they'd come from. My father was named Harry and a sister was Carrie and they never knew for sure whose name was being called by their parents. Everyone was cramped, contained. He grew up knowing the story of his own father, who had been studying to be a rabbi in Volozhin, at the famed Yeshiva in the center of his village, and ended up in a Williamsburg undershirt factory instead. Over and over the lesson was that you could count on nothing. Parents could not protect children, communities could not protect themselves. Vigilance was everything, though it didn't always work. And sticking to your own, which also didn't always work. Only marriage to Katie Tatarsky, whose family had a background in Kosher slaughter and who gladly worked beside him during their first years together, got my father's father out of the sweatshop and off Keap Street to posh Eastern Parkway at the northern tip of Prospect Park. A good marriage and cleanliness, hard work, and business sense, and maybe a few words of Italian.

Nothing my father learned in his first two decades contradicted these lessons. He was sweet to his sisters, dutiful to his parents, loyal to his brothers, and did not strain against the limits in ways anyone remembers. Except when he learned to ride a horse.

A horse! Cossacks rode horses, Polish landowners rode horses, but people in families like my father's did not ride horses. When my father learned to ride, he learned English saddle, the gentleman's way. He had jodhpurs and thigh-high boots, a straight back, etiquette. He may have been jockey sized, but on horseback he cantered and galloped with elegance and never raced. On horseback, he was not a warrior, not a baron, not a jockey, and not fooling around. This was his violin playing. Despite the problem of his eye and limited view of the horizon, he catapulted himself to gentlemanship by learning the equestrian's stylish manner and physical skills. Riding English saddle was riding with rules and structure, the antithesis of free-form cowboy riding. My father was deeply drawn to rules, to forms that held. He liked to see the lines and lanes. What he took from his father's religion was belief in commandments, leaving the faith behind.

Whatever was missing for my father from musicianship was present in horseback riding. And while he never taught his two sons to speak Yiddish or slaughter chickens, he did teach us to master the English saddle.

By 1928, when my twenty-year-old father was supposed to be an Olympian, the world he lived in had transformed so fully that I can grasp his loathing of change. Already behind him were World War I, Prohibition, the Jazz Age, the first talkies, and Lindbergh's transatlantic flight. The Great Depression was palpable in the country's economic chaos. Hitler, Mussolini, and Stalin had assumed power. Brooklyn boomed, its population doubling during the time my father had been alive, its downtown erupting with skyscrapers, its underground alive with subways and sewers. Things moved faster, further, and with less control on the part of the family, which was itself beginning to come apart as Carrie got married, then George got married, then their father developed diabetes and heart trouble. My father opened a Kosher retail market in a building owned by his parents, reaching out to the Chinese restaurants and the Italians and the Germans, even selling rabbits alongside fowl. The Place was bustling, the waterfront thriving, the Mafia moving in on Red Hook, and the whole world had altered.

My father's response, after his inevitable move to expand the trade, was to hunker down and do only what he knew how to do well. His wholesale supplier remained his father and brother, though their prices were not the best. He went to The Place from before dawn till after dark six days a week, ate dinner at his mother's table, and followed his father's Golden Rule for domestic and business success: open the doors early and keep the floors clean. On Sundays he rode a horse in Prospect Park.

He didn't read. He didn't sing or dance (or listen to violin music). He didn't play games. No hunting, no fishing, no nights in tents under the stars, no sleeping late. He never flew in a plane. He didn't go to war. He was never west of the Poconos, east of Connecticut, or north of Lake George in upstate New York. He went to Cuba for his honeymoon, then was never south of Delaware, where he'd gotten a ticket for speeding.

He had no favorite television shows. I remember being with him and my brother in the car one Sunday morning when he turned on the radio. I didn't know the car's radio actually worked. Then, as he listened to a man telling stories in a mixture of English and Yiddish, my father suddenly cackled. Threw back his head, almost brushing the roof with his cigar, and let out this noise that I had never heard him make before. He knew how to laugh! This was no less remarkable than seeing him gallop toward first base.

He didn't drink wine. He didn't eat sauce. He didn't wear vests. Shirts did not hang loose and were always tucked in sharply. Hats were not worn at angles, belts did not flap, socks did not sag, shoes did not come untied. Public toilets were flushed with your foot, after which you lathered up like a surgeon, then turned off the rest room light switch with your elbow.

What he did, my father did with ritual precision. He dressed in black and white. He tied a Windsor knot with quick and dazzling flourishes of his hands like a magician or, I suppose, like a butcher. The material came together with a whisper in its perfect triangular slipknot. He was meticulous and strict whether stropping a razor, sharpening a knife, parting his sparse hair, shining his shoes daily, or preparing the tip of his cigar for its holder. On the rare occasions when he smoked his meerschaum pipe instead of a cigar, the procedures for unfolding a pouch of Mixture #79 and preparing the pipe's bowl were mesmerizing. I saw him use a parallel process when opening his miniature bottle of Scotch in the box seats behind third base at Ebbets Field. It seemed to take two innings to get ready for his one massive swig, and I still don't know what he did with empty peanut shells. He bought me baseball cards on Friday nights after shutting his market, always exactly five packs. He got his hair cut every Thursday, visited his mother every other Sunday and his father's grave on the last Sunday of the month, bought a new black Buick every two years. My father's showers ended with thirty seconds of an ice-cold farewell rinse and a snorting of loose mucus. His shaves ended with two pats of Old Spice, his peeing with two shakes and a dip of the knees, and his cough with a brisk swipe of wrist. Goodnight was two quick pecks to the forehead and a "See you tomorrow, buddy."

Just as there was a Kosher way to slaughter fowl, and a proper way to ride a horse that honored the bond between animal and man, and a sequence that led a person from the desire for a smoke to the pleasure of the first puff, there were ways to conduct any aspect of living. A Rabbinic tradition that could specify how many steps a person took from his bed in the morning before washing at least his fingertips *(nagelwasser)* led him straight to rules for how much he should tip the maitre d'hotel, the busboy, the waiter, the hatcheck girl, the carhop. It was an ongoing, Talmudic process of commentary on the mutable intricacies of life. How to talk and listen, shake hands like a man, cut and chew food. When to pay bills. How to learn in school. At the ballpark, you sat behind third, not first. You didn't say "You're welcome"; you said "Don't mention it." You didn't get sick. You lived in an apartment building among fellow Jews in East Flatbush.

My father devised a set of rules based on principles snatched from the thin air of his vanished childhood world. This was precisely when his own family had gone secular and remade their sense of life. With nearly genetic rigor, he believed in following the Talmudic path of maxim, careful adherence to rules of conduct, axioms and edicts. He needed structure and form, like poets need meter and rhyme, to set him free.

But sometimes the family rules were so convoluted that a boy couldn't follow them without getting lost. It was forbidden to eat pork except in Chinese restaurants or a certain diner on Sunday mornings, or when my father brought home *salsiccia* from the Italian butcher next door to The Place. If you didn't wash your hands after going to the toilet in the evening, you had to change your pajamas. At the dinner table, it was forbidden to reach for food or eat quickly, and a specified number of chews was required before swallowing. Except at Lundy's on Sunday. At Lundy's it was only possible to order one appetizer of steamed clams, even though steamers were my father's favorite item, my brother's favorite item, my favorite item, and none of us particularly cared about the rest of the Shore Dinner except the biscuits. Those first ten minutes of a meal there were a great free-for-all in which the quickest male ate the most steamed clams; shells, butter, and clam broth filled the air around our table and no one spoke except my mother, who commented on the action like Red Barber doing play-by-play. After the appetizer was finished, the original rules applied.

Yet for all his distorted mastery of childhood lessons and adoration of his parents, and despite his desire to create a family modeled on the one he loved, my father found himself in a life he couldn't stand. It was clean, industrious, solvent, tightly confined, and it didn't work.

He did what he thought he was supposed to do, but always a bit late and askew. He married, but not till he was thirty and then to a woman ill suited to the life he offered. Admiring earthy, hardworking, no-nonsense women, he chose a would-be aristocrat, pampered and yearning for a life of privilege, who turned his home into a stage set with maids and fancy furnishings he could ill afford. He sought refuge in family and found instead constant agitation. His wife wanted to talk about Shakespeare and Beethoven, the customers who came into her parents' shop when she was a child, the importance of ermine; he wanted to talk about Joe Louis and Rocky Marciano, the price of pullets, Mafia hits. Loving the sense of community, he married a woman whose favorite word was *exclusive*. Wanting companionship, a wife who would willingly labor beside him and who would ease his workaday hardship, he was lonely and on his own. They shared virtually nothing except an address. He tried to stay away from the black market in poultry and nearly priced himself out of business while his mother and brother were forced to raise rents on the building that housed The Place. He saw that supermarkets were destined to absorb his clientele and city development to carve up Red Hook, but waited too long to let go of his market and ended up working for his brother-in-law, selling women's dresses.

The family story is that my father married on the rebound. He was disappointed in early love, turned his frustrated energies to work, and married at last out of desperation. I've never been told any details about this mystery woman, the love of his life, when he lost her or why. The Rebound Story is possible, I suppose, but doesn't go far enough. Lost love alone is not a compelling explanation for his particular marital choice, for selecting as mate a woman who considered herself so far above him and vastly his superior. I think my father was confused in his feelings about class. His parents had taken him from teeming, immigrant Williamsburg to a quiet six-story apartment only a few blocks from the park. Success was evident in upscale accouterments and their contrast with the family's original status. This was a standard of measurement my father fully accepted. Where and how a family lived was apparently the key. He remembered his sisters enthralled by the Botanical Gardens, close enough to seem their own. Sunday mornings, his father took the younger children for a row on the park's lake, walking there from home. He remembered family china, gleaming sterling silver, crystal, new carpets and wallpaper. These were clearly good things, elevating things, worth striving for on behalf of your family. But I don't believe he cared about them himself, drawn as he was to a rawer set of pleasures. He was, I believe, theoretically attracted to the pretensions of sophistication, the idea of a quieter life, an urban idyll with flowers and rowboats on peaceful lakes, shaded bridle paths on which to ride horses in high style, the concept of English saddles, and the furrier's daughter speaking of Salvador Dali and

Sibelius as though they were personal friends. But his heart wasn't in this stuff. Theater bored him, art held no appeal, he was too tired for concerts and recitals and grand openings and fashion shows. He was boisterous at heart, a spirited man's man who worked hard to fetter himself with a prissy, pseudoclassy life he didn't enjoy. I think he lost touch with what he truly wanted, perhaps when his great romance failed, perhaps in the year he spent at home recovering from the loss of his eye and felt the world shrink around him. Maybe he never knew, focused as he was on the family business. Or maybe he just wanted to take his parents' success to the next level, providing these things for his own family in lieu of having what his heart desired.

There is one photograph I have—and only one—in which he looks crazed with happiness, off balance, out of control, childlike. It is the mid-1930s and he is sitting with a bunch of men his own age on a docked boat in Sheepshead Bay. They all have their arms around each other, smokes in their mouths, hats on cockeyed, leaning every which way, roaring with laughter. I never saw him like this. I think he was miserable with the life he'd put together for himself.

He gave Sunday mornings to his sons. By the time I was old enough to join them, my father and brother had worked out a routine that remained in effect till we left Brooklyn in 1957.

We would rise early and speak in whispers to avoid waking Mother. We peed quietly against the inner rim of the toilet, dressed fast, walked tiptoed, and put on our shoes only after leaving the apartment. We took the stairs down instead of the elevator to make our getaway faster. In the strange silence of Sunday mornings on Lenox Road, we stuffed ourselves into the Buick's front seat and, it seemed, flew over to Toomey's Diner for breakfast. I loved sitting squashed between my brother and father as we raced down Flatbush.

In Toomey's I had nothing to do but watch my face melt in the ripples of chrome that circled our red leather stools as my father ordered flapjacks, fresh-squeezed orange juice, and sides of bacon all around. The soles of my feet turned upside down in the stool's silvery pedestals as I spun in a slow, silent circle and snuck glimpses of the other customers. Every table had its own private jukebox. Some people used so much syrup on pancakes that their breakfasts looked like stew. The diner's air was thick with breath and smoke, grease and sweetness. My father and brother sat with their elbows on the red Formica counter, planning the rest of our morning, but I didn't join in. I didn't care what we did, only that we did something, and it was more fun to watch people sop up syrup or egg yolk with pinches of toast and drip onto their shirt fronts. There was always a sign proclaiming Special Today with nothing else written on it, which I interpreted as Toomey's announcement that these Sundays were important, that this today was a Special Today. There were grains of rice hiding within the salt, giant pyramids of cereal boxes at each end of the cook's window, toothpicks in small glasses available just for the taking. On winter mornings, when we ate in the dark, the whole world outside Toomey's windows glowed pink, then blue in the sudden shift of neon. If I closed my eyes and forced myself to stop listening to particular conversations, the whole place seemed to swell with one great sound like a prayer on High Holidays at the synagogue. We ate fast and finished everything, making noise as we chewed and slurped, all etiquette temporarily suspended, as though being in such a place liberated my father to be himself. As we left, I liked to linger long enough to watch Toomey skewer our bill and slam his cash drawer shut.

Then, depending on the season, we went to Prospect Park to ride horses or sleds or to Coney Island for a round of thrill rides, games of skill, and occasionally a tour of Steeplechase. We walked in and out of the great crowds, sometimes went onto the boardwalk. I remember the sound of loose change in my father's trouser pockets and his cigar smoke mingling with sea smells. He didn't tell stories of the old days, but I had the feeling he had been here often in the past. He sashayed.

Once a month, we drove out to Long Island and visited my

grandfather's grave. I had never known this man, who died nine years before I was born, and seldom heard anyone speak of him, but he was a fixture on the monthly schedule. Going to the cemetery was always strange, no matter how often we did it. We rolled slowly down the small road inside the cemetery, tires loud on the gravel in the surrounding silence, and parked at the very edge of the property. As soon as my father stepped into the family plot, passing beside the great stone marker with the family name on top, he would take off his glasses and plop down on the marble bench beside his father's grave. My grandfather's headstone bore my brother's name, and I hated to see it there above the grave. But I couldn't look at my father, whose face was unrecognizably soft as he leaned forward, forearms on thighs, hands dangling over his knees, mumbling to his father in ways that sounded to me like the essence of grief. One time, I remember my brother suddenly running toward the headstone and vaulting over it, using his hands like a gymnast to push himself over the top. My father seemed to grab him before he even landed, spinning him around into the full force of a backhand slap.

Around noon we were home again, back in the apartment for a few hours of hissed arguments between my parents about where we had been, what we should wear, where we should go next week. Then it was time for us to leave and visit living relatives. We might drive into Manhattan and see my mother's parents in their apartment on West Seventy-second Street; we might drive to see my father's mother in her Brooklyn Heights apartment, where she moved after my grandfather died. Either trip seemed the same to me: an angry, smoke-filled, crawl through traffic in the sweltering Buick with its windows closed so my mother's hair would not get messed up, after which we would eat overboiled chicken and vegetables in a cramped dining room and then go somberly home. The background noise was always the same. If only my mother had gotten ready on time, we would have beaten the afternoon traffic; if only my father had stopped yakking or the children had not acted like show-offs we would have beaten the evening traffic. I especially liked the Sundays when we visited aunts and uncles scattered throughout Brooklyn, Queens, and Manhattan, where there were cousins and food that didn't sag onto my plate in a way that reminded me of my grandparents settling onto the sofa. A couple of Sunday afternoons a year, we left my mother at home again and went to a ball game at Ebbets Field. Those were days when she wanted to sleep some more or work on the greeting cards that she designed using buttons for faces and snips of cloth for hats to create pouting females who haughtily wished people well. Each card was too precious to send or sell, but she was building up her inventory. At least one Sunday a month we all stayed home until it was time for dinner in a restaurant, Lundy's or Key's or Ruby Foo's. During that time my father paced like a caged turkey, agitated, talking in staccato bursts, pecking at his cigars, rattling pages of newspaper. He napped, thrashing in the sheets, went out for a walk by himself around the block, met neighbors in the courtyard for a chat about business. The long afternoon gave my parents ample time to work up their mutual fury before we left for a seething drive to the restaurant.

No one seemed to visit us at our apartment. My mother hated the mess guests left. Since she didn't cook and the maid was off on Sundays, the only way to feed them was to order food from a restaurant. This my father hated. One of his rules was that you gave guests home-cooked food, chicken from his market or meat from one of the Italian butchers he worked beside in Red Hook. Restaurant food you ate in restaurants, which, as he said, any idiot knew.

This was the usual rhythm of my father's life, his one day of rest gradually turning into his day of greatest aggravation, his time with the family enjoyed in inverse proportion to the time spent alone with them. Being together without togetherness. He'd gotten exactly what he thought he wanted, a family living well in a nice neighborhood with all their needs met and all the latest trappings, and it brought him no pleasure. It made him feel trapped.

We did what many Jewish families did with their Sundays in

Brooklyn in the 1950s, working the Coney Island-Prospect Park-Ebbets Field-cemetery-relatives-restaurant circuit. But my father did them without spark except in those rare moments that remain frozen in my memory: when he mopped egg yolk off his plate, galloped up behind my brother to rescue a hat blown off by the wind, toppled off the sled with me at the end of a long ride downhill, rose to cheer at a clutch double to left by Carl Furillo.

My father looked old at forty-seven. I saw it then and can see it now in photographs. Of course all fathers look aged to their eight-year-old sons, but mine was gray and bald and lined and too exhausted to play with me. We didn't play catch or cards, didn't tell riddles and jokes. His pallor and grimly set mouth still haunt me in dreams. I remember seeing a photograph of Truman Capote near the end of his life, heavy and tired, eyes half shut, closing down before the world. He looked *exactly* like my father. Same shaped face and body, the mouth and jowls, the expression; my macho old man's ravaged twin.

My father never stopped being accident prone. There are family stories of chicken coops dropping on his nose and hands, teeth knocked out, sliced skin where his knife slipped, toes busted against unseen stoops, fingers mangled in great sliding doors. He dented the car, broke his eyeglasses, dropped bottles and cups and dishes.

For the last hundred years, since well before the term "accident-proneness" was first suggested by the British researchers Farmer and Chambers in 1926, students of the mind have recognized that certain people show increased liability to incur accidents. Flanders Dunbar in 1954 posited an unconscious need for physical trauma as the psychodynamic root of such behavior. Although accident-proneness usually abates as a person ages, my father's got worse. He was increasingly drawn to punishing his body. After 1957, when he sold his market and moved us to Long Island, a series of accidents accelerated in pace and bodily damage until he died four years later. It was, I think, as purposeful as hanging himself from a basement pipe.

Freud was long fascinated by the subject of a person's unconscious intention being expressed in the form of accidents. In his 1899 book *The Psychopathology of Everyday Life*, he examined bungled actions, slips of the tongue or pen, errors, chance occurrences, and the accidents people commit during normal daily life. He believed that "certain shortcomings in our psychical functioning and certain seemingly unintentional performances prove, if psychoanalytic methods of investigation are applied to them, to have valid motives and to be determined by motives unknown to consciousness." To Freud, an accident was no accident at all, but rather the "carrying out of an unconscious intention." Further, he felt that "many apparently accidental injuries that happen to such patients are really instances of self-injury." The more severe an accident, the more it expresses an intent toward self-destruction. "I have learned of more than one apparently chance mishap," Freud wrote, "the details of which justify a suspicion that suicide was unconsciously allowed to come about."

In my father's case, it is not necessary to be a Freudian or firm believer in psychological interpretations of personal calamity to see his story clearly. Once his Brooklyn-based life and work ended, his accidents grew more self-destructive; they were so reckless and avoidable that his purpose seems evident.

By late 1956, he knew he would have to sell his market. The cost of doing business escalated dramatically after the war. Supermarkets emerged, eroding his customer base; the Mafia dominated the food industry in Brooklyn, squeezing his supply and distribution; and the Brooklyn Battery Tunnel and Brooklyn-Queens Expressway cut the neighborhood both apart and off. Also by late 1956, my father knew we would have to move from our apartment. The new Downstate Medical Center began construction directly across from our front door, in the vacant lot where my friends and I played war games. Word spread that our building would be taken over for use as dormitory space.

On Sundays we drove out to Long Island, visiting realtors and looking at houses. My parents discussed what my father might do next. All he'd done was kill and sell poultry. The idea of working in a grocery or supermarket appalled him. He had no interest in learning bookkeeping or design as his brothers had done. He wondered about developing a line of clothing for short men, opening a restaurant that specialized in all kinds of fowl, or using money from the sale of his market to buy and train racehorses. But none of that really appealed to him. He was lost, a man nearing fifty with no training or education who had been his own boss in a dead industry.

In the fall of 1957, we rented the upstairs half of a private home in Long Beach, a summer resort on the south shore of Long Island. My father began commuting to Manhattan, where he worked for my mother's brother in a factory producing dresses for the city's haute couture establishments.

Within ten months, my father was crippled. It is risky to ascribe motive in an auto accident, but in the space of a few minutes he made a half-dozen wrong decisions, putting himself in escalating danger. He had a flat tire in heavy traffic on Rockaway Boulevard during the dawn commute. As though seizing on an opportunity, he pulled off to the right shoulder, ignoring the turn-out available for such purposes thirty feet ahead. He shut off the lights, leaving the car in semidarkness less than a yard off the road. Then he dodged across six lanes of heavy traffic to a stranger's home, where he called the AAA for assistance. Instead of waiting safely on the porch, he dodged traffic again, walked behind his car, turned his back to oncoming traffic, and began to open the trunk. He was hit by a car that hopped the curb and slammed into him, flinging his chest into the still-unopened trunk, shattering both legs between the bumpers. For a week, it was not clear that he would live. Then it was not clear that he would ever walk.

The family story is that he gave up then, didn't really want to pull through, but love of family brought him around. He was hospitalized, except for a brief two-month period when he was in traction at home, for the next two years. His life force did seem to vanish. He had no rules for how to be disabled and no interests to occupy him while literally chained to his bed. After several surgeries, he progressed from bed to wheelchair to canes to walking with a built-up shoe, then went back to the factory. For a half year.

On the Veteran's Day holiday in 1961, he went with a group from the local synagogue to spend a weekend at a hotel in upstate New York, joining my mother and her new acquaintances for a quick vacation. It might have been more out of character for my father to join a theater troupe, but not much. After having spent the previous three years inactive and recuperating from his injuries, he used the occasion of this trip to, essentially, march himself to death. He rode horses several times each day, dragging a different cluster of men out with him into the cold air. He played horseshoes and shuffleboard, a round of badminton, walked with great effort along wooded trails to participate in a nature hike, and never rested. He drank and ate wildly. No one was going to see him weak. On the vacation's last evening, after another full day of activity, he lay beside the pool under a sun lamp till fully overheated, then moved quickly to the pool and dove in.

Witnesses said they thought he was waving at them, kidding around in the deep water. Like the character in Stevie Smith's poem, who was "much further out than you thought," my father was "not waving but drowning." His final message to others, like most messages in his life, was misconstrued. After a frantically fun-loving weekend, he seemed to those who might have saved him only to be "larking." The family story is that my father had a heart attack upon entering the water and then drowned. But there was no autopsy and no proven history of heart disease and there are other possibilities: a cramp or the weakness of an unfit convalescent or his lifelong lack of skill as a swimmer. He was pulled from the pool, briefly revived, said "I can't catch my last breath," and died. He was fifty-three.

I turned fifty-three in the year 2000. For most of my life since my father's death, I believed that I too would die young, victim of a heart attack. In the first of many modifications of the family story, I took up long-distance running instead of sprinting. I watched my cholesterol; I moved to the country. But still my father haunted me, in sadness as well as high cholesterol numbers. At eleven when he was injured and fourteen when he died, I was always too young to be of much help to him.

Finally, I have found a way. By examining the possibility that my father's death, like his auto accident or his many earlier accidents, was anything other than preordained or accidental, I have begun to let him talk to me at last. In reconsidering the stories and myths, in thinking about his life, I am letting memory rather than legacy take over. One way to live a life of my own, it turns out, is to grasp the essence of my father's story and live beyond it.

A few years ago, my Uncle Sidney, the family archivist, unearthed an audiotape made at his son's Bar Mitzvah in 1955. One by one, everybody in the family comes up to the microphone to speak a few words for posterity. I am there, joining my cousin Michael in a mock play-by-play of a Dodgers game. My mother's father is there, though this was not his family and he had no idea who the Bar Mitzvah boy might be ("He seems like a nice fella and I vishes him gut"). When my father spoke, I had no memory of his voice. It was shocking to hear him sound like a stranger. Actually, like a Groucho Marx gone serious, wondering why the hell he had to come up and speak into Sid's silly machine. After playing the tape through, I decided to make a copy for myself before returning the original to my uncle. What happened, though, was that I erased it. By accident.

10

The Year of the 49-Star Flag

In the fall of 1959, when I was twelve, the idea that I might never actually get to be five feet tall drove me wild. I wasn't even close. When I looked at my parents next to other parents, I felt doomed. My mother was four feet, ten inches, and my father only five inches taller. Further, my mother's mother could barely reach the sink in her tiny Manhattan apartment, and my father's mother had only grown sideways since she left Bialystok as a young girl. My brother was a normal-sized twenty year old. But he didn't look like the rest of us and kept insisting that he and I had very different genes, which he said explained why only I turned out to be obnoxious.

Doctor Robbins, whose family supplied cardboard boxes for my father's market in Brooklyn, reported that my feet were relatively large for my height. He said this meant I was going to grow just fine. Average height, he kept assuring me, staring over my head. Nothing to worry about. Meanwhile, I was always at the front of lines arranged by size in school, was shorter than almost every girl, and it felt that I had to peer upward just to look a toy poodle in the eye.

Whenever I entered a room, I jumped to touch the transom, slam-dunking balled-up socks or just leaving my fingerprints up there. It seemed to bring the world down to size. Before going to bed every night and as soon as I awoke every morning, I hooked my feet under the bed frame and reached as far back as possible, stretching with all my might. I dangled myself from a chin-up bar and held on until ten of my forty-five-rpm records had played through. I went on walks along the shore of the small barrier island where we had moved two years earlier, filling my lungs with heavy salt air, holding my breath, hoping to force my various organs outward so they would expand my body from within. I drank so much milk and ate so much cheese for my bones and beef for my muscles that it's a wonder I didn't have a heart attack by age fifteen.

The world was slow in 1959. None of the literature talks about that phenomenon, but I remember it clearly. Weeks lasted forever. Everything was transforming except me. Classmates were developing practically before my eyes, of course, but that wasn't all. It seemed to me that I could feel life itself, and the possibilities life held for me, inching away like the line of wet sand at the beach behind our house when the tide turned, leaving me stranded. Wherever I looked, there were markers to measure how the world was changing. The flag, for example. Alaska joined the union on January 3 to become the forty-ninth state, the first new one since Arizona in 1912. On July 4, two days before my birthday, there was a fancy new flag, but then Hawaii was admitted in August and yet another new flag, this one with fifty stars, would come into use exactly one year later. It served to symbolize for me the importance of 1959, a once-in-a-lifetime year. Grow now or it's all over. I mean, even the flag was growing.

In school, we talked about what was happening in the South, integration and riots, and what was going on in the North, strikes everywhere. Slow, demonstrable progress, evolution in action, rites of passage. I suddenly realized that the word "flux" was not a euphemism like "goldarn" but a real word to describe the process of change. I used it every chance I got, hoping to coax my own changes along. There were satellites overhead and fallout shelters underground, monkeys in space and Barbie dolls in store windows. Edsels were discontinued by Ford after only two years on the road, and rear-engine Corvairs were introduced by Chevrolet. Things were in flux, all right. Major league baseball was thriving in California, seven astronauts were chosen for orbital flight, and people who weren't astronauts could circle the globe on Pan Am even though no one was allowed to go to China anymore. Fidel Castro had marched on Havana, where my parents went for their honeymoon in 1938, their one and only trip out of the country, and it looked as though Communism would be swimming right over to Miami, so we were no longer friendly with Cuba, which meant that my father had trouble getting his cigars. It was impossible to figure things out, to get a picture of the future. The world felt unsafe as we learned to shield ourselves from nuclear blasts by hiding under our seats at school. Though the universal watchwords were "wait and see," who had that luxury?

All that whiz, that flux, and I was at a standstill. I would measure myself against the pencil mark behind the bathroom door after every shower. It became impossible to answer the question adults always seemed to ask about my aspirations in life because I was frozen in time, holding out to see what would become of my hopes for playing major league baseball. There weren't many players in the size category to which I seemed consigned. Even Albie Pearson, the outfielder famous for being tiny, was five feet, five inches, well above anything I could realistically imagine. And he had gotten traded by the Washington Senators in May, after his batting average slumped to .188, for a player half a foot taller.

I was obsessed. Then my mother started arranging lessons for me. Lessons in everything, with particular emphasis on skills I had no desire to learn, as though she had decided I needed distracting, or maybe it was focus. Lessons so that I could start to grow, even if the growing was not the kind that mattered to me.

When Mr. Angelo Capobianco came to our house the first Monday afternoon in September, I thought it was some kind of stunt my mother was pulling. What had she done, hire a dwarf guitar teacher to make me feel better? He was exactly my height. So was my new Stella guitar, which I could barely grip. To reach the top E string without muffling the other five, I had to curl my left wrist and stretch my fingers so far that I thought the act might deform me before I could master my first chord.

Mr. Capobianco, however, had colossal hands, the kind that belonged to a basketball player, dangling from the ends of his stumpy arms. Those hands, and the prodigious ears that permitted him to hear each of my mistaken notes more clearly, and his sluggish tongue that was as awkward with English as I was with music suggested to me that Mr. Capobianco's body parts had been scrounged, perhaps in Italy during the war. I was spellbound by him, especially when he tuned the guitar and played a quick number that required his talons to move at the speed of light. Look out, Duane Eddy! There was no way I was going to learn how to play the guitar from this man, but I looked forward to the first ten minutes of each weekly lesson just to see him again.

I had the same feel for music that Mr. Capobianco had for baseball. The one time I sought to engage him in conversation as we marched down the hallway to my room, asking what he thought about the amazing season Wally Moon had just had while playing leftfield for the Dodgers, he looked at me as though I'd asked him for a handful of lunar dust.

About three months after the lessons began, Mr. Capobianco mentioned as he was leaving that I was the worst student he had ever had. He said this conversationally, in the same way he might have mentioned that tagliatelle was his favorite pasta. After so many weeks of watching his frustration mount, I had expected him to shout at me, but he never did. He would just get red, look away from where I contorted myself around the neck of the guitar, and sigh. When he finally categorized my playing, his winsome tone and those words spoken in a spookily unaccented English were much more of a shock. I was used to being yelled at and retreating into my private world of meditations on the Dodgers; his expression of wonder at my ineptitude was something altogether more unsettling.

It might have helped if I had practiced between lessons, but there were too many other demands on my attention. For one, I had to prepare myself for musical stardom. Buddy Holly had died in February and there was a real need for new talent. I would stack ten more records on my phonograph, strap on the Stella, open my closet to expose the full-length mirror, swivel my hips, and avoid touching the guitar strings while lip-syncing to my favorite hits, Holly's "Rave On" or Dion's "Teenager in Love" or "Problems," in which I managed to do both Everly Brothers' parts simultaneously. Every set of ten songs included one ballad, maybe "Donna" or "Lonely Boy," when I would stand closer to the mirror and practice sneering as I sang. The idea was to find the sultry rebel hidden somewhere deep inside my absurdly sweet-little-boy looks, but the result more closely resembled a sufferer of heartburn. Each set also included one instrumental number, maybe Johnny and the Hurricanes or The Virtues, demonstrating my expertise and finesse as I gracefully changed chords while picking air above the strings. Because the guitar was so big for me, I would switch to my black and white baseball bat after a few songs, just as great performers changed their instruments between numbers. I could really gyrate with my little Louisville Slugger guitar. All this used up my allocated practice time, and then I would run outside to play Wiffle ball with friends. The idea of actually getting competent on the guitar didn't occur to me.

Some days, as an extended form of my music homework, I experimented on my hair by mixing hot shower water and massive amounts of brylcreem to see what effects could be achieved. With black hair slicked close to the skull and a part so melodramatic it looked like a scar, I resembled Milton Berle more than Dion.

Instant success as a rock 'n' roller was no longer a distant fantasy. Last year, right on the boardwalk here in Long Beach, five guys singing doo wop were discovered by Bob Shad, who owned his own record label. He just sat down on one of those benches overlooking the beach, put his feet up on the railing, ate a hot dog while watching the young ladies in bathing suits, and listened to Claude Johnson and his pals gathered over by the ski ball stalls where they could sing and catch the good echo. They were very good; all the kids knew about The Genies. Shad introduced himself and arranged a recording session for a song Claude wrote with another member of the group, Fred Jones. They cut "Who's That Knocking" and it became a genuine Top 100 Hit during the winter of 1959. So I knew it could happen right outside my door, in a spot where I myself had stood many times. I was getting myself ready.

After a while, I realized that I didn't need to hold a guitar in order to achieve stardom. A guy could sing a cappella, or just croon into a mike while his less famous associates played instruments and sang backup.

Since I had never asked for a guitar or lessons, I didn't feel disappointed in the outcome. Or surprised. Playing music was my mother's territory anyway; I had no desire to go there. It wasn't enough for me to take up a different instrument and leave the piano to her. I didn't want to be speaking the same language, period.

So music was out and finally even my mother acknowledged that. But I did like those plastic guitar picks, which I thought might be fun to collect. There were so many varieties, like marbles only prettier to my eye and much easier to store. I preferred the picks that looked like wood grain when you held them up to the light.

Before the year's end, I had stored my guitar in the back of my closet. The only time I ever saw Mr. Capobianco again was in La Seranata, the Italian restaurant where my mother often took me to eat dinner when she got home late. He pretended not to know me when I waved, turning full attention to his steaming plate of eggplant Parmesan.

At the same time that she had found Mr. Capobianco, my mother also enrolled me in dance lessons. If I'd ever wanted or needed dance lessons, these were coming about five years too late. Dance lessons were for 1954. The kinds of dances people were doing in the fall of 1959 required, if anything, antilessons. They were about dancing by yourself. When the music played, you essentially did whatever you felt like doing. Since the few times I went to dances the only thing I felt like doing was leaving, Mrs. Rothstein's instruction had about as much chance of success with me as Mr. Capobianco's had.

Nevertheless, Wednesdays after school I rode my bicycle across town to Mrs. Rothstein's studio, which had opened in the building where an old discount store used to be. Even the building reeked of failure and old-fashioned ways. I was not the kind of boy who considered cutting his lessons; I might create a fantasy world of my own where I did whatever I wanted to, but if I was supposed to go to dance lessons in my mother's world, I went to dance lessons. We were a collection of wallflowers, all of us. If we had been normal kids in 1959, the last place we would have allowed ourselves to be seen was at the dance studio.

This was prime football-playing weather, but instead of being with my friends running patterns on the street, I was taking lindy and fox trot lessons. What next, the Charleston? I had to lie to my friends, who believed that I was going for medical treatments on my knobby legs. There was no way I could let them know the truth, that while kids on *American Bandstand* were doing the stroll, or perfecting the slop, or throwing in a little skip to turn the slop into the pony, or waving their arms to make it the monkey, I was going one-two-cha-cha-cha.

This was also the time when I was preparing in secret for my appearance on a quiz show. I knew that a twelve-year-old contestant would be unusual, but I felt that our family had connections. First of all, my father's cousin Seymour was a buyer for *The Price Is Right* on nbc, so we were in the business. Further, the year before we had moved from Brooklyn to Long Island, my brother had had a tutor named Mr. Ludwig who was actually a contestant on *The $64,000 Question*. Using the sort of logic that my mother always used, I imagined that all it would take was a call to Mr. Ludwig, backed by a call to cousin Seymour, and I would get right on the show. Or on *Twenty-One*, where Charles Van Doren had appeared.

Of course, not just yet. The United States Senate was currently investigating quiz shows over the issue of providing contestants with answers, and the major shows were no longer actually on the air, but that didn't stop me from preparing for the time when they returned.

In his book *The Fifties,* David Halberstam writes about "the belief that seemingly unexceptional Americans did indeed have secret talents and secret knowledge." This belief guided producers in their development of the quiz show as prime time entertainment and certainly guided me in my quest to find the hidden guitar-playing solo-dancing rock singer, or the athlete, or the grand-prize-winning contestant. So what if I was tone deaf or too small to play the sports I loved or had not read much more than The Hardy Boys?

My category would be either baseball or rock 'n' roll. That explained why I had to spend so much time immersed in both.

As though a dam had been switched on, the great sea of child's play suddenly shrank on the Monday following Thanksgiving. Late that afternoon, my Bar Mitzvah date was selected at a meeting in the rabbi's office. A blotter in the form of a calendar took up the entire surface of his desk. He seemed worried over the crammed schedule, with so many baby boom boys cued up for their ceremony of initiation.

On September 10, 1960, two months after I would turn thirteen, I was going to stand next to the rabbi in front of the congregation, do what was required of me, and thereafter be counted as a "son of the commandments." I would become a man.

I was signed up for Bar Mitzvah lessons beginning in January. Apparently there was no end to the things I had to learn in the year of the 49-star flag.

But this was the big one. My parents had been saying for years that the Bar Mitzvah would be the most important event in my young life. They told me it was a ritual that every son's parents, and therefore every son, looked forward to eagerly, the coming of age, and I should stop all my complaining. It was an honor. Whenever

I felt overwhelmed by having to attend Hebrew school right after a full day of public school, or by going to services every Saturday morning, they would remind me of where this was all heading. At thirteen, life would change for me; I would be an official adult and a member of the community. This was like the flag again. I now had another demarcation for the start of something I wasn't sure I could grow into on time.

Next to my Bris, which fortunately I did not remember, my Bar Mitzvah would represent life's major rite of passage until marriage. Afterward, I could be included in a minyan, a prayer quorum, my presence counting the same as any of the old men with prayer shawls draped over their heads, praying for all the dead from the Holocaust. I would be *responsible.* So I had better not fool around.

I had two conflicting thoughts about this milestone. On the one hand, I wondered if it might be the thing to trigger my adult growth spurt, though I knew that several of my friends were already "men" in the senses that mattered most among us. They were already developing serious bodies; their voices were falling apart and being reassembled in a much lower register; they were getting hair in places that, on my own body, were remaining stubbornly bald and were getting muscles in places that remained all bone on me; and their concern over the scope of my baseball card collection was fading. On the other hand, I wondered if I would be able to see over the pulpit when I stood up there with the rabbi and the cantor to say my portion of the Torah. My first question, after shaking Cantor Mendelssohn's hand and being welcomed to his tutorial, was whether there would be a stool for me to stand on during my Bar Mitzvah.

Although these lessons were all about becoming a man, I never felt more like a child than when I was sitting with the cantor, who was more famous among the boys for his cheek pinching than for his gorgeous tenor voice. Every time I mastered the melody of a small section of my Torah portion, he would grab my face between his thumb and index finger and try to remove it. This was a very poor incentive to mastery. I was happy to please him but dreaded the reward.

Lessons took place at the synagogue two afternoons a week. Two other afternoons, I was to come to the synagogue after school and stay there to study. While this blessed task took care of my dancing lessons, and my own performances had taken care of my guitar lessons, it was hard labor to be spending a couple of hours four times a week trapped in the synagogue.

My task was to learn in Hebrew the lengthy Torah passage that I would read on September 10, comprehend its meaning, and master the special melody by which it was to be chanted. Singing lessons! I knew on the first day that nine months would be cutting it close, that the amount of Hebrew and the intricacies of the melody would push my limited faculties to their limits.

Curiously, there was nothing in my lessons about matters of the spirit, about faith, even about duty or accountability or community. It was like geometry class, the strange scrawls of text replacing theorems and formulas. Boys like me, who had attended Hebrew school at the synagogue for the last two years, were assumed to know something about Jewish history, festivals and holidays, as well as be able to read Hebrew. We couldn't translate it, but we could sound out the words. In theory, I suppose the pieces were there, but nothing about my religion truly held together for me. Rather than a coherent system of belief in or reverence for a supreme being, a grounded way of life, Judaism seemed to be another in a long line of rule-laden, judgment-oriented programs whose requirements I had to follow, whose lessons I had to master, if I knew what was good for me. My Judaism meant nothing to me, and the Bar Mitzvah that would welcome me into its fold was just another hurdle I had to clear. The intimate setting and personal contact with the impressive young cantor provided by my Bar Mitzvah lessons turned out to be like sessions with Angelo Capobianco, another overworked taskmaster.

Herman Wouk, in his classic introduction to Judaism entitled *This Is My God: The Jewish Way of Life*, describes the "disagreeable process" of preparation this way: "Countless boys who barely knew the Hebrew alphabet were schooled to parrot foreign words in a strange musical mode, by dint of coaching stretched over a year or more." I may have had a bit more Hebrew than the typical boy Wouk writes about, but my reward for that was to be given more to say during my Bar Mitzvah ceremony.

Only a few months before my lessons began, a situation comedy that my friends and I loved premiered on CBS, *The Many Loves of Dobie Gillis*. In this show, Bob Denver played a beatnik named Maynard G. Krebs whose fluent tongue would always get hung up on one particular word: WORK! Maynard G. Krebs and his cry WORK! was my first thought after seeing how much study and practice it would take to get ready for my Bar Mitzvah. Cantor Mendelssohn wondered why I looked up from the text and began to laugh.

It had never occurred to me that my mother, in arranging all these lessons, was providing daylight custodians. Though I didn't know at the time, she had even gotten special dispensation from the rabbi for me to spend those two afternoons studying at the temple. If she had thought of numismatics, I'm sure she'd have signed me up for coin club on Thursday afternoons, entirely filling my week's bill.

Because she was gone from noon till 7:30 every day visiting my father, who had been in a hospital in Queens since late autumn of 1958, recovering from his automobile accident. She had only recently learned to drive at age forty-eight, which enabled her to spend every day with him. Borderline diabetic, borderline Kosher, he was a finicky, eccentric eater and wouldn't touch hospital food. For breakfast, he would eat two dry slices of the Thomas' Protein Bread that my mother left in the hospital refrigerator. Lunch and dinner were homemade meals my mother brought with her each day, a truly heroic endeavor because she had always refused to cook.

These were days when children were not permitted as visitors in a hospital. We were seen as carriers of germs, noisy and rambunctious, and the rules said that even visits to parents were forbidden. Once only, after my father had been hospitalized for about a month, was I permitted to see him, and that was because I had simply ceased to believe he was alive. He had vanished from my life on a November morning and I kept demanding to be taken to his grave. Nothing anyone said could convince me that he was not dead, so an exception was made for me. Two minutes, don't touch anything, and leave when you're told.

He was in a bed rigged with heavy hardware, a cross between a small gym and a crib. His spread legs were suspended from wires that dangled from the bed's superstructure. A small trapeze hung above his chest so he could lift his torso. The bed itself had cranks and pulleys and adjustable bars and a metal table that could swing in front of his face. As I approached his bed, the smell overwhelmed me, blood and sweat and waste and vomit and disinfectant, a mixture of odors that forever defined loss for me. At first I could not see his face, and my attention was riveted by thick metal pins sticking through his heels. Flesh puckered around their points of entry, crusty and inflamed. From ankle to waist, his body was draped in cloth so I could see nothing more of him, but those heels told me all I needed to know.

I stood beside his bed and strained to kiss my father as he strained to lift himself far enough to be kissed. His glasses were off and his face was a mass of scabs and scars, swollen and discolored. But it was recognizably his, so at least I knew they weren't pulling a trick on me. He was pale wherever he wasn't bruised and his expression was one of deep concentration, as though focused wholly inward on his pain. I had never seen him sick before, in bed for anything other than sleep. He tried to talk, but his breathing was labored and all he could manage was a breathy whisper.

"I'll be home soon," he said. "We'll play catch again before long, buddy."

Even I knew that was an empty promise. I also knew that we hadn't played catch since about 1953. But I shook my head and tried to smile at him. He sagged back onto his pillow, closing his eyes. As though that were a signal, my mother whisked me from the bedside and out of the ward to the elevators. I didn't have a chance to say goodbye to him. The last image I had was of my father shut down.

At first, my parents' friends visited us at home to lend support. They brought casseroles and hams and roast chickens, sacks of fruit and nuts, packs of soda, cookies and cakes that I wasn't allowed to eat. Someone brought me a fountain pen and fancy stationery, suggesting I might keep in touch with my father that way. A man who clearly did not know my father very well brought a hardback copy of the new novel by Boris Pasternak, *Doctor Zhivago,* for us to bring to the hospital. On the flyleaf he had drawn a cartoon of my father, glasses and characteristic cigar in place, standing with his trousers sagging around his ankles, his rear end being examined by a doctor with a stethoscope who says, "You'll be good as new in no time, Mr. Skloot." Just like Dr. Robbins assuring me I would grow. The house was filled with talk about donating blood, but when I asked to be included they all laughed. What else could I give my father? Instead of taking me seriously, there were whispers about what to do with me, conversations I overheard by hiding behind the kitchen door overlooking our sunken living room.

"It will help him grow," someone said. My heart lurched; *No,* I thought, *God couldn't be that mean.*

"He's too young to be alone so much," my mother kept saying. "He'll need things to do."

So near the end of 1958 our family structure and routine had altered in a flash. Its fallout filled 1959 as we waited for life to sort itself out. With my brother working in Manhattan, my father in the hospital, and my mother gone each day until late evening, I was swamped with lessons from instructors I did not know and who did not seem interested in knowing me. Arcane knowledge would occupy my mind, which was already cluttered with baseball and rock 'n' roll trivia. Remote guides would occupy my time with teachings that had little application to my life. Clearly, I had things to learn, and just as clearly I needed to discover them by myself. Perhaps by offering me the opposite of what I really needed, my mother gave me the chance to identify and address those needs for myself.

Finally, in midwinter my father came home. He would be with us for a few weeks before moving to the local hospital for additional surgeries. His legs had healed wrong and would have to be rebroken, starting the whole process of recovery over again.

By then I had discovered a box containing the clothes he wore when the accident occurred. Evidence for the trial. Unmarked, its flaps neatly folded together, it was irresistible there in the corner of the garage. I lifted out his torn trousers, caked shoes with laces limp under the tongue, socks and shirt, tie, everything stained and stiff with his blood. I had also discovered a manila envelope full of pictures a news photographer had taken while my father lay behind the car. His elbows were on the ground and his arms were raised as though warding off the air. I tried to see the expression on his face, but the details were not clear enough. About three months after the accident, I rode my bicycle to the deli owned by the man who had hurt my father. There was a huge line of people at the counter, buying their Sunday morning breakfast feasts, the bagels and lox, smoked sable and sturgeon, whitefish chubs, cream cheese that they would bring home to their families in a bag with Pincus Deli written in large red letters. I tried to see inside the store, to catch a glimpse of him. I didn't want him to cut his fingers off accidentally in the meat slicer, or to burn himself on the grille where the franks were cooked, or to choke to death on a fishbone. I couldn't even muster up hatred for him. But I wanted to see his face. The white-haired man wearing a stained apron who looked up just as I looked in smiled at me, holding up his long knife in salute. Before I turned away, he beckoned me inside with an arch of eyebrows.

This was when the sleep disturbance began. I could not make it through the night without sitting bolt upright in bed, heart racing though the nightmare imagery had vanished. My subsequent wanderings through the house disturbed my mother, desperate for sleep as another hospital day loomed. Even when my father got home, I couldn't sleep.

His bed was moved into a corner of their room. A huge hospital bed was installed in its place next to my mother's twin bed, separated from hers by the gaudy table holding its two-headed lamp. My father was still strung in traction, immobilized from the waist down. My mother had to manage his bedpan, his shaving, his cleanliness and feeding.

I watched everything. I hovered in the background and heard the scrape of a razor on my father's face, the moans and grunts and sighs as he shifted positions, chewing and swallowing, the sound of bladder and bowels. As though in counterpoint, the bed clanked and rattled with each move. In time, I stepped forward and asked to help. I combed my father's hair, or what was left of it, noting to myself how gray it had grown in the last year, careful to get his part straight so he would smile when I held up a mirror. I cleaned the shaving basin, amazed at the living mess of stubble and soapy water. I pulled over a chair and table to set up a game of Gomo-Q for us, the first time we had ever played a board game together. Gomo-Q required a player to place five marbles in a row while blocking an opponent's efforts to do the same. In order to detect rows on the board, my father had to lean way over amidst his rigging, compensating for his sightless right eye. I had never really seen his vision limits in action before. After school, I would stand at the side of his bed, leaning back against the wall, and tell him about my day, another thing we had never done before.

It was a brief idyll, but I still could not sleep through the night. At 2:00 or 3:00 in the morning, I would tiptoe down the hall and slip into the extra bed in their room. From there, far against the wall, I could hear their mingled breath and get back to sleep. Then he was taken away again. My mother said I had to learn to sleep in my own bed.

The day before my Bar Mitzvah, a Friday, my mother took me to get a haircut. The sides were clipped very short, the back was razor sharp, the part was precise, and the little pompadour perfectly weighted to hold its shape. I looked so square that I hoped none of the girls invited to the celebration would show up.

My father, back from his additional surgeries, had healed well enough, with the help of regular physical therapy, to begin working again in Manhattan. Wheelchair bound, or supporting himself for a few minutes at a time on crutches, he would be driven into the city by my brother every Monday morning and stay with him at the Cooper Union all week, returning home on Friday nights. My brother, who also worked in Manhattan, loved to have my father to himself those five days, and they both returned to Long Beach cheerful, bearing a bunch of new records or five packs of baseball cards as a gift for me.

This Friday, though, they came home grim. The Bar Mitzvah and especially the party afterward, which was to be at the Coral Reef Beach Club near our home, was all my father could think about. He asked me if I was sure I knew my portion of the Torah. He wondered about my clothes for tomorrow. He wanted to see the prayer shawl that his mother had bought for me in Israel, to make sure it was still clean. He wanted me to go to sleep right after dinner. He was making me very nervous.

First thing in the morning, he wanted me to go to the barber for a haircut and a fresh combing. This, finally, was too much. Though I was grateful that he was alive, that he was home and mobile again, that he had been spared any more suffering, and though I remained as frightened of his temper as I was prior to his weakening through injury, I said "No."

He stared at me from the doorway to my room, where he sat in his wheelchair hunched forward like a racecar driver.

"What?"

"I got a haircut yesterday. I can comb my own hair."

"I want you to look right."

"Dad, I can do it myself."

He began to wheel himself over to the bed. This meant serious trouble. I sat up, turned to put my legs down on the floor, and was determined not to back down. The joints of his fingers cracked as he rotated the chair's wheels. I looked at him steadily and he held my stare. The chair stopped inches from my legs. As I watched, his face slowly softened. He looked up at my hair.

"Maybe you should have slept sitting up, buddy."

As I write this now, I am fifty, exactly the age my father was when he had his accident. I am perhaps an inch taller than he was, and I look very much like him despite my beard. Some memories of that time remain so clear they seem to have happened last week—helping him use the parallel bars that stood where the extra bed had stood as he learned to walk again, watching him negotiate the ten steps up to our door from the street, seeing him graduate from crutches to canes to a built-up shoe as he began walking again, meeting him at the train station when he came home from the city.

Those last two years of his life, before his sudden death, were filled with powerful images for me. But nothing is as vivid as the moment he let me off the hook, let me comb my own hair on the morning of my Bar Mitzvah, judging that I had learned enough in the last few years to be dismissed from childhood.

3

A Measure of Acceptance

Kismet

My brother, Philip, was buried on the morning of my fiftieth birthday. Earlier that week, he had decided to stop dialysis treatments, so his death was not really a surprise.

But it was a shock. My sister-in-law called just after dawn and I snatched up the phone, turning on my knees, naked, to lean over the bed as though in prayer. Elaine said hello, then issued a sound I did not at first recognize. The phone in our bedroom is an ancient, staticky cordless with a replacement universal antenna that falls off whenever I pick up the unit, so I assumed that the sound was just her voice breaking up over the thousand miles between us.

But Beverly knew at once what she heard coming through the unit and the bones of my skull. She bounded out of bed, ran into the next room, picked up the phone in there, and began comforting Elaine before I could let the truth seep in.

We had last seen Philip two months earlier. During that visit, for the first time, he had begun to speak about dying. On Friday night, he interrupted a dinner-table discussion of the virtues of root vegetables to say he thought he had about six months left. Provided he continued receiving dialysis four times a week. "I'm okay with this. I've had a good life." He gestured toward Elaine, and his left hand landed on top of his buttered bread, which made him chuckle, then shrug, then eat the chocolate chip cookie he had been hiding in his right hand.

Near the end, when he weighed 264 pounds, my brother was a vestige of his former self. He sat quietly in his recliner or wheelchair, listening, a mellow smile on his face, gray hair flattened in back and spread like a fan above his ears. When he spoke his voice was deeper and slower than it had ever been, tamped down. What he had to say was offered in counterpoint, as comment on what he heard rather than as part of the main melody.

Philip was fifty-seven. In his apartment, he liked to strip right down to basics, white boxer shorts and V-neck T-shirt, or maybe a pair of loose sweatpants while the air conditioning blasted. Without the black wraparound shades, he kept his sightless eyes closed. Without the false teeth, he kept his mouth shut but loved to work his gums sideways across each other. His skin, stippled with odd growths, bore the soft ocher shade of renal failure and stung whenever he was touched. There was a hump at the base of his neck. He could barely walk, soles numbed, muscles atrophied, balance in shambles. He needed help to stand and could not get himself up off the toilet or take a shower by himself. He had trouble breathing and when he slept, slumped in the recliner, his face erupted in tics.

He looked exactly like our grandmother Kate in the months before she died in 1965. She was then seventy-nine.

In his heydays my brother weighed 375 but moved with uncanny grace, as though the planet held him in place with a different kind of force than the rest of us. He was a successful gambler, a savvy player of games, an unlikely ladies' man. He knew odds; he counted cards. Over the years, he sold pressure-sensitive papers or envelopes or shoes or metals, always expanding his territory, on the go. When he could no longer walk well or see well enough to drive, he sold computer hardware by phone, what he disdainfully called "Inside Sales." He was the kind of guy you instinctively trust, a sell-sand-to-the-Saudis type, and his word was good. He was the joke a minute sort, the life of the party, suavely smiling, cigarette cupped in his palm, wise to the ways of the world. Even blind, he would give his wife directions when they drove together through the streets of San Francisco, saying "Turn left here" or "Bear right at that Texaco station." He knew what he knew. He loved the spotlight, the lead, and he was never very interested in blending into the background.

For casual wear, my brother favored brightly colored shirts and contrasting golf slacks. He claimed visual space, flaunting his size, proclaiming that he had nothing to hide. I have a photograph of Philip posed beside his tall, slender wife before a fancy evening out; he is wearing a red sports jacket with fuchsia accents, a fuchsia tie, and red shoes to go with the white shirt and red-and-white-checked slacks. As always, the thick black hair is carefully pompadoured.

To eat with him was to witness pleasure carried to the level of torture. Restaurant owners and chefs fawned over him, the maitre d'hotel and maitre de cuisine lavishing attention on his vast table of friends, waitresses bringing free desserts and aperitifs. He tipped everyone twice. I remember eating a five-course dinner with him one Saturday night at an Italian restaurant in New York's east Village, Mario's, then stopping for doughnuts on the short drive to his home in New Jersey, then watching him eat a sandwich before going to bed. My sleep that night was one endless nightmare. Early next morning, there was a full table of traditional Jewish Sunday brunch foods, bagels and nova with cream cheese, smoked sable and sturgeon, whitefish chubs, lox wings, ruggelach.

Afterward, we drove to the batting range and swatted line drives in the blistering August heat. I weighed less than half of what he weighed, but felt rotund as Babe Ruth and was not sure I could manage a swing without my arms thumping my belly.

Our grandfather Philip, my brother's namesake, was born in the old country in the fall of 1880. The old country was Russia or Poland or Lithuania, depending on the year in question, though in the late nineteenth century it was part of the Russian empire designated as the Pale of Settlement by Tsar Alexander III, the only place where Jews were legally authorized to settle. The Skluts came from Volozhin, between Minsk and Vilnius, in what was known as White Russia and is now part of Belarus.

Volozhin was and remains a small town. But its renowned Jewish Academy or Yeshiva was known throughout the Jewish world, a place that was led by such great rabbis as Rav Chaim or Rav Joseph Baer Soloveichik and that attracted Talmudic scholars. The Hebrew poet Hayyim Nahman Bialik and essayist/fiction writer Micah Joseph Berdichevsky studied there.

As Paul Johnson notes in his book *A History of the Jews,* "In the last half-century of imperial Russia, the official Jewish regulations formed an enormous monument to human cruelty." It was a preview for Nazi policy. To be a Jew in Volozhin was to be constantly at risk from Poles, Cossacks, Catholics, Tsarist loyalists, Nazis, and to survive required both vigilance and resilience.

Beset by violence, transformed by invasion the way a cell is transformed by a virus, Volozhin's destiny was to be always under attack. Like a human body perpetually challenged by pathogens, the community's collective defense mechanisms became rewired, organized to be continually on alert. We became a people focused on self-defense, locked in to patterns of resistance, guarded even when there was no threat.

Prayer, communal solidarity, the development of niche skills, bribery, conversion—these were typical external forms of coping. In *A Promised Land,* Mary Antin's classic 1912 memoir of eastern European Jewish life and immigration, a sense of resignation underlies Jewish creativity in the face of continued calamity: "But what can one do? the people said, with a shrug of the shoulders that expresses the helplessness of the Pale. What can one do? One must live."

At constant risk, people either adapted or perished. Current theories about evolutionary biology suggest that there would have been internal forms of coping as well, biological adaptations to prolonged stress that mirrored the external adaptations, ultimately weakening the body as they preserved it, overburdening the immune system. In time, a pattern of neurologically mediated behavior evolved that closed off responses irrelevant to self-protection. In a sense, my brother and I came from people whose biological adaptation to stress had a self-destructive component. Programmed to biologically circle the wagons, our immunological responses were maladaptive—we eat ourselves up with worry. This was the secret baggage brought to America from the old country, and whether or not the theory is correct, the metaphorical implications are compelling.

After increasingly anti-Semitic restrictions imposed by Alexander III, and an escalation of pogroms, four Sklut brothers left Volozhin in 1892. Two settled in South Africa, where the family name became Sloot; the other two, Eliahu and Samuel, came to New York, where they were processed at Ellis Island as Skloot. The name refers to a mason's tool used to chop the rough edges off stone.

Grandfather Philip, a scholarly former student prepared to enroll at the Volozhin Yeshiva, a reader of books and nascent arguer of interpretive points, the would-be leader of a congregation, went to work in an undershirt factory. Shortly afterward, his father—our great-grandfather Eliahu—died of a heart attack. Eliahu was in his midfifties when he died. He never got to see his younger son save enough money to own his own grocery store or marry an émigrée from Bialystok named Kate Tatarsky and open his own live Kosher poultry market.

Like Eliahu, grandfather Philip's life was short and his end sudden. A diabetic, he died of a heart attack in his eldest daughter's arms in 1939. He was fifty-nine. And like those of the two generations before him, our own father's life, also etched with diabetes, ended suddenly at fifty-three.

It is easy to look at this pattern and conclude that our destiny is to die young of the complications of diabetes and perhaps heart disease. It is fate, Kismet. The three generations of fathers we know about all apparently did so. Whether due to evolutionary biology's maladaptive changes or to long-standing genetic tendencies, we are genetic patsies and there is not much we can do.

In essence, this was my brother's view. He ate wildly, almost contemptuously, in the face of his inheritance. He smoked to the same rhythm, often four packs of cigarettes a day. Aggressively sedentary, he was an accomplished napper, a spectator and kibitzer of fine style and volume. He was resigned to the inevitability of early death and chose to live high while he lived. In a sense, he converted; he joined the enemy.

My own view was the exact opposite. I dieted fanatically, buying ever more sensitive bathroom scales and kitchen scales, measuring and apportioning nearly everything I took in, keeping elaborate diaries of my running with details added of sleep and weight and estimated calories burned. Never smoked, logged nearly twenty-five hundred miles of running a year, ate all the miracle foods from oat bran to salmon to Egg Beaters omelettes, and took all the supplements. I worried and wrote poems about dying young and had a will drawn up before I had anything of value to leave behind. I also thought I was managing stress, having developed all those outlets for it, but of course was so intense about this that it made my brother laugh.

There was something romantic about the assumption of being marked for an early end. Like Mickey Mantle, our hero when we were growing up, or like settlers beyond the Pale who hear Cossacks in every shift of the wind, my brother and I felt shadowed by mortality. Philip, adopting the Mantle method, went for broke, living it up in the terms that made most sense to him; I became something of a genetic ascetic, denying nearly everything that my brother emphasized. He was a hellion and I was a good boy. We were, as ever, quite a team.

But the truth of the matter is that genetic tendencies toward diabetes, heart disease, and obesity, however evolved, are not necessarily death sentences. Geneticist Steve Jones writes in *The Language of Genes* that "a harmful gene can sometimes become obvious only when the environment changes." Both Philip and I have a genetic predisposition to diabetes, but it is not a genetic sentence to the disease unless we create the right environment for the harmful gene to flourish.

According to *The Merck Manual,* 80 to 90 percent of the people with type II diabetes mellitus, the common adult-onset, non–insulin dependent form of the disease that my brother developed, are obese. In these cases, the body still produces insulin—the hormone responsible for absorption of glucose into cells for energy production—but in insufficient amounts to meet the body's needs, especially when the body is overweight. Not only is it possible to prevent, or at least to delay, the onset of diabetes, but the disease can be controlled through careful management of diet, exercise, and the use of drugs. My brother did none of these things, either before or after diabetes began to change his life.

I remember visiting Philip in Fremont, California, in 1984. He took me on a sightseeing tour of the area, driving up into the hills of Alameda County and the Sunoi Regional Wilderness, weaving all over the road in his struggle with fading eyesight. After dinner at his favorite restaurant, which included a double order of zabaglione—a beaten egg yolk, sugar, and liqueur concoction—for dessert, he insisted on driving home. Suddenly, he pulled onto the shoulder of the highway, sighed, and just made it over to the passenger seat before falling into a sleep that approached coma.

In 1991, Philip flew up to visit me in Portland, Oregon. He was the last to emerge from the plane, and I was glad he could not see my reaction. He was gray haired and his teeth, which had steadily begun to spread into gaps, were now a gleaming row of ill-fitting chompers that distorted his mouth. His eyeglasses where thick and sturdy as mugs, with a special insert in the right lens for magnification. Only his right eye had vision, but he obviously could not see well enough to walk with confidence and held his arms poised in front of his chest like a wrestler. He was hungry after the flight and wanted to stop for a sweet roll before we left the airport.

The last meal we ate together in a restaurant, in early spring of 1997, culminated in Philip's ordering baked Alaska. He had not liked his appetizer of raw clams, nor his shrimp cocktail, and had not been able to finish his salmon. Wheelchair tucked under the table's edge, he signaled for the waitress all throughout the meal, wanting dessert before our entrées had arrived, lost in time, and unaware that we had been seated for just twenty minutes. He could not get enough water, though he was not supposed to drink much in the days between dialysis. He was edgy, unable to listen to conversation, and his usual smile was gone. I knew that we were seeing the end of Philip's journey, when even a fine meal could no longer please him. Only when his dessert arrived did he settle down, and when it was done he smiled in turn at each of us.

One Monday evening in the fall of 1958, my brother announced that he wanted to audition for a local theater production of *Kismet* on Thursday. "What else am I going to do?" he asked.

He figured he would play Hajj the poet-beggar and get to sing "Fate!" in his rich baritone. *What fate, what fate is mine?* Hajj had easy songs to put over on an audience, Philip thought, songs that took acting talent rather than operatic pipes. It would be a cinch. Or maybe he would play the Caliph, lighten up the voice a little so he could be the beau and croon the great love songs like "Stranger in Paradise."

We had moved from Brooklyn to Long Island the year before, following his high school graduation, and Philip knew no one in the town where we lived. Stranded, he said, just like Hajj. So it would be method acting. Being in the play might be a good way to make friends, to meet girls. Especially girls, since he was spending all his free time now driving to and from Brooklyn for dates and was too tired to get up for work in the mornings.

At nineteen, he was finished with his half-hearted attempt at college, where playing intramural football had gradually become his major. Employed in the Manhattan garment district, he was learning the children's dress business from our mother's Uncle Sam, who owned Youngland. Philip wanted to sell but had to begin by sweeping floors. He hated it. He would drive into the city from our new Long Island home every morning at 7:00, leaving a half hour after our father, who worked only a few blocks from Young-land. They would arrive back home in their separate cars at nearly the same time, ravenous for dinner, but would never commute together, for reasons they seemed to agree upon without ever having to talk about them. After dinner, there was nothing for him to do but sit around the house and bicker with our parents or play endless games of Careers with me. He hated that too.

I was eleven and my job for Wednesday afternoon was to prepare Philip's audition song for him. He was not supposed to sing anything from *Kismet* and had chosen Tennessee Ernie Ford's hit from three years earlier, "Sixteen Tons." I had to listen to the record and write down the lyrics. And they had better be perfect, even if I had to listen to it a thousand and one times. *Some people say a man is made out of mud. A poor man's made out of muscle and blood.*

"What's this?" he asked on Wednesday night, when I handed him the page of lyrics. Certain lines had a heavy *X* in the margin.

"Snaps. You have to snap your fingers there when you sing."

He shook his head. "I'll do the snapless version. You never see an Arab snap his fingers when he sings."

Kismet, which opened on Broadway in December 1953, has an unusual pedigree. Basing a musical's book on an existing novel or play was a Broadway tradition—the Gershwins did it with *Porgy and Bess,* Rodgers and Hammerstein did it with *Carousel* and *South Pacific.* The script of *Kismet* is based on a popular World War I–era play by Edward Knoblock, set in Baghdad, that used the grandeur of the Arabian Nights as background for romance between a beggar's daughter and noble Caliph despite the machinations of the Wazir. But unlike the great musicals of the period, the score of *Kismet* was completely unoriginal. Its music actually came from mid-nineteenth-century Russia, composed there by a chemist and professor of medicine named Alexander Borodin. Its lyrics, however, were written nearly a century later by two Americans, Robert Wright and George Forrest, who made a theatrical career out of putting words to the melodies of dead composers. They had already turned Edvard Grieg's music into *The Song of Norway,* Sergei Rachmaninoff's into *Arya,* and Victor Herbert's into *Gypsy Lady,* so their formula was well tested. In *Kismet,* they applied lyrics to Borodin's *Polovtsian Dances* for "Stranger in Paradise," "He's in Love," and "Not Since Ninevah." They used a love duet from the opera *Prince Igor* for "The Olive Tree" and another melody from earlier in that opera to create "Rhymes Have I." The notturno of Borodin's String Quartet No. 2 in D major was used for "And This Is My Beloved," and a theme from elsewhere in the quartet gave them "Was I Wazir." Symphony No. 1 yielded "Gesticulate," Symphony No. 2 produced "Fate," and *In the Steppes of Central Asia* turned into "Sands of Time." Listening to a recording of Borodin is like listening to Wright and Forrest's overture. At a Portland Chamber Orchestra performance of the D Major Quartet, I drew angry stares for singing along with the notturno.

Clearly, *Kismet* is a classic of adaptation. Taking the genetic code of Borodin's music, grafting it onto an ancient Middle Eastern fable, and writing fresh lyrics, Wright and Forrest did something wholly new with what they were given. They created an alternative destiny, a new life out of Borodin's material, giving it quintessentially American features. Fittingly, the winner of Broadway's Tony Award in 1953 for excellence in musical composition was Alexander Borodin, who had died in 1887.

Philip's audition for *Kismet* was a success in the sense that he got a part in the production. But he was cast as the Wazir and had only one song to sing. He would be going to rehearsals every night for two months just to sing one song! I knew he would hate that and thought it was my fault.

But I was wrong. He reveled in the cruelty of the character, the wicked minister of state who dismembered suspects arm by arm and ear by ear and joint by joint, who sealed an embezzling tax collector in a pot of glue and hung seven hundred men "by their fuzz" in a prison pen. *Was I Wazir? I was!* Philip played the Wazir as a Cossack, modeling the role on those stories we had grown up with, tales of vicious torturers who preyed on Jews. I read him his cues in our living room and saw how hard he worked. Eyes bulging and fists clenched like our mother's when she was angry, voice going flat like our father's when he was about to erupt, he used everything he knew. In performance, he was riveting; with his sinister and musical laugh, his relish in delivering the song, even in his death by drowning, he stole the show. *I hacked and hatcheted and cleft until no one but me is left!*

Kismet has an underlying motif of sensory confusion, of difficulty in figuring out how to read the signs. "Fate," Hajj sings, "can be the trap in your path." It can "weave the evil and good in one design." *Is it good? Is it ill? Am I blessed, am I cursed? Is it honey on my tongue or brine? What fate what fate is mine?*

I cannot listen to the soundtrack without chills. It speaks to something so deep within me, a mix of fraternal memories and fears and pride that seem never to have released their hold. I also hear in the exotic music and backstory a theme that has dominated our lives: the mysteries of fate, of kismet, as played out in the blood. My brother and I share a legacy of bad genes and confusion over what to do about them.

I have never forgotten a childhood dream about my brother. It probably occurred in 1953, when I was six, since I woke up in the room we shared in our Brooklyn apartment. I got out of bed and went across the room to his, carefully leaning over his body to determine whether he was still there and still alive.

The dream was set in that room, which was four stories up above the building's enclosed courtyard and looked down a brick alcove onto the space where we played stickball. My brother, glasses off, dressed in an undershirt and pajama pants, was clinging to the window ledge. He was calling to me. I tried to get out of bed, but the covers were too heavy. Just as he lost his grip, I managed to squirm free and run to the window. But the air was thick, like the ocean at Long Beach, where we went on hot spring afternoons, and I could not move fast enough. He began to drift away, floating like a feather rather than plummeting to the courtyard. His right hand still reached for me; his eyes were fixed on mine. He was silent, all his hopes grappled to my outstretched arms that could do nothing for him.

Beverly and I began visiting Philip regularly in 1995. Every three months, we would fly to San Jose on a Thursday afternoon and stay until early Monday morning. It was the end game. We all knew that, but since he never spoke about being terminally ill, we only discussed such matters out of his hearing.

At first, he would be sitting in his wheelchair at the gate to greet us, duded up in shades and windbreaker, head tilted back to hear what Elaine whispered as she bent over the chair's back with her hands on the grips. He loved to hug Beverly, this tall and willowy blonde sister-in-law of his that he had never actually seen but clearly approved of. We would head for the baggage claim together, me with my cane and Philip being pushed in his chair, and he would lay out the weekend's plans for where we'd eat each night.

A rhythm developed through the next two years. Thursday evening we would dine at a vegetarian restaurant in San Jose, in honor of Beverly's preferences, and Philip would joke about his passion for bok choy. I had never known him to compromise when it came to food, but he was elegant in his consideration now. On Friday we would drive him to dialysis in the morning, dropping him off at 9:00 and returning at 1:00. Then we would bring him home, keep him company as he ate a sandwich and napped until the food programs came on television at 4:00. We prepared dinner on Fridays, since Elaine worked all day. Saturdays were for rest and then dinner at fancy restaurants in San Francisco; Sundays were for dinner with their two grown children.

Gradually, time fell apart. Philip was no longer able to meet us at the gate, waiting instead in the car while we got our baggage. We began eating in restaurants closer to their apartment on Thursdays and then, by mid-1997, went straight home and ordered take-out dinners. Friday, his stays at the dialysis center got shorter, until at last he was there for less than an hour, gradually diminishing his treatments and growing ever sicker as the toxins normally removed by dialysis built up. After being hooked to the machine through an in-dwelling catheter directly above his heart, Philip would doze for a few minutes. Awake, he could not remember how long ago he had arrived but believed that he had to get home immediately. Neither the attendants nor the nurses nor the doctors nor I could convince him that he had been there only a half hour. He slept for six hours afterward instead of three and could not eat the dinners we prepared. On Saturdays, he could not venture out for the trips to Monterrey or to San Francisco, as before, and on Sundays he could barely stay awake during the family visits. He talked less and less.

Then over dinner the last Friday we saw him, Philip spoke about being okay with death, about having a good life, and stuck his hand in the butter. He was surrounded by pill bottles and the apparatus for injecting himself in the abdomen with insulin. He was surrounded by cookies. He was surrounded by family and love. He was surrounded.

One morning in September 1997, about two months after my brother died, I was sitting on the living room couch, listening to music. It was just after breakfast. Across the room was the collage of photographs I had assembled on the weekend he died. One showed my brother, aged eight, holding me in his arms shortly after I was born. He is dressed in an undershirt and striped pajama pants, sitting on the edge of his bed, and has unwrapped me like a gift. My discarded blankets lie next to him. Not quite smiling, hunched there in a room crowded by the crib crammed against the wall behind him, Philip looks confused but resigned. *Am I blessed? Am I cursed?* In a second photograph, I stand between him and our cousin Phyllis, both squatting before a parking lot fence through which the rear ends of late-1940s Oldsmobiles and Chevrolets can be seen. Philip is displaying a white windup-toy dog to the camera, obviously something just given to me, and Phyllis holds a plastic dog bone. They are both smiling and I have the same resigned, confused look on my two-year-old's face that Philip had in the earlier photo. The final image was taken a half year ago, after our last restaurant meal with Philip. He is at the head of the table, his wife beside him with her hand clasped in his, and a single red tulip juts from its vase, tilted toward them as though drawn to their warmth. I am next to Elaine, looking across the table at my wife. We are all smiling. We seem almost giddy at being together. There is nothing held back and there are no questions in the air. His expression says *I've had a good life.*

As the sun rose just high enough above the oaks to shine into our windows, the notturno from Alexander Borodin's D Major Quartet began. Its exquisite, tender theme—the movement essentially has only one theme, repeated and varied among the strings for eight minutes—was announced by the cello and floated across the air. For the first time since my brother died, I began to cry and could not stop until the music ended.

My brother had been dying for so long that I had time to prepare myself. As his physical presence dwindled, memories of him loomed everywhere. The transition to holding onto him as pure memory was relatively simple. But somewhere along the way, I had skipped a step, held my grief in and instead built a shrine to my brother's dogged destiny.

Now I see it all tinged with regret, even anger, because his death was unnecessary. Through the years of excess, he could be provoked to fury by any suggestion that he temper his behavior; at the end, he acknowledged his mistakes and worried about the fate of his son, whose habits are a direct copy of Philip's. The riddle of *Kismet* remained unsolved for my brother. The honey on his tongue was in fact brine, and what he construed as good was ill. He sought to embrace in life the very things that would kill him. That, rather than the more mundane genetic inheritance or the facts of renal failure, is the real end of the story.

"For he counteracts the powers of darkness
by his electrical skin & glaring eyes."

Christopher Smart, *My Cat Jeoffry*

12

Counteracting the Powers of Darkness

Whenever my mother spoke of me as an infant, her story began the same way: "He was born with impetigo." She said this with a wrinkling of the nose and shake of the head, eyes closing against the awful vision. "Blisters!" she would whisper, still shocked at the memory, "Rings of them all over his inner thigh. A contaminated baby. Can you imagine?"

My childhood was marked for her from the very outset by filth. "It took weeks to get him cleaned up." Of course, the fact that a fetus contracts impetigo's staphylococcus bacterium from its mother was never considered relevant. All that mattered was that I emerged polluted by germs and was permanently tainted in her eyes, one more agent of the powers of darkness.

It would be difficult to overstate my mother's loathing of stain, grime, infection, disease, or any other manifestation of what she considered Dirt. She was hyperconscious of the stigma associated with uncleanliness and its echoes of the ghetto, of the lower classes. Her fear of pestilence was like a tormenting memory of epidemics and quarantines that she never actually endured. Maybe it was a genetic inheritance, since nowadays so many oddball behaviors are viewed as gene induced. For sure, the sight or stench of rot was her living nightmare. She let everyone know she was an Uptown woman, born and raised on the opposite end of Manhattan from all those typhus-and-cholera-ridden former Old World shtetl dwellers like my father's people.

Sepsis had replaced Cossacks and Nazis in her imagination of terror. Soiled hands, spilled drinks, crumbs, dust, sand, even outside air were all potential miasmic hazards, capable of breeding affliction. My mother could be reduced to tears by the sight of fingerprints on the walls or a drip of gravy on her tablecloth. She despised leftovers. Any food that might disguise contamination was distrusted—stews, chowders, casseroles. One of her commonest utterances was the world *vile!* stretched out to the length of a full sentence. "That place?" she would say, referring to a neighbor's unkempt apartment. "Vile!" Playing outside, I was not supposed to perspire or accept drinks from my vile friends or pick things off the ground. I kept my hands to myself. The greatest threat was The Unseen. Our apartments required constant vigilance. I was not allowed to bring playmates home, or to take more than one item from my toy chest at a time, or to enter the living room unless my mother was present. If I wanted something to eat, I asked for it, barred from opening the refrigerator until I was an unstoppable adolescent. Windows stayed shut and locked, especially in summer, which was polio season. Once, when I returned from the hospital with my broken fibula in a cast, she kept me standing outside the door until all the loose plaster had been brushed away. Though she lived for forty years within walking distance of the beach, my mother never set foot on the sand because of what might lurk there and how tenaciously it clung to the toes. Like the Sanitation Police of 1890s New York City, she exercised absolute authority over contagion in her domain. She kept dust cloths tucked into the pockets of her housecoat and carried her feather duster like a billy club from room to room. No one was permitted to eat anywhere but at the kitchen table or to touch anything after coming indoors until the washing ritual was complete.

My brother and I learned to scrub up like surgeons before every meal. We mastered the intricacies of a sterile field even before we learned to read. The great trick was to wash the backs of our hands as intensely as the fronts, fingertips to forearms, while leaving the bathroom spotless. Not a simple task for toddlers.

After washing, we went through two tableside inspections—one for the initial wash, one for the automatic rewash—before our mother allowed us to eat. Once, as a test, I turned on the faucet but did not stick my hands under the water during a second round of washing, and when I passed inspection it was impossible not to reveal my ruse. That cost me dinner and a week's worth of TV.

My mother viewed my father's trade as profaned by Dirt. Her ongoing contempt for him was, I think, grounded in disgust over his work, his defiled labors at the chicken market. She saw him as, well, befouled. My father's nails were always caked with dried blood, stained beyond the quick, and it was not unusual to find stray feathers somewhere on his person. He smelled, beneath the currents of Old Spice, like day-old sawdust and raw gizzards. In one of my earliest memories, he comes home from work and marches past me into the bathroom, where I hear the water running in the sink and do not see him again until the next morning. I must have fallen asleep before he came out for dinner, but it feels more accurate to remember him washing up through the entire night.

It is hardly surprising that I did not have a pet when I was a child. Well, once, for about seventeen hours. On a Sunday afternoon in early summer, my father bought me a chameleon at Ebbets Field. He did not actually intend to get me a chameleon, but between games of a Dodgers-Giants doubleheader he gave me some money to buy whatever I wanted at the concession stand near our seats. Holy smokes, I was free to wander! I strolled past hats and wall pennants, baseballs, yearbooks, food vendors, and froze when I saw the cart where a man was selling real live lizards. The man saw the look on my face and smiled, beckoning me over with his finger. Not only was I a dinosaur freak, I was also tired of sleeping with a beat-up old hand puppet that I kept under my pillow. At seven, even I knew I was too old for that. I knew what these little cuties were: chameleons were masters of disguise, ideally suited for camouflage in the face of danger, which more or less made them cousins to me. *Whatever you want, buddy.*

I placed the chameleon's box under my seat for safekeeping and my father never noticed it. He was busy working to open a miniature bottle of whiskey with a penknife, tongue protruding from the corner of his mouth, and then Game Two began. I remember him using a rolled-up program like a megaphone to cheer when Duke Snider hit a home run onto Bedford Avenue. I picked it up at the end of the game to save for my collection and saw that it was stained with tobacco. Dirt! I could not decide whether the risk of bringing the ruined program into my mother's domain was worth the pleasure of adding it to my collection, especially since I was already loaded with contraband. What the hell, the program might distract her; I added it to my haul. When we left the stadium, my father draped his arm across my shoulders and never asked what I was carrying.

The instant we crossed the threshold of our apartment, my mother said, "What's that?"

My father brushed past without registering her question. But I halted like a spotlit criminal. The program was now jutting out of my jacket pocket and I held the box in both hands, staring at the holes in its top. Guilty, two counts. The chameleon moved and both my mother and I noticed the box shift in my hands. I wondered if the chameleon had turned all white against his white walls. At the moment, as I stood before the gleaming white apartment door, that sounded like a brilliant move.

"Just a chameleon," I said.

My mother screamed as though she'd been attacked. "Just a chameleon! Oh my God!"

She put her fist in her mouth and ran into the bedroom, slammed the door, and began shouting at my father. "How could you do this to me? Just a chameleon!" She turned the water on full force and began to scrub her hands. "Vileness! Why not a rat! A cobra that spits in your eye!"

I was sent to bed without dinner, which was all right because I'd eaten well at the ballpark, and without my chameleon, which I hadn't yet named but was thinking of calling "Rainbow." The closed box was placed atop newspaper on the kitchen floor, in a corner beneath the window, with the understanding that tomorrow I would either give it to a friend, release the chameleon in the nearby vacant lot opposite King's County Hospital, or flush it down the toilet.

But in the morning, the chameleon was gone. At first I suspected that my mother had thrown the box down the incinerator after I had fallen asleep, except that she was in a panic herself, searching the apartment, threatening divorce, threatening to have me locked away at King's County, where evil children were kept in darkened rooms beside murderers without food or water until they reached the age of twenty-one.

We found the chameleon during a delayed breakfast, after the room-to-room search failed to turn it up. A peculiar smell began to emerge from the toaster as we sat in silence. When I looked inside, the chameleon was black even though the toaster itself was shiny silver. Adaptability apparently had its limits.

In 1953, when I was six, baseball cards became my most vivid companions. I did not collect them in the sense of assembling a complete set, or keeping them in the order of numbers printed on their backs, or using checklists to ensure that I had every card issued. These were not at all like stamps or coins to me; they lived. I did not risk losing them to friends in flipping contests and I certainly did not keep them in pristine condition. I had fun with them the way my friends frolicked with their pets, down on the floor, talking to them, gazing at their faces, using them as playmates.

I teased Dodgers catcher Roy Campanella about the way he wore his hat, but secretly smashed and folded my own Dodgers hat until the crown resembled Campy's. I asked Pirates pitcher Paul La Palme if his teammates ever called him Paula, chatted with Phillies pitcher Ken Heintzelman to find out why he looked so depressed, and practiced the unsmiling glare of Yankees first baseman Joe Collins. I liked to sniff the cards, which held a scent of bubble gum from their packaging, and sometimes stood the cards in a line against a wall with a gap left in the middle of the group, where I would place a photograph of myself carefully trimmed to match the size of the cards. Just one of the guys, Dodgers shortstop Floyd "Scooter" Skloot, born July 6, 1947.

I grouped my cards by teams, each team housed in double rubber bands with the catcher on top and pitchers on bottom, and stored them in a set of my father's old cigar boxes. I traded cards with friends solely to assemble a particular team's starting lineup. Pitchers were expendable and it made no difference to me whether a card was rare or a player was a star; if I needed George Crowe to complete the Boston Braves infield, I would gladly trade away an extra Cleveland Indians pitcher like Bob Feller even if his card was more "valuable" because he was great. Then, when I had a complete team, at least one player for each position, and had memorized the statistics on the back of each card, I would play my invented games on the carpet of whatever room I found myself hiding in. Cards arrayed in the classic diamond shape of the infield and arc of the outfield, I lost myself in the world of imagination, living out a game of my own devising.

Penny baseball was, for me, both too dull and too random. My brother had showed me how to use a penny as the ball and a pencil as the bat, swatting the penny and seeing whether it landed close enough to a fielder's card for him to "catch" it. But no matter how I tried to rig the results, a penny could roll anywhere. A slugger might dribble silly ground balls that got snagged in the shag carpeting, while the weakest hitting shortstop socked one off a bedroom wall. I already had enough of the random in my life.

Instead, abandoning props, I held a batter's card upright and would envision the pitcher winding up and delivering, then twitched the card to imitate a swing, made the sound of a ball cracking against the bat, and played out the results, moving my batter down the baseline, leaping across the carpet to a fielder who was chasing the ball, all the while announcing the action. There was no plan of how a game would unfold, just intuitive responses to the players' looks and needs, to the dynamics of the moment. This was not a game of chance but a game of dreams. A coherent world, incorporating chance and destiny, under my total control. A full nine innings could take two or three hours easily, especially as I got older and began keeping box scores and statistics. I used a composition book to record each player's performance, accumulating a season's worth of statistics, making notes of spectacular moments such as the time Mickey Mantle hit a home run clear out of the bedroom and into the distant foyer. My game of dreams was safe and relatively clean, even if it did take place on the apartment floor, and I had the records to prove it existed. Everything was calm here. No one got sick or hurt, no one endured a prolonged slump, no one was traded. They all got to play and eventually thrive; I unconsciously saw to that.

Despite my mother's efforts, I was a sickly boy, my childhood garlanded with a daisy chain of tonsillitis, ear infections, colds, asthma, measles, recurrent mononucleosis. By the age of ten, I had developed a seasoned terror of delirium that equaled my mother's response to Dirt. I missed school in great chunks. Then, as an adolescent, I broke the leg, the wrist, the rib; was knocked unconscious, scalded by coffee grounds, run over by a Packard, nearly drowned in a canal, bitten by a dog, stung on the eyelid by a bee.

My illnesses and injuries enraged and terrified my mother. She once removed a thermometer from my mouth, studied its findings, muttered "103.6" and slapped me across the face. I was the only child I knew who got punished for being sick, put to bed without television or books or even baseball cards, denied dinner and a goodnight kiss.

It was all very confusing. Being ill or hurt seemed just other forms of being bad, being contaminated, something I should be able to control but could not. I felt guilty, soiled, helpless.

I remember having one dream repeatedly. Dressed in my pale blue one-piece pajamas that made me look like a miniature Lone Ranger, I would descend a staircase into a roaring subway station.

The trains flashed by and I entered a car by simply passing through its skin like a germ. Though the exterior had seemed spotless and gleaming, inside the cars were filthy. I stood there swaying, unwilling to grab a pole for balance. I had no idea where I was headed, but in the flickering glow that came through the train windows I watched myself slowly dissolving, losing more and more of my body with each strobe of light. My hands, my arms, my feet. The conductor spoke over the loudspeaker in a voice I recognized as my mother's, shrieking the same message over and over: "YOU ARE ON THE WRONG TRAIN YOU ARE ON THE WRONG TRAIN."

In 1954, when it was announced that we would receive polio vaccinations in the school gymnasium, I was astonished to see my mother sign the permission slip. She was actually agreeing to let them inject me with polio germs! The whole thing made no sense to me, no matter how often the concept of immunization was explained. I knew a trick when I saw one. Lining up with my classmates, I knew exactly what to do. It was easy to slip out of line and drift over to the nurse.

"Did you get stuck yet?" she asked. Aha!

I nodded, eyes filling with tears at the very thought. She slapped a Band-Aid on my left arm and I went back to class.

Within an hour, the principal came into our room. He carried a vial in one hand, looking grim, and whispered to the teacher before turning to glare at us. "Did anyone here miss his vaccination?"

I looked out the window. The light seemed to flicker. The principal left.

About six months later, our neighbor's teenaged son contracted polio. My parents shook their heads as they discussed this over dinner and said how glad they were that I had gotten vaccinated. Children were at the greatest risk, and if a child got sick then his parents were at risk. The next morning, I confessed.

The whole family had to go to the doctor's office for gamma globulin injections. I was made to watch as first my father, then my brother bared their buttocks for shots. Because he was so large, my brother had to lie there while the doctor unscrewed the syringe and screwed on another. The stubby needle top jutted from his flesh.

In the 1950s, we did not have Nature in Brooklyn. With the exception of Prospect Park and Botanical Gardens, which my mother would not visit, it was as though the city itself had enacted her dirt-free policies. At least that is the way I recall things.

My core memories of childhood contain nothing but concrete, brick, cement, steel. Brooklyn is surrounded by the water, jutting into the Atlantic at Coney Island, bordered by the Upper and Lower New York Bays to the west and Jamaica Bay to the east, separated from Manhattan by the East River. Brooklyn had beaches, which had sand, which got tracked into houses laden with vileness. No, for us the borough was so densely urban that the notion of "land" or "sea" never arose. Earth was the name of the planet, not the surface of the world; soil, like dirt, was a bad thing.

Though I cannot picture them, there were a few trees in front of our apartment building. There they are in a wrinkled snapshot, confined within a low brick wall crowned by cement that extrudes iron spikes in one neat row like a hedge. The "backyard" was a small concrete plaza enfolded within the building's wings. The building itself, which took up half a block, loomed over everything, our downtown mountain. When I looked straight up at clouds, I would see the exotic urban flora of fire escapes, a network of aerials and exhaust turbans at the roof's edge. Across the street, where the State University of New York Health Sciences Center is now located, there was a vacant lot strewn with rubble that seemed to me to be our forest. I sliced open my knee playing war games there with friends and knew I must not go inside until the bleeding stopped, must hide the wound though it needed a stitch and left an inch-long scar.

Our family seldom traveled together outside the city. Brooklyn, Manhattan, Queens, and the Bronx were the borders of our world. When a cousin moved to King's Point on Long Island, barely outside the New York City limits, our visits there seemed like foreign vacations.

There was one wildly exotic trip to Washington DC, and Silver Springs, Maryland, where my father's cousin Bert lived. En route, my father was ticketed for speeding in Delaware, which seemed to sour him on further exploration. The eight millimeter films he shot to commemorate this trip were all double exposed, as though such travel were indeed a ghostly illusion, a trick of memory, and life really took place only in the familiar city. We stayed put behind the double-locked doors of our apartment fortress. We had paintings and statues instead of houseplants, china with images of vines painted on it, candy bowls in the shape of shells or leaves, gelatins molded to look like flowers.

It is true that, when I was an infant, we did go to the beach at least once. There is a photograph in which my mother is holding me up, face toward the camera, with her arms stretched to their fullest in front of her body so that I dangle out there like a load of trash. I may have been sandy, or soiled my massive diapers, or had a runny nose. Clearly I was not cuddly at the moment and was being exhibited before the camera like a dangerous substance. Avoid close exposure to this creature. I do not appear happy; my face looks like the face of a fifty-year-old grouch.

My only experience of the natural world occurred when I was sent to sleep-away camp for eight weeks every summer. From 1951, when I turned four, until 1962, when I turned fifteen, I was shipped north to the Pennsylvania mountains, the New Hampshire woods, or rural upstate New York accompanied by my brother and cousins, and was visited one weekend each summer by my parents. These were grand lakeside adventures, surrounded by forests and mountains, and they only underscored the fact that Nature and Home were essentially separate worlds.

Now, of course, my home is in the woods. Holed up here with Beverly and our three cats, I am nearly as far from my childhood home as it is possible to be while still living in "the Lower Forty-eight."

The nearest town has a smaller population than the block I grew up on in Brooklyn. Its principal commerce is four antique shops that change ownership annually; to buy groceries or get a haircut or do our banking we drive a dozen miles north. I am in the middle of nowhere. Nature, with its inevitable Dirt, encroaches continually here, the forest eager to reclaim this tiny clearing for itself, and the nights teem with insects, birds, rodents, amphibians, and sneaky mammalian life.

A few years before we got together, Beverly had built this small round house in the center of twenty hilly acres of rock-strewn basaltic land. It is an hour west of Portland and an hour east of the Pacific coast, in wine country, and we are officially Tree Farmers, with mostly second-growth oak, maple, and fir, with some wild cherry, cedar, and one skimpy madrona that we transplanted ourselves from beside the road.

The property is overrun with poison oak and wild blackberries whose slender early summer blossoms litter the driveway now with petals and the promise of a good August harvest. There is wild rose, hazelnut. Earlier this week, looking out our dining room window while sitting down to dinner, I saw a mother skunk with her four kits shuffle past the compost heap. Bees batter the screens all day, working hard at the hyssop and rosemary. I routinely share the grounds, and sometimes the house, with mice, voles, moles, rats, frogs, lizards, snakes, and squirrels. During the middle of the night, several years ago, a bat came into our bedroom through the cat door.

In short, I am living in a place that embodies my mother's worst nightmare. It also confronts me with childhood terrors I caught from her like that case of impetigo. She can hardly bear to hear me describe the life I lead, interrupting my accounts to ask "But can you get *The Tonight Show?*" or "How do you keep the place clean?"

The dark is darker here, but the light is lighter, and I think that combination is what draws me most powerfully. Country life is supposed to be quiet, and sometimes is, but it is also loud with life, a Brooklyn of insect and animal life. It is impossible to control. I am isolated and exposed but feel completely safe.

Daily life reminds me again that the powers of darkness are different for everyone. That is what makes them so sinister, so elusive. We must all learn to fend for ourselves, condemned to go solo against our own demons. To put it another way, no one's darkness can truly be shared and no one's light works in someone else's darkness.

When I got sick in 1988, it seemed at first to be almost too exquisitely ironic. Of course someone from my background would eventually be faced with a kind of Ultimate Dirt, a viral predator. Even the random can seem poetic, or at least ironic.

While Beverly, a social worker, spends her days assisting the elderly, the dying, and the temporary residents of a psychiatric hospital unit, I am here under the protection of three cats. Cats, I have come to learn, can be our allies in the fight against the powers of darkness. The electrical skin and glaring eyes that Christopher Smart, writing from the madhouse, spoke of in his poem about Jeoffry the Cat are certainly part of the arsenal. We all need electrical skin and a good glare. That sensuous alertness and fullness with which my cats move around the property demonstrates the integrity of a life lived directly. As Smart says later in his poem, a cat "counteracts the Devil, who is Death, by brisking about the life." Bursting from stillness after prey, leaping up trees in exuberance, adding the occasional banshee howl to the act, my cats defiantly brisk about the life. Then they sleep. Theirs is life as haiku, utterly simplified in form yet resonant with implications.

But the work of these cats is not simply in the expression of feline energy as a corrective to my own limitations. Yes, I knew I must simplify my life and I did. But I also had to learn what was within my powers as a person irretrievably altered by brain damage. My mother, it seems, was essentially right to believe in the threat of the unseen, though her tactics of vigilance and will were largely futile. After getting sick, I had my subway dream again for the first time in over thirty years, but the voice over the loudspeaker was garbled.

Since moving here the dream has not returned and I have never felt more certain that I am on the right train.

My ability to protect myself—not only against a virus but against the ensuing failures of normal daily function—has been compromised to the point where I seldom leave home. It would be easy to surrender to the powers of darkness. But cats are resourceful in making certain that we face up to our worst fears, which is the surest way to counteract them.

The answer to my mother's question about how we keep the house clean is *we do not.* Cats, famous for personal cleanliness, their finicky licking of themselves and each other, track in all sorts of Dirt, bringing dried fir needles, twigs, bark dust, mud, deadlife. This, however, is our dirt, not theirs. When they greet us, our cats roll in the dirt, dusting their sleek, dark coats a dull gray. When they vomit, they are careful to do so on the carpet or bed before exiting through the cat door. Their work is rich with symbolism, tapping into my dream matter to bring the imagery of my unconscious to light. Last winter, I woke up from a nap, sat at the edge of the bed, and reached for my shorts only to find a live garter snake coiled in the crotch. Early this spring, in the deep middle of the night, we were awakened by the sort of scream that makers of horror flicks covet. Something flitted across our bed and upstairs, where we heard a sound like a modest square dance. One of the cats had brought in a live rabbit and released it near the sofa; by the time we got up there, the three of them, aligned in a neat triangle, had it frozen in their headlights. By now, I have learned to keep a pair of thick gloves by my bedside to catch such wildlife—a throwback to my old infielder days. We managed to save the rabbit, at least temporarily, and set it free in the woods. On the way back inside, I looked up and realized that the night was aglow. Far from city lights, high on a hill under an almost full moon, I saw the sky as a dazzle of stars and clouds and had no trouble finding my way home.

13

What Is This and What Do I Do with It?

The dream is just beyond reach. I remember the sea, a dune that seemed to rise forever, a windblown nimbus at its tip I thought might be God. But even that now seems wrong. Memory is close, but I cannot grasp it. The beach may have been behind my childhood island home on the east coast, except the moon had risen in the wrong place. The dream was in color, though I know the human eye does not see colors in moonlight. There was action, a narrative that brought me to the shore and turned my face toward light, but it has slipped away too, like sand through fingers, now that I am awake.

The feeling of forgetting is still eerie, even though forgetting is normal for me. I don't get used to it. The feeling seems sensory in essence, like first hint of hunger. I get memory pangs, my whole being closing around the vacancy as I try to recall an event, a name, a face, a place in time. With my memory systems as they are, simple recollection is as fluid as waking from a dream, with things that I believe to be vital vanishing as I reach for them.

I know viscerally what Harvard psychiatry professor J. Allan Hobson means when he writes in *The Chemistry of Conscious States* that "the poor memory we have of dreams once we awaken from them is similar to the memory lapses experienced by Alzheimer's patients." I live in a strange zone between the elusiveness of dream and the abyss of Alzheimer's. Nothing terrifies me quite as much as being around the demented, in whom I can see a dreaded future.

But Beverly and I are going to New York to see my ninety-year-old mother. She lives in a beachfront retirement hotel in Long Beach, off Long Island's south shore, a few blocks from the apartment building she lived in for the last three decades. A fire four years ago caused her to relocate overnight. She shed most of her hoarded belongings with astonishing willingness and embraced life in her new home, free of memorabilia and happy as long as she had a boyfriend to occupy her time. So far, she has been through three. They seem not to last long, each dying within a year from the start of the romance. Now she has settled on a much younger man, Irv, who is eighty-two.

Flying cross country always disorients me, my already tenuous relationship with time spinning further out of control, fatigue making my symptoms flare. My mother is disoriented too; by phone it has become apparent that she is slipping further into Alzheimer's fog, and she has been asking to see us. So I am going home, into the source of memory, and have asked my twenty-eight-year-old daughter to join us from Pittsburgh.

My mother is sitting in the lounge, holding hands with Irv. Irv is asleep, lulled by the voice of the activities coordinator reading the Sunday paper to a group of residents who sit with their backs to the lovebirds. My mother looks in the direction of the door, where I have just appeared as though materialized from the mists of her past.

She shows no recognition. I turn to tell my wife and daughter I have found her, then turn back to see my mother pointing toward herself and mouthing the word *Me?* I wave. She yanks Irv to his feet. They totter and steady each other, then he hands her an aluminum cane and we all meet under the lintel.

After the embraces, my mother says, "I couldn't remember what you looked like." For the first time, her eyes meet mine. "But as soon as I saw you, I knew."

We settle on the sun porch with its view of boardwalk joggers and surf. We give her the gift she has requested over and over during our phone conversations, a box of assorted Godiva truffles, and read her the card we have all signed with love. My mother tells Irv, "You can't have any of these."

"Whaaat?" he says, winking at us.

My mother scans the room and announces, "This is the happiest day of my life!"

"I'm glad we came," I say.

"What's the relationship?" Irv says. "Who are these people?"

My mother tilts her head in my direction. "This is my grandson, you stupid man."

"She's gorgeous," my mother says, gazing at Beverly. "You two should get married already."

"We are married," I say again. "Today is our seventh anniversary."

Her eyes widen. "Oh, congratulations!" Then she frowns, looks at my daughter, Becka, and says, "Seven?" I can see that we have brought her nothing but further confusion. Everyone is either too old or too young. Then I see her do something I have not seen her do before: she restrains herself. Or maybe she simply forgets.

Smiling at her granddaughter, my mother says, "She's gorgeous." Then memory comes flooding in, visible as a sudden glint of life in her good eye. "Wait a minute, this is the one with the Italian boyfriend! Quateero, right? He was here. He came to see me."

"His name's Gualtiero," Becka says. "We were here in the fall."

"I met him! Quateero. He's from Italy and he has a sister who went to Israel to do something. Teach, maybe. He's a very good-looking man." She reaches for Becka's hand and says, "You two should get married already."

"Actually," Becka says, "we're talking about that."

"Good! I'll make the centerpieces."

But the glint has gone out of her eye. Ruined by macular degeneration, my mother's vision has slowly clouded over and further encouraged her to dwell inside the chaos of her thoughts. I take her hand.

"You look great," I say, and she does. For ninety, she radiates surprising physical health despite remaining fifty pounds overweight, despite a lifetime of Chesterfields and a refusal ever to exercise.

"He has a sister in Israel. Why would an Italian girl go to Israel?"

"She went there to study," Becka says.

"He was so handsome. I remember he came to see me. We got along so well; I almost stole him from you. He has a sister who went to Italy to teach Jewish to the children there."

At that, my daughter nods and refuses to look at me or at Beverly. My mother, however, is looking from face to face. At first I think she's trying to remember where she's seen us before. Or perhaps just struggling to bring someone, anyone, into focus. Then I see she is pursing and smoothing her lips, a gesture I remember from childhood; she is trying to figure something out.

"Why don't you two get married?" she asks me. "She's gorgeous."

"We are married. Today's our seventh anniversary."

"Seven. That's nice." She looks again toward my daughter. "So where is the mother?"

I let this question resonate for a moment. "Well, Becka's mother and I got divorced."

My mother nods. "Who was she, again?"

"Betsy."

"No, I mean your first wife."

"Her name was Betsy. This is Beverly."

"And who's that?"

"Becka. She's your granddaughter."

I can see that this would be hard to follow even without her increasing symptoms of Alzheimer's disease. It's like an Abbott and Costello routine: Beverly Betsy Becka. A good thing my daughter doesn't call herself Becky.

As though picking up the knot of confusions and trying to find the magic strand, Irv asks, "What's the relationship?"

At this point, my mother is so lost that she doesn't even try to answer. She senses movement around her and sighs. "It's lunchtime."

We have been through lunch at the Manor many times in the four years since my mother moved there. So we know the drill: we must wait outside the dining room doors until everyone else is seated, then move in slow procession through the tables as my mother introduces us to everyone we have already met. I am always afraid that the residents will choke on their salads as they try to stand, speak, and chew at the same time.

Since no one remembers who we are, the entrance is always freshly received, like curtain time before a new audience, though it feels well rehearsed to us. "This is my family from Oregon." I have now made the acquaintance of Rose Gitler at least a dozen times, her face lit each time by the joy of finally meeting Lillian's son the author, and her tremulous voice affirming how much she loves my mother. We meet the waiter, the woman who used to live in the same apartment building as my mother before the fire forced them out, the activities director, the man in a Yankees cap who once tried to dance with my mother, the girls with whom my mother no longer plays cards because they're all jealous that she has Irv.

We take our seats at the special table reserved for residents with guests. Irv immediately begins issuing warnings. "Watch out for the bread, it's stale. Don't eat the cookie till the end. The salad dressing could kill you; go easy on it. Start asking for coffee now and maybe you'll get some before they clear the table." He is at his most lucid. But my mother is strangely silent, allowing him to speak an unprecedented string of sentences before interrupting him.

"Where are you staying?" she asks me.

"Brooklyn."

"Brooklyn?" she picks up her fork and puts it back down. "Why Brooklyn?"

"That's where I was born. I haven't visited in about forty years, and we thought it would be nice to see the old haunts." I was hoping that a tour of my childhood neighborhood would help trigger memories that had disappeared in the virus-frazzled wiring of my brain.

"You were born in Brooklyn?" She looks at me and frowns, her brows knitting. "I am so forgetful!"

She is poised where forgetting and the awareness of forgetting coexist. I know this to be a painful place myself, and know as well that my mother's memory is far more ravaged than my own. I pick up the tiny glass of fresh orange juice and down it like a shot of whiskey.

"Yes, at Brooklyn Jewish Hospital. In 1947."

"And who was your father?"

I open my mouth but cannot speak for a moment. Having talked to her by phone every week throughout the last year, I expected my mother's short-term memory to be fragmented. She would routinely call me back to re-ask the questions that she originally called to ask, and which I had already answered multiple times. She couldn't find the pens and pads I'd sent, couldn't remember when we said we were coming to New York or where she'd written down the information. She could not get straight the time difference between New York and Oregon and several times called me at 5:30 A.M. But at least she remembered that I had sent her pens and pads, that we were coming to visit her, that she had a son in Oregon. She seemed more amnesiac than senile. And she remembered her parents, her late brother's success in the fashion business and—with a little prodding—my daughter's name. So I believed her long-term memory might still have some integrity.

I look toward Beverly, who is a hospice social worker, then look back at my mother. "Harry was my father. You remember him, he owned the chicken market." My father's market is one of the places we intend to visit. I was astonished to learn from a friend of the family that the building still stood and was still a chicken market.

"Poultry, dear. It was a poultry business." She has a half slice of bread in her hand now, holding it above the plate. "I would never refer to it as a chicken market." She starts to put it in her lap like a napkin but then replaces it in the bread dish. "Was he your brother's father too?"

I nod. It is the first time she has mentioned my brother, who died three summers ago. This is all much more than I had bargained for, a mixture of grief and confusion and fear that has subdued both my appetite and my wits. I wonder if she has forgotten my brother's name. "He was Philip's father too, yes."

My mother shakes her head. I am not sure if she thinks I have it wrong, if she is frustrated with herself for failing to remember, if she is signaling some sort of regret, or if she is thinking about something else entirely now.

"So when were you born?"

"In 1947."

"1947! What year is this?"

"2000. I'm about to turn fifty-three."

"So am I," she says, and smiles, looking to see if Irv has heard.

So some things are still intact. This was a joke, not a glitch of memory. For a moment, I am intensely relieved by the familiar patter that used to drive me crazy.

As lunch is ending, we propose to take my mother for a Sunday drive. Does she need anything? We could go to the mall at Roosevelt Field and buy her stockings, a dress, shoes. We could go to the cemetery where her two husbands are buried, and then cross Long Island to the cemetery where her parents are buried, a trip she has requested in previous years. Is there someplace she would like to go?

She shakes her head, then points across the table to Irv. "Can he come?"

"If he wants."

"He wants." My mother is still working on her plank of red snapper, shooing the waiter away every time he checks, threatening to stab him with a fork if he dares to reach for her plate. Like most of her fellow residents, she has not risked eating her corn on the cob and has only nibbled at the succotash. The rest of us have pushed our plates aside.

My mother was always a slow eater. She used mealtimes for extended harangues, or reports to my father of improper behavior by me or my brother, or accounts of the times when she had eaten far better cuisine. Now, though she proclaims it to be excellent, she seems listless about her food. Until dessert arrives. The waiter sets a small silver cup of chocolate ice cream in everyone's cleared place but begins to carry my mother's portion away since she has again forbidden him to remove her dinner plate. In a flash, she turns left and barks, "You come back here!"

This is the voice I remember from dinners past. The tone as well. It is obviously something the waiter has also heard before. He puts the ice cream down but does not lift her dinner plate. She waves him away and beams.

We are the last to leave the dining room. At the front desk, my mother introduces us to Rose Gitler again, then sends Irv downstairs for his overcoat and hat. As we wait, I think about where to drive, since my mother says she needs nothing and wants to be sure we bring her back in time for tea at 4:00.

This outing, I know, is essentially for me, not for my mother. I cannot face the familiar routine of three hours in her room, where—over and over—we will look at her surviving collection of costume jewelry; where Beverly and then Becka will be asked to try on her mink coat, the one made for her by her father and bearing her name embossed on the lining, in case either wants to take it home; where my mother will show us the teetering pile of notes she maintains beside her phone and will search for a functioning pen, and then the cycle will begin again.

She no longer receives much mail—all her bills, checks, and tax documents are sent to me in Oregon, where I manage her affairs on-line—so the endeavor of sorting through clutter, which kept us occupied up there in years past, is no longer necessary. I took over those functions after finding twelve months' worth of unopened letters, unpaid bills, and uncashed checks on her desk the first year she was in the Manor. So for the last three years, our visits have amounted to little more than a continuously repeating floor and fashion show in her tiny room during the hours between lunch and tea. This time, I would have driven her anywhere she wanted just to avoid her room.

Irv returns. We start toward the elevator that will take us down to street level when my mother says she needs to go up to her room. It will only take a minute. I feel a sense of doom. We were so close to getting out.

Somehow, the room is even smaller than I remember. All four of her paintings hang crookedly on the wall above her bed as though rattled by an earthquake. My mother's chair faces the television and is almost flush to the screen because her sight is so poor. Becka turns it around and sits; Irv sits in his customary visitor's chair beside her and my mother perches on her bed. The only other chair is the Roosevelt Chair, a crown-topped, button-backed Hitchcock that came from FDR's summer house at Campobello and was bought at an auction to benefit polio research in 1957. We all know enough not to sit in it. Though the chair takes up a goodly percentage of the available floor space in the room, and there is nowhere for us to sit except the floor, neither Beverly nor I gives it a second thought.

Then my mother is up, headed for her closet, and holding out the heavy mink coat made for her by her father forty years ago. The women are to try it on while my mother goes to the bathroom. Then we can leave.

"Oh, and there's something I need you to do," she says to me.

On her table is the wooden plaque from Israel that I remember from my childhood. The plaque holds two stones from Mt. Sinai in form-fitting, recessed holes. Both in Hebrew and English, it is noted that these stones were brought down from the mountain in 1954. The trouble is that one stone is no longer snug in its hole, but lies on the table beside the plaque, its surface agleam with an overlay of white.

"What happened?"

"I don't know," my mother says. "The rock fell out. I put some glue on, but it won't stay."

She shuts the bathroom door behind her. I turn to Beverly, who is far more adept at repairs than I am, and she joins me by the window to study the plaque. I remember that my mother's Israeli cousin, Hannan Gayor, gave it to her as a gift. In my mother's versions over the years, Hannan has been upgraded from Brigadier General to Ambassador to United Nations Representative, though I believe he may actually have been a freelance translator after completing his compulsory military service. He had also been born in Czechoslovakia, Hungary, Austria, and Belgium. Beverly flips the rough gray stone over. The white on one side looks like paint. She sees a small bottle on the table beside the plaque. It is White-Out fluid for correcting typos, not glue. My mother has slathered the stone's face in White-Out — only God knows why she had White-Out or where she found it — and tried unsuccessfully to fit it back into the slot.

When turned to the proper side, the stone fits snugly. It stays in place without glue while the plaque is held up to her wall. But it shines a brilliant white in the sunlight coming through her window.

My mother is delighted. She allows Beverly to restore the plaque permanently to its place, then says, "Is it time for tea yet?"

"No, but we're going for a drive."

"We are?" she seems wary. "Why?"

"It'll be nice to get outside, won't it? See the sights, do something different."

"Can he come too?"

"If he wants."

I realize how important Irv is to my mother's normal, moment-to-moment functioning. They ground one another. Even if neither of them knows what day or town it is, they know their routine. They are a team. And even if she instantly forgets what he says, or he cannot tell her what part of Long Beach they are in, they talk and listen, they make their way.

Under the circumstances, the only place I can imagine to take them is to the Borders Bookstore in Westbury. To me, bookstores are a safe haven; today my need to be around books is increasing by the moment. My mother can manage only a very short walk, insists that there is nothing she needs, and just wants to be back to the Manor by 4:00. She doesn't care where we go. The bookstore is about a forty-minute drive; we can sit in the coffee shop and the three of us can rotate browsing breaks while leaving two behind to keep my mother and Irv company.

But it does not work like that. My mother is pleased to sit in the shop and sip her coffee, is even more delighted to hear that cookies are available, but refuses to touch anything unless we are all there together. Fair enough.

Beverly tries to find out what Irv would like to drink. Tea? Coffee? Soda? What kind of soda? The more she probes, the greater Irv's winks and nods become. He says, perhaps in Italian, *"Tutu bene."* Then he shakes his head but says, switching to French, *"Mais oui."* Then it's Yiddish, and a shrug: *"Tahkeh."*

"He wants coffee," my mother says.

With the drinks and a mixed plate of cookies in front of us, suddenly things calm down. My mother seems content. We go over, again, where we're staying and why, who is married to whom and for how long, and when we are leaving to return to Oregon.

"Where are we?" Irv asks.

"Westbury."

He nods. My mother says, "He never knows where he is. I don't see how he could have been a pilot."

"You were a pilot, Irv?" Beverly asks, smiling at him warmly.

"Sure."

"Where did you fly?"

He lifts his hand and flutters it in front of his eyes. "Around."

"Did you like flying, Irv?"

He nods and winks. "It gave me a lift."

There it is again. Both of them do that, just when I am sure there is no hope. A flash of wit, almost self-mocking, reflecting the simple joy of a mind at play. *There's still someone home in here, Kid.*

Then my mother says, "There used to be a theater in Westbury," and I am stunned. She remembers *that* and not my father or my dead brother? Pretty soon, I expect Rod Serling to make an appearance outside the store window. Then my mother lifts her cup and says, "I have no idea what I'm drinking."

"It's coffee," I tell her. "Do you want some more milk in it?"

She shakes her head. Then she picks up an oatmeal raisin cookie, looks at it, turns to Becka, and says, "What is this and what do I do with it?"

Beverly, born and raised in Portland, Oregon, has never been to Brooklyn. Becka was there only once, as a very small child, when I drove with her and my mother up Flatbush Avenue on an aborted search to locate the old neighborhood. During that trip, my mother and step-father argued so heatedly about where a certain Chinese laundry was located that I decided to head for the relative safety of the cemetery instead. So I have not been back since shortly after we moved away in 1957, when I was ten.

I wanted to see the apartment building in East Flatbush where I spent my first decade, find the site of the chicken—I mean poultry—market my father owned, and locate Toomey's Diner, where we used to eat Sunday breakfasts on the way to Coney Island or Prospect Park. I wanted to explore the park, perhaps find the stables where we used to ride. There would be vast changes, I knew that, but each of these talismanic places was still standing and it was important for me to find them again.

As I drove toward East Flatbush, a poem by my mentor and friend Thomas Kinsella kept popping into my mind. It was a great relief to find that anything remained intact in my mind and that I could still recall something as important as a few stanzas of poetry if I wished to. Especially in competition with the Sunday traffic, reggae music, and horn blasts from the street where I used to ride a trolley to shop with my mother.

In *Personal Places*, Kinsella had written:

There are established personal places
that receive our lives' heat
and adapt in their mass, like stone.

These absorb in their changes
the radiance of change in us,
and give it back

to the darkness of our understanding,
directionless
into the returning cold.

I believed these Brooklyn places were of this kind and that there would be a sort of feedback loop between the changed apartment building or ramshackle poultry market and my own damaged memory. Despite age and time and destructive forces, they would bolster one another, these ancient personal places and my lesion-pocked brain, creating an understanding that would resonate for me. In the face of my mother's losses and the loss of my mother, in the face of my own functional failures, memory would endure: I would see it with my own eyes, in the form of these places, and be—what? Soothed, healed, restored. It was like visiting a shrine.

But the only "radiance of change" I found was illuminated by complete transformation. My old apartment building was recognizable in shape only. Its brick face had been covered over, leaving only the iron-studded brickwork at its front intact. The concrete courtyard in back, where I played punchball and stickball, was locked tight, impenetrable and apparently planted with a few scraggly trees. My old school, four blocks away, was undergoing massive reconstruction. The diner on Empire Boulevard, refaced in the sort of red brick that used to grace my old apartment building, retained its name but seemed to crouch in its hostile, graffiti-riddled surroundings like a trapped fox. The park was virtually sealed off. Then, with the help of Beverly's expert navigation, we found the Elite Poultry Market and parked across the street. Only the *I* and final *E* remained of the first word. Becka and I got out to look inside the small slit in its front wall. No longer a wholesale business, it had no coops against the perimeter and no sign of customers, only a few terrified chickens and ducks running over the floor and, in the back, one shadowy man killing and plucking fowl. It stank. It seemed to be collapsing in on itself. From the parking lot where an Italian butcher shop used to be, a man approached and seemed to ask what we wanted.

"My father used to own this market," I said. "He sold it in 1957."

The man nodded and walked away. "I no born," he said.

Becka has returned to Pittsburgh. She is going to move ahead with her plans to be married, having spent the last few days reaching a decision. As she left us and walked into Penn Station to catch her train, I saw that the nimbus of light from my dream was around her form. I understood that it is my daughter who, in the richness of her heart and mind, in her love for us and for her fiancé, embodies the radiance of change I had been looking for. Amid all the instability of memory in this family, she was taking us all into the next place.

Driving back to the Manor on our final evening in the East, Beverly and I swing through the center of Long Beach to scout for restaurants. My mother has said she would not mind eating Chinese food and I am looking for familiar establishments. I left here for good in 1965, but a surprising number of shops and eateries remain from the old days.

Next to my mother's bank I see a sign for Sui Szechuan and recognize the place at once. It used to be Wing Loo's. They sponsored my recreation league softball team one summer. Beverly and I check the menu and agree this is the perfect place. We will order my mother her favorite item, shrimp with lobster sauce, and know she will be delirious with joy as she takes an hour to clear her plate of every morsel.

My mother is waiting for us at the front desk of the Manor. She introduces us to Rose Gitler, whose face is lit by the joy of finally meeting Lillian's son the author. She tells us that she just loves my mother, then, to my astonishment, actually pinches my mother's cheek and survives to walk away.

"Where's Irv?" I ask.

"I sent him downstairs to get his overcoat and hat." She looks around. "Where is that man?"

"Who?"

"Irv."

"You sent him downstairs to get his overcoat and hat."

"He never remembers a thing. I have to help him."

At Sui Szechuan, we are the first diners of the evening and sit in the middle of the restaurant. Irv offers to hang my mother's coat on the rack, but she is cold and wants to keep it around her shoulders. I watch Irv walk past the coat rack and stop short, just before leaving the restaurant. He returns to the table, still carrying his coat and hat.

"I have to go to the bathroom," he says.

"Here," I say, "let me hang your things up for you."

I offer to read the menu to my mother but she refuses, picking up her own menu and glaring at it. "I can't read this," she says.

"How about shrimp with lobster sauce?"

"Do I like that?"

Irv returns and studies the menu closely. Then he puts it down and pours himself a cup of hot tea. After one sip, he carefully spoons ice from his water glass and slips it into the teacup. He opens a packet of Equal sweetener.

"This envelope is half-empty already," he says.

"Do you know what you'd like to order?" Beverly asks him.

Irv picks the menu up again and says, "I used to like won ton soup."

"Then you should have some."

"No, I don't think so."

Irv leans toward Beverly and goes through the winks and language thing while I order for my mother. *Tutu bene. Mais oui. Tahkeh.* Then says he'll have what she is having.

When the waiter leaves, Irv asks where we are.

"We're still in Long Beach, Irv."

"Where are you staying?" my mother asks.

"Near the airport."

"Which airport?"

"Kennedy."

Irv suddenly says, "I used to work there."

We all turn to him. "You flew out of Kennedy?" Beverly asks.

"I was a mechanic."

"Why are you staying near the airport?" my mother asks.

"Because we have to catch a flight at 8:30."

"A flight? You're going home?" I nod and take her hand. "But you just got here."

"We were here Sunday too. It's been a whole week already."

My mother clearly does not think so but again restrains herself. I am seeing a version of her that I have yearned to see for as long as I can remember.

"What section are we in?" Irv asks, looking up from his tea.

"The no-smoking section," Beverly says.

Irv nods. "I mean what part of town?"

"This is Long Beach, Irv. The center of town. We're right across from the railroad station."

"*Tutu bene.*"

My mother pronounces herself delighted with her combination plate, mixing together the fried rice and shrimp with lobster sauce, eating slowly. Irv removes every trace of shrimp from his plate, piling them on a side dish, and mixes the rice and lobster sauce, eating with such gusto that his shirt is quickly covered with stains.

It is clear that we have caught my mother—and Irv—at some sort of cusp. They are beginning to disappear from view but are still recognizable as themselves, their quirks magnified, the essences distilled, but nevertheless *there*. The irrevocable damage that defines Alzheimer's progress has reached a stage of inevitability, has crested and is about to accelerate downward. We are seeing a last clear view of who they are.

This trip home has taught me that I was wrong about the resonance of those personal places I wanted to visit. My mother, who had absorbed so much of my life's heat over the years, is still giving something vital back to me, reflecting in the changes she endures with genuine grace something of the changes I am trying to endure as well. She is moving in a world grown darker because of the failure of her vision, and because of the dimming of her fierce fires. She is always cold. But she is still making a life for herself, helping Irv and being helped by him regardless of their limitations.

The waiter comes to take our plates but my mother is not finished. She banishes him with a look. When he returns with dishes of pistachio ice cream, I watch her face and wait for him to dare leaving without placing dessert in front of her.

14

A Measure of Acceptance

The psychiatrist's office was in a run-down industrial section at the northern edge of Oregon's capital, Salem. It shared space with a chiropractic health center, separated from it by a temporary divider that wobbled in the current created by opening the door. When I arrived, a man sitting with his gaze trained on the spot I suddenly filled began kneading his left knee, his suit pants hopelessly wrinkled in that one spot. Another man, standing beside the door and dressed in overalls, studied the empty wall and muttered as he slowly rose on his toes and sank back on his heels. Like me, neither seemed happy to be visiting Dr. Peter Avilov.

Dr. Avilov specialized in the psychodiagnostic examination of disability claimants for the Social Security Administration. He made a career of weeding out hypochondriacs, malingerers, fakers, people who were ill without organic causes. There may be many such scam artists working the disability angle, but there are also many legitimate claimants. Avilov worked as a kind of hired gun, paid by an agency whose financial interests were best served when he determined that claimants were not disabled. This arrangement was like having your house appraised by the father-in-law of your prospective buyer, like being stopped by a traffic cop several tickets shy of his monthly quota, like facing a part-time judge who works for the construction company you're suing. Avilov's incentives were not encouraging to me.

I understood why I was there. When the Social Security Administration had decided to reevaluate my medical condition, eight years after originally approving my claim of disability, it exercised the right to send me to a doctor of its own choosing. This seemed fair enough. But after receiving records, test results, and reports of brain scans, and statements from my own internal medicine and infectious diseases physicians, all attesting to my ongoing disability, and after requiring twenty-five pages of handwritten questionnaires from me and my wife, scheduled an appointment for me with Avilov. Not with an independent internal medicine or infectious diseases specialist, not with a neurologist, but with a shrink.

Now, twelve years after first getting sick, I can say that I've become adept at being brain damaged. It's not that my symptoms have gone away: I still try to dice a stalk of celery with a carrot instead of a knife, reverse *p* and *b* when I write, or draw a primitive hourglass when I mean to draw a star. I place newly purchased packages of frozen corn in the dishwasher instead of the freezer; after putting crumpled newspaper and dry pine into our woodstove, I strike a match and attempt to light the metal door. Preparing to cross the "main street" in Carlton, Oregon, I looked both ways, saw a pickup truck a quarter-mile south, took one step off the curb, and landed flat on my face, cane pointing due east.

So I'm still much as I was in December 1988. Along the way, though, I learned to manage my encounters with the world in new ways. Expecting the unexpected now, I can, like an improvisational actor, incorporate it into my performance. For instance, my tendency to use words that are close to—but not exactly—the words I'm trying to say has led to some surprising discoveries in the composition of sentences. A freshness emerges when the mind is unshackled from its habitual ways. In the past, I never would have described the effect of that viral attack on my brain as being "geezered" overnight if I hadn't first confused the words seizure and geezer. It is as though my word-finding capacity has developed a buckshot associative function to compensate for its failures of precision, so I end up with *shellac* instead of *plaque* when trying to describe the gunk on my teeth. Who knows, maybe James Joyce was brain damaged when he wrote *Finnegans Wake* and built a whole novel on puns and neologisms that were actually symptoms of disease.

It's possible to see such domination of the unexpected in a positive light. So getting lost in the familiar woods around our house and finding my way home again adds a twist of excitement to days that might seem circumscribed or routine because of my disability. When the natural food grocery where we shop rearranged its entire stock, I was one of the few customers who didn't mind, since I could never remember where things were anyway. I am more deliberate than I was; being attentive, purposeful in movement, lends my life an intensity of awareness that was not always present before. My senses are heightened, their fine-tuning mechanism busted: spicy food, stargazer lilies in bloom, birdsong, heat, my wife's vivid palette when she paints have all become more intense and stimulating. Because it threatens my balance, a sudden breeze stops me, so its strength and motion can register. Attentiveness may not guarantee success—as my pratfall in Carlton indicates—but it does allow me to appreciate detail and nuance.

One way of spinning this is to say that my daily experience is often spontaneous and exciting. Not fragmented and intimidating, but unpredictable, continuously new. I may lose track of things, or of myself in space, my line of thought, but instead of getting frustrated I try to see this as the perfect time to stop and figure out what I want or where I am. I accept my role in the harlequinade. It's not so much a matter of making lemonade out of life's lemons, but rather of learning to savor the shock, taste, texture, and aftereffects of a mouthful of unadulterated citrus.

Acceptance is a deceptive word. It suggests compliance, a consenting to my condition and to who I have become. This form of acceptance is often seen as weakness, submission. We say "I accept my punishment." Or "I accept your decision." But such assent, while passive in essence, does provide the stable, rocklike foundation for coping with a condition that will not go away. It is a powerful passivity, the Zen of Illness, that allows for endurance.

There is, however, more than endurance at stake. A year in bed, another year spent primarily in my recliner—these were times when endurance was the main issue. But over time, I began to recognize the possibilities for transformation. I saw another kind of acceptance as being viable, the kind espoused by Robert Frost when he said, "Take what is given, and make it over your own way." That is, after all, the root meaning of the verb "to accept," which comes from the Latin *accipere*, or "take to oneself." It implies an embrace. Not a giving up but a welcoming. People encourage the sick to resist, to fight back; we say that our resistance is down when we contract a virus. But it wasn't possible to resist the effects of brain damage. Fighting to speak rapidly and clearly, as I always had in the past, only leads to more garbling of meaning; willing myself to walk without a cane or climb a ladder only leads to more falls; demanding that I not forget something only makes me angrier when all I can remember is the effort not to forget. I began to realize that the most aggressive act I could perform on my own behalf was to stop struggling and discover what I could really do.

This, I believe, is what the Austrian psychotherapist Viktor E. Frankl refers to in his classic book, *The Doctor and the Soul*, as "spiritual elasticity." He says, speaking of his severely damaged patients, "Man must cultivate the flexibility to swing over to another value-group if that group and that alone offers the possibility of actualizing values." Man must, Frankl believes, "temper his efforts to the chances that are offered."

Such shifts of value, made possible by active acceptance of life as it is, can only be achieved alone. Doctors, therapists, rehabilitation professionals, family members, friends, lovers cannot reconcile a person to the changes wrought by illness or injury, though they can ease the way. Acceptance is a private act, achieved gradually and with little outward evidence. It also seems never to be complete; I still get furious with myself for forgetting what I'm trying to tell my daughter during a phone call, humiliated when I blithely walk away with another shopper's cart of groceries.

But for all its private essence, acceptance cannot be expressed purely in private terms. My experience did not happen to me alone; family, colleagues and friends, acquaintances were all involved. I had a new relationship with my employer and its insurance company, with federal and state government, with people who read my work. There is a social dimension to the experience of illness and to its acceptance, a kind of reciprocity between Self and World that goes beyond the enactment of laws governing handicapped access to buildings, or rules prohibiting discrimination in the workplace. It is in this social dimension that, for all my private adjustment, I remain a grave cripple and, apparently, a figure of contempt.

At least the parties involved agreed that what was wrong with me was all in my head. However, mine was disability arising from organic damage to the brain caused by a viral attack, not from psychiatric illness. The distinction matters; my disability status would not continue if my condition were psychiatric. It was in the best interests of the Social Security Administration for Dr. Avilov to say my symptoms were caused by the mind, were psychosomatic rather than organic in nature. And what was in Social Security's interests was also in Avilov's.

Anyone who observes me in action over time can see that I no longer have "brains." A brain, yes, with many functions intact; but I'm not as smart or as quick or as steady as I was, or as a man my age and with my education should be. Though I may not look sick and I don't shake or froth or talk to myself, after a few minutes it becomes clear that something fundamental is wrong. My losses of cognitive capability have been fully measured and recorded. They were used by the Social Security Administration and the insurance company to establish my total disability, by various physicians to establish treatment and therapy programs, by a pharmaceutical company to establish my eligibility for participation in the clinical field trial of a drug that didn't work. I have a handicapped parking placard on the dashboard of my car; I can get a free return-trip token from the New York City subway system by flashing my Medicaid card. In this sense, I have a public profile as someone who is disabled. I have met the requirements.

Further, as someone with quantifiable diminishment in IQ levels, impaired abstract reasoning and learning facility, scattered recall capacities, and aptitudes that decrease as fatigue or distraction increases, I am of scientific use. When it serves their purposes, various institutions welcome me. Indeed they pursue me. I have been actively recruited for three experimental protocols run by Oregon Health Sciences University. One of these, a series of treatments using DMSO, made me smell so rancid that I turned heads just by walking into a room. But when I do not serve their purpose, these same institutions dismiss me. Or challenge me. No matter how well I may have adjusted to living with brain damage, the world I often deal with has not. When money or status is involved, I am positioned as a pariah.

So would Avilov find that my disability was continuing, or would he judge me as suffering from mental illness? Those who say that the distinction is bogus, or that the patient's fear of being labeled mentally ill is merely a cultural bias and ought not matter, are missing the point. Money is at stake; in our culture, this means it matters very much. To all sides.

Avilov began by asking me to recount the history of my illness. He seemed as easily distracted as I was; while I stared at his checked flannel shirt, sweetly ragged mustache, and the pen he occasionally put in his mouth like a pipe, Avilov looked from my face to his closed door to his empty notepad and back to my face, nodding. When I had finished, he asked a series of diagnostic questions: did I know what day it was (hey, I'm here on the right day, aren't I?), could I name the presidents of the United States since Kennedy, could I count backward from one hundred by sevens? During this series, he interrupted me to provide a list of four unconnected words (such as *train, argue, barn, vivid*) that I was instructed to remember for later recall. Then he asked me to explain what was meant by the expression "People who live in glass houses should not throw stones." I nodded, thought for a moment, knew that this sort of proverb relied on metaphor, which as a poet should be my great strength, and began to explain. Except that I couldn't. I must have talked for five minutes, in tortuous circles, spewing gobbledygook about stones breaking glass and people having things to hide, shaking my head, backtracking as I tried to elaborate. But it was beyond me, as all abstract thinking is beyond me, and I soon drifted into stunned silence. Crashing into your limitations this way hurts; I remembered as a long-distance runner hitting the fabled "wall" at about mile twenty-two of the Chicago Marathon, my body depleted of all energy resources, feeding on its own muscle and fat for every additional step, and I recognized this as being a similar sensation.

For the first time, I saw something clear in Avilov's eyes. He saw me. He recognized this as real, the blathering of a brain-damaged man who still thinks he can think.

It was at this moment that he asked, "Why are you here?"

I nearly burst into tears, knowing that he meant I seemed to be suffering from organic rather than mental illness. Music to my ears. "I have the same question."

The rest of our interview left little impression. But when the time came for me to leave, I stood to shake his hand and realized that Avilov had forgotten to ask me if I remembered the four words I had by then forgotten. I did remember having to remember them, though. Would it be best to walk out of the room, or should I remind him that he forgot to have me repeat the words I could no longer remember? Or had I forgotten that he did ask me, lost as I was in the fog of other failures? Should I say, "I can't remember if you asked me to repeat those words, but there's no need because I can't remember them"?

None of that mattered because Avilov, bless his heart, had found that my disability status remained as it was. Such recommendations arrive as mixed blessings; I would much rather not be as I am, but since I am, I must depend upon on receiving the legitimate support I paid for when healthy and am entitled to now.

There was little time to feel relieved because I soon faced an altogether different challenge, this time from the company that handled my disability insurance payments. I was ordered to undergo "a Two Day Functional Capacity Evaluation" administered by a rehabilitation firm the company hired in Portland. A later phone call informed me to prepare for six and a half hours of physical challenges the first day and three hours more the following day. I would be made to lift weights, carry heavy boxes, push and pull loaded crates, climb stairs, perform various feats of balance and dexterity, complete puzzles, answer a barrage of questions. But I would have an hour for lunch.

Wear loose clothes. Arrive early.

With the letter had come a warning: "You must provide your best effort so that the reported measurements of your functional ability are valid." Again, the message seemed clear: no shenanigans, you! We're wise to your kind.

I think the contempt that underlies these confrontations is apparent. The patient, or—in the lingo of insurance operations—the claimant, is approached not only as an adversary but as a deceiver. *You can climb more stairs than that! You can really stand on one leg, like a heron; stop falling over, freeloader! We know that game.* Paranoia rules; here an institution seems caught in its grip. With money at stake, the disabled are automatically supposed to be up to some kind of chicanery, and our displays of symptoms are viewed as untrustworthy. Never mind that I contributed to Social Security for my entire working life, with the mutual understanding that if I were disabled the fund would be there for me. Never mind that both my employer and I paid for disability insurance with the mutual understanding that if I were disabled, payments would be there for me. Our doctors are suspect, our caregivers are implicated, and *we've got our eyes on you!*

The rehab center looked like a combination gym and children's playground. The staff was friendly, casual; several were administering physical therapy, so the huge room into which I was led smelled of sweat. An elderly man at a desk worked with a small stack of blocks. Above the blather of muzak, I heard grunts and moans of pained effort: a woman lying on mats, being helped to bend damaged knees; a stiff-backed man laboring through his stretches; two women side by side on benches, deep in conversation as they curled small weights.

The man assigned to conduct my Functional Capacity Evaluation looked enough like me to be a cousin. Short, bearded, thick hair curling away from a lacy bald spot, Reggie shook my hand and tried to set me at ease. He was good at what he did, lowering the level of confrontation, expressing compassion, showing concern about the effect on my health of such strenuous testing. I should let him know if I needed to stop.

Right then, before the action began, I had a moment of grave doubt. I could remain suspicious, paranoia begetting paranoia, or I could trust Reggie to be honest, to assess my capacities without prejudice. The presence of patients being helped all around me seemed a good sign. This firm didn't appear dependent on referrals for evaluation from insurance companies. It had a lucrative operation, independent of all that. And if I could not trust a man who reminded me of a healthier version of myself, it seemed like bad Karma. I loved games and physical challenges. But I knew who and what I was now; it would be fine if I simply let him know as well. Though much of my disability results from cognitive deficits, there are physical manifestations too, so letting Reggie know me in the context of a gymlike setting felt comfortable. Besides, he was sharp enough to recognize suspicion in my eyes anyway, and that would give him reason to doubt my efforts. We were both after the same thing: a valid representation of my abilities. Now was the time to put all I had learned about acceptance on the line. It would require a measure of acceptance on both sides.

What I was not prepared for was how badly I would perform in every test. I knew my limitations but had never measured them. Over a dozen years, the consequences of exceeding my physical capabilities had been made clear enough that I learned to live within

the limits. Here, I was brought repeatedly to those limits and beyond; after an hour with Reggie, I was ready to sleep for the entire
next month. The experience was crushing. How could I comfort-
ably manage only 25 pounds in the floor-to-waist lift repetitions? I
used to press 150 pounds as part of my regular weekly training for
competitive racing. How could I not stand on my left foot for more
than two seconds? You shoulda seen me on a ball field! I could hold
my arms up for no more than seventy-five seconds, could push a
cart loaded with no more than 40 pounds of weights, could climb
only sixty-six stairs. I could not fit shapes to their proper holes in
a form-board in the time allotted, though I distinctly remember
playing a game with my stepson that worked on the same principles and always beating the timer. Just before lunch, Reggie asked
me to squat and lift a box filled with paper. He stood behind me
and was there as I fell back into his arms.

I may not have been clinically depressed, as Dr. Avilov attested
earlier, but this evaluation was almost enough to knock me into the
deepest despair. Reggie said little to reveal his opinions. At the time,
I thought that meant he was simply being professional, masking
judgment, and though I sensed empathy I realized that could be a
matter of projection on my part.

Later, I believed that his silence came from knowing what else
he had to make me do. After lunch and an interview about the Activities of Daily Living form I had filled out, Reggie led me to a
field of blue mats spread across the room's center. For a moment, I
wondered if he planned to challenge me to a wrestling match. That
thought had lovely symbolic overtones: wrestling with someone
who suggested my former self; wrestling with an agent of THEM,
a man certain to defeat me; or having my Genesis experience, like
Jacob at Peniel, wrestling with Him. Which, at least for Jacob, resulted in a blessing and a nice payout.

But no. Reggie told me to crawl.

In order to obtain "a valid representation" of my abilities, it was
necessary for the insurance company to see how far, and for how
long, and with what result I could crawl.

It was a test I had not imagined. It was a test that could, in all honesty, have only one purpose. My ability to crawl could not logically be used as a valid measure of my employability. And in light of all the other tasks I had been unable to perform, crawling was not necessary as a measure of my functional limits. It would test nothing, at least nothing specific to my case, not even the lower limits of my capacity. Carrying the malign odor of indifference, tyranny's tainted breath, the demand that I crawl was almost comical in its obviousness: the paternal powers turning someone like me, a disabled man living in dependence upon their finances, into an infant.

I considered refusing to comply. Though the implied threat (*you must provide your best effort . . .*) contained in the letter crossed my mind, and I wondered how Beverly and I would manage without my disability payments, it wasn't practicality that made me proceed. At least I don't think so. It was, instead, acceptance. I had spent the morning in a public confrontation with the fullness of my loss, as though on stage with Reggie, representing the insurance company, as my audience. Now I would confront the sheer heartlessness of the System, the powers that demanded that I crawl before they agreed temporarily to accept my disability. I would, perhaps for the first time, join the company of those far more damaged than I am, who have endured far more indignity in their quest for acceptance. Whatever it is that Reggie and the insurance company believed they were measuring as I got down on my hands and knees and began a slow circuit of the mats in the center of that huge room, I believed I was measuring how far we still had to go for acceptance.

Reggie stood in the center of the mats, rotating in place as I crawled along one side, turned at the corner, crossed to the opposite side, and began to return toward the point where I had started. Before I reached it, Reggie told me to stop. He had seen enough. I was slow and unsteady at the turns, but I could crawl fine.

I never received a follow-up letter from the insurance company. I was never formally informed of its findings or given documentation of my performance, though my disability payments have continued.

At the end of the second day of testing, Reggie told me how I'd done. In many of the tests, my results were in the lower 5 to 10 percent for men my age. My performance diminished alarmingly on the second day, and he hadn't ever tested anyone who did as poorly on the dexterity components. He believed that I had given my best efforts and would report accordingly. But he would not give me any formal results. I was to contact my physician, who would receive Reggie's report in due time.

When the battery of tests had first been scheduled, I'd made an appointment to see my doctor a few days after their completion. I knew the physical challenges would worsen my symptoms, and wanted him to see what had resulted. I knew I would need his help. By the time I got there, he had spoken to Reggie and knew about my performance. But my doctor never got an official report either.

This was familiar ground. Did I wish to request a report? I was continuing to receive my legitimate payments; did I really want to contact my insurance company and demand to see the findings of my Functional Capacity Evaluation? Risk waking the sleeping dragon? What would be the point? I anticipated no satisfaction in reading that I was in fact disabled, or in seeing how my experience translated into numbers or bureaucratic prose.

It seems that I was of interest only when there was an occasion to rule me ineligible for benefits. Found again to be disabled, I wasn't even due the courtesy of a reply. The checks came; what more did I need to show that my claims are accepted?

There was, I suppose, no real need for a report. Through the experience, I had discovered something more vital than the measures of my physical capacity. The measure of public acceptance that I hoped to find, that I imagined would balance my private acceptance, was not going to come from a public agency or public corporation. It didn't work that way, after all. The public was largely indifferent, as most people, healthy or not, understand. The only measure of acceptance would come from how I conducted myself

in public, moment by moment. With laws in place to permit handicapped access to public spaces, prevent discrimination, and encourage involvement in public life, there is general acceptance that
the handicapped live among us and must be accommodated. But
that doesn't mean they're not resented, feared, or mistrusted by the
healthy. The Disability Racket!

I had encountered the true, hard heart of the matter. My life in
the social dimension of illness is governed by forces that are severe
and implacable. Though activism has helped protect the handicapped over the last four decades, there is little room for reciprocity
between the handicapped person and his or her world. It is naive
to expect otherwise.

I would like to think that the insurance company didn't send
an official letter of findings because it was abashed at what it'd put
me through. I would like to think that Dr. Avilov, who no longer
practices in Salem, hasn't moved away because he found too many
claimants disabled and lost his contract with the Social Security
Administration. That my experience educated Reggie and his firm,
and that his report educated the insurance company, so everyone
now understands the experience of disability, or of living with brain
damage.

But I know better. My desire for reciprocity between self and
world must find its form in writing about my experience. Slowly.
This essay has taken me eleven months to complete, in sittings of
fifteen minutes or so. Built of fragments shaped after the pieces
were examined, its errors of spelling and of word choice and logic
ferreted out with the help of my wife or daughter or computer's
spell-checker. It may look to a reader like the product of someone
a lot less damaged than I claim to be. But it's not. It's the product
of someone who has learned how to live with his limitations, and
work with them. And when it's published, if someone employed by
my insurance company reads it, I will probably get a letter in the
mail demanding that I report for another battery of tests. After all,
this is not how a brain-damaged man is supposed to behave.

15

Jangled Bells:
Meditations on *Hamlet* and the Power to Know

I am standing at the bottom of the stairs, my attention caught by a bookcase where I keep biographies and essay collections. The storage room door is open behind me; in the bathroom across the narrow hall I can hear clothes still spinning in the dryer. There is a small green light shining from the base of my computer in the den, and to my left a yowling Zeppo has just come into the bedroom through his cat door in search of food. I have absolutely no idea why I am standing here.

There is a novel in my hand, its pages folded around my index finger to mark the place where I stopped reading, so I didn't come downstairs to raid the bookcase. We have finished dinner, so I'm not after a can of soup or box of rice in the storage room. The laundry is not done yet, so I'm not here to fold clothes. I don't have to use the toilet. It's too early for bed and I don't feel sleepy; if I was headed for my den to write something down I have forgotten what it is.

Now what do I do?

It is not a question of being unable to make up my mind. Essentially, I don't know my own mind. This has become a familiar situation. I recognize the grim slowness of mind, the slow grinding of this patchwork brain I am left with. It is the still new-feeling vehicle I now use to make my way in the world, the one for which I had traded down.

The person I knew as myself had always been decisive. At least for the first forty-one years. Look at a situation, analyze it, consider alternatives, factor in what my gut was saying, and choose. I didn't dither. For seventeen years, I worked in the field of public policy, helping governors and legislators make decisions, advising corporate executives, taking action. I worked for one state budget director who had a passion for Shakespeare and used to call the practice of excessive analysis "Hamletting." He hated Hamletizers. When he promoted me, he said it was because I was resolute.

Now I waffle. There is a gap between thought and action. No, a gulf. I think, but not always clearly, and I no longer trust my thought processes. Like Hamlet, I am out of fashion from myself. I find myself wandering along our gravel driveway unsure whether I was headed out to the car or in to the house. I tell Beverly that I will bring the peach pits down to where she is waiting, when I mean to say I'll bring the beach chairs. I open the armoire where we keep our television and music system and am confused when I can't find the skim milk I was looking for. This week, when there was no dial tone on my bedside phone, I went upstairs and checked the other phones, which were also dead, then checked to be sure the answering machine was on, then tried the microwave, then turned on the kitchen faucet and thought, *What the* HELL *am I doing?*

No longer confident in how this new version of a mind works, I find myself, like Hamlet in the throes of his tortured decision making, "a dull and muddy-mettled rascal." I am a stranger, or rather a newcomer, to my own mind. Worse, I am stuck in my head "like John-a-dreams, unpregnant of my cause," obsessed with the effort at clarity. This is not good for the self-esteem. Trying to sort things out in my teeming brain, I feel like Hamlet during his torturous "O, what a rogue and peasant slave am I" soliloquy, when thought finally comes to a stop and he seems to stand outside himself, muttering, "About, my brains!" as he tries to jump-start his mind.

Our problem, me and Hamlet, is how to know, how to be sure of our powers of reason. We are no longer masters of our identity, unable to tap its source, cut off from the flow of comprehension. Stumped, we mutter, "There is something in this more than natural, if philosophy could find it out." That's what makes Hamlet indecisive and what makes me stand in the downstairs hall wondering what the hell I'm doing there. I quickly reach the limits of what I can know, stranded there without a sure sense of direction. The more I ponder, the more confused I get.

We may have gotten to this point by different routes, but we have both become unrecognizable. And not just to ourselves. Transformed, as Claudius says of his cousin/son, so that "nor th' exterior nor the inward man / Resembles what it was."

I spent the entire spring of 1969 reading *Hamlet*. This was my final semester at Franklin and Marshall College and I was taking English 32, Shakespeare Seminar, which devoted three entire months to the study of one play. The professor, Edward Brubaker, was also a director in the Green Room Theater on campus and had cast me, two years earlier, in my first Shakespearean role—as Pompey the bawdy tapster in *Measure for Measure*. Maybe, I had thought, this class would be a lark, as in my senior year in high school when the whole football team took a chef's course offered by our coach through the home economics department. It was difficult to imagine Brubaker's scholarly side, but I was looking forward to being around him once more before my college career was over.

So while student protests against the war in Vietnam spread among American campuses, and the war itself moved from the slaughter at Hamburger Hill to an empty promise of Vietnamization, and while the trial and sentencing of Sirhan Sirhan was taking place and an artificial heart was being implanted in human chests and probes were landing on Venus, I was lavishing vital attention on a drama written around 1600. We acted scenes, tried out all the roles, read commentary, discussed nuances, wrote papers. The semester seemed too brief and, looked at from a distance of three decades, absurdly self-indulgent.

Hamlet's native habits of mind, no doubt bolstered by his studies in Wittenberg, were familiar enough to any college senior. It was easy, especially in 1969, to experience a mind meld with the Danish prince, losing ourselves in analytical folly, playing at existential despair, burdened by the darkness of the world around us, dressing all in black. How can anyone decide anything on this insane, abandoned planet? I felt drawn to join the demonstrations on campus, but I also felt drawn to this one last orgy of study. Stay sheltered in school rather than face the larger kingdom of discord. I wanted to write, and write about the life around me, but I also wanted to continue acting, to continue exploring the possibilities of theater, and I wasn't alert enough to see how they all might come together in the streets. I wanted to get on with my life, but the life I wanted to get on with involved more school rather than a tour of duty in the war zone, so the best thing to do was complete my undergraduate degree and secure the grad school placement I'd been offered, which hinged on my graduating with distinction. Finish my gloomy honors thesis on the novels of Thomas Hardy, ace the Shakespeare seminar, concentrate. But I also wanted to direct a play as well as act in one, and I desperately wanted to find a new girlfriend, and my mother had recently remarried (not, however, to my father's brother) and moved to Italy, where she wanted me to live for the coming summer.

I played at tormented uncertainty but had made my decisions and stuck by them—take the seminar, finish the work, turn away from the turmoil outside, do without Italy in order to work. But Hamlet and his inner life were really holding my attention. I believe I identified with the wrong characters and for the wrong reasons. I knew that playing the role of Hamlet was beyond my technical skill and experience, that I was more suited to playing clowns and sidekicks. I also refused to see anything of myself in his character. Brood? I don't brood. True, my father had died, but that was ages ago and I felt I'd come to terms with his loss. True, my mother had remarried, but I felt myself freed by that. True, I would rather stay in school than face the hard world outside, but that position made sense when the world outside was engaged in a war I opposed. No,

I was drawn to Laertes. Fiery Laertes, a man of action, the romantic and daring lad, athlete and scholar, loyal brother, independent but loving. Ah, yes. At that point, I neither saw through Laertes—so childish and impulsive, so limited in his soul—nor through myself. Leaping into the open grave, dueling with the hero, falling for Claudius's dark plans but then coming clean. I could do naive. Plus, I had the notion that he was short, like me. Now the idea of playing Laertes just tires me out.

The other character I was interested in playing, Horatio, remains a role to covet. What a good friend Horatio is, steadfast and courageous. He can tell Hamlet the truth, can defend and support him, offers to die for him rather than let his buddy drink poison. And he has some grand speeches—"the morn in russet mantel clad" or the piercingly simple "Now cracks a noble heart" followed up with "Good night, sweet prince, / And flights of angels sing thee to thy rest." The older I get, the more appealing that role becomes.

Now I think it might be fun to try acting Hamlet after all. Provided, of course, that I didn't have to learn any lines, because the lesions that score my brain have shattered its system of memory. A few years ago, agreeing to portray the lead role of a detective in a fund-raising production at our local library, I ended up having to carry the script around with me to recite my lines. Hamlet obviously has the opposite problem. He cannot forget anything and moves through his days haunted by events, obsessed by the Ghost's message, tormented by recollections of his privileged childhood and his noble father. Hamlet's brain overflows with remembered speeches from plays he has seen, with bits and pieces of literature available to him for quotation or allusion as his mind ricochets.

But I strongly identify with his sense of lost capacity. Our brains have become destabilized (and my mental powers measurably lessened) and far from "infinite in faculties." Ophelia, after listening to one of her beloved's zanier rambles, is horrified at the evidence of Hamlet's diminishment. Saying, "O, what a noble mind is here o'erthrown!" she zeroes in on the fact that all his powers are "quite, quite down." Looking at him, she recognizes that his "noble and most sovereign reason" is "like sweet bells jangled, out of time and harsh."

This is true. I am here to confirm that unclear thought fills the brain with noise like the sound of jangled bells. A cacophony of half-realized messages, "wild and whirling," like the words Hamlet utters to Horatio in an outer manifestation of the way his inner world sounds.

Not knowing how to think means not knowing how to act. If we cannot reason our way through a situation, we are left to rely on instinct or reflex, like an animal. Deprived of reason, divided from ourselves, we become, as Claudius says of the deranged Ophelia, "mere beasts." Which is the same notion that torments Hamlet: "What is a man / If his chief good and market of his time / Be but to sleep and feed? / A beast, no more." He wants for himself, and admires in others, the ability to act rationally: "Give me that man / That is not passion's slave, and I will wear him / In my heart's core."

It would be method acting at its most basic for me to play Hamlet in his fallen mental state. With a teleprompter, of course, and a cane.

I don't wish to overstate my identification with Hamlet. He does not, for instance, seem brain damaged. His disturbance is presented as less organic than psychic in origin. But who can say for sure? Mood, Hamlet's melancholy, can induce chemical changes to the brain. Or melancholy can be triggered by circumstances such as those he faces. Neuroscience is quite clear on the way traumatic situations cause the release of stress hormones that inhibit the brain's hippocampus but excite its amygdala, thus altering the balance between emotion and memory, action and thought. Further, a sufficient number of such hormonal storms can produce permanent changes.

Hamlet has suffered a trauma that, though different from a viral attack, "hath put him / So much from th' understanding of himself" that he no longer feels comfortable in his own head. I am not so much suggesting a medical diagnosis as responding to his behavior in a way that recognizes certain common signs. As he says, "For, by my fay, I cannot reason."

Rereading the play, I see with self-reflexive clarity that Hamlet is devastated by his loss of cognitive command. In mourning for his father, outraged by his mother's behavior and his uncle's treacheries, distraught over the appearance of the Ghost, unable to make a decision about revenge, confused over his feelings toward Ophelia, he is in a terrible quandary. But the worst, I think, is that he hardly recognizes himself anymore; this student from Wittenberg, a believer in the nobility of man's reasoning and the infinite capacity of his faculties, is suddenly incapable of clear thought. It is a terrible thing not to trust your own mind.

But there are some things we simply cannot think through. Claudius knows this; it is behind his argument in the play's second scene, when he urges Hamlet to stop his excessive grieving. Such behavior is "to reason most absurd." Rather than ponder his losses, Claudius believes, Hamlet should ponder the absurdity of grieving too long. That's something a person can get a handle on; the meaning of mortality is not. While we may never solve the mystery of our fathers' deaths, we can see through the futility of protracted grief. Of course, Claudius fails to understand that grief is grief, and no more subject to reason than fear. But the foundation of his logic is clear: there are limits to what we can understand, so let's get on with life.

Western culture has long viewed reason as invincible. Not only invincible, but central to our humanity. When things are working right, when all is in balance, we believe the head is "native to the heart." This notion ignores the primacy of the human heart, by which we usually mean emotion or feeling, as a tool of knowledge. Or rather, of wisdom. We have been taught to fear the estrangement of head and heart, to welcome the dominion of the rational. The loss of brainpower is among our greatest horrors. In my case, it was a virus that was responsible for "breaking down the pales and forts of reason." You can see the shrapnel marks on my brain. Yet all is not in ruins. I have gradually learned, for instance, that a part of me *knows* what my brain may not. When I tell Beverly that I need to go downstairs and *deviate* when I mean to tell her I need to *meditate*, I have actually said something vital and true about my need to change the frame of mind I am in, to angle off the normal path. I must abandon the frustrating loop in which my brain has become entangled at exactly the point when I most need to meditate. Put another way, when I begin losing track of things, or of myself in space, it is the perfect moment to slow down and figure out what I want or where I am. To deviate.

This intimation of acceptance is where I part company with Hamlet. He cannot accept his inability to reason through a course of action, his mental powerlessness in the face of all the evidence before him. He keeps testing to convince himself the Ghost is "real," an exquisite irony when you think about it—he must apply rational proofs against the most irrational of manifestations. Hamlet flat out cannot bear the failure of his reasoning, and it leads to tragedy.

The issue of acceptance suggests a way to distinguish comedy from tragedy. Some things, life-changing and profoundly alien to our sense of Self, we can neither master nor alter. Hamlet needs to master and alter; when he cannot, it drives him to tragic action. "There is," Hamlet tells us, "nothing either good or bad but thinking makes it so." He has so convinced himself that reason's failure is proof of madness that he begins to play at being mad, knowing others believe him so. Hamlet reduced to instinct and emotion has become unacceptable to himself.

My situation, I have come to see, is essentially comic in nature. Beverly and I recently bought an inflatable, two-person kayak in our ongoing pursuit of activities to do together, activities that would get us outdoors and give me a modicum of exercise. The logic was sound. We live close to several rivers and sloughs, the kayak is sufficiently portable to make a spontaneous trip possible, and its two seats allow me to rest if I must while Beverly—as usual—does most of the work involved in getting us where we're going. At the time I got sick, I had been a fanatical long-distance runner, so getting out in a kayak might even make me feel some of the same rush I had loved when training on remote, wooded trails.

Of course it didn't work that way. After extensive reading in the various guidebooks and one round of practice on a small, sheltered lake, we launched the kayak on the south fork of the Yamhill River and headed upstream. I wore my lucky Brooklyn Dodgers hat to shield me from a sun that resolutely refused to look upon what we were doing. With the ropes that are used to guide the rudder tied around my feet, I was sitting in the back, where I could occasionally contribute to the paddling. As Beverly shouted instructions about which way to turn, I jerked each foot in turn, hopelessly confused over using my right to steer us to the left, and soon we were spun sideways and carried back where we had begun, swept downstream by a current that our guidebooks insisted on calling mild.

Another fine mess. Yet we had achieved the main goal. We'd had great fun, been outdoors, and fully exhausted ourselves. True, we had done so through laughter rather than exercise, but the result was nearly the same and, in many ways, even better for the spirit.

Though I am sometimes a stranger to myself and not always sure I can do what I set out to do, though I sometimes feel trapped in an unscripted vaudeville skit and often cannot think my way out of a problem, deafened by the jangling bells of confusion, I find myself thriving within the limits of a changed life. Beverly and I can joke about my shenanigans, so I don't feel stressed when they happen. If I say "stink" instead of "skunk," I can look in her sparkling green eyes and think, *Well, it* is *funny.* If I come to a stop in midsentence, rifling through the tatters of my lexicon, she will find the missing word for me in a way that is graceful rather than intrusive, an expression of love rather than impatience. When I topple backward while searching the vegetable bin in our refrigerator, she helps me up and kisses me into balance. So I find myself focused on what's important, not what's incidental. I accept myself as both diminished and different, but also as viable, which is what Hamlet cannot do.

As a young actor, studying the play scene by scene, Hamlet's "To be or not to be" soliloquy was the one I admired most. It showed a mind engaged with the fundamental question of existence, trying to decide whether and then how to exist. Great poetry, noble ideas. But when I return to it now, I am not convinced that Hamlet is actually considering suicide, that his situation is one—even as he returns to it in a subsequent soliloquy—that he would seriously elect to resolve by "self-slaughter." His suicide soliloquies seemed to me to be a pose. The real question at the heart of his speech, it seems to me, concerns how to be, how to live, especially when you find yourself at the end of your ability to know.

Now I think the best speech, the speech offering clearest evidence of Hamlet's access to truth, is a taut one-liner. Though early in the play, it shows Hamlet at the place where his ability to know has reached an end, a place from which he will not be able to move again. It is spoken almost half-heartedly, without the snideness or self-loathing that soon follows, but it contains the simplicity of real belief and the direct language of insight. "There are more things in heaven and earth, Horatio, than are dreamt of in your philosophy."

Lethe, the river of oblivion, rolls
Her watery labyrinth, whereof who drinks
Forthwith his former state and being forgets,
Forgets both joy and grief, pleasure and pain.

John Milton, *Paradise Lost*

The Watery Labyrinth

One of my jobs as a child was to be my mother's memory bank. As we stormed down Prospect Parkway in the black Buick, she would say, "Remind me to call Irma Brown when we get home," and she meant it. I was accountable if Irma went elsewhere for lunch the next day. The charged context worked wonders on my ability to encode these memories. Remembering is essentially a process of deep naming; the more we elaborate upon the selected details, giving them visual associations or smells and tastes, pinning them down, the more likely we are to recall them. Pointing out the passenger window, my mother would say, "Now, remember the phone number on that sign across the street. I want to call about a dining room table." My father in the driver's seat would cough and add, "For God's sake, don't forget." I seldom did. I knew I was even supposed to remember things I wasn't told to remember, like the name of our waiter at Key's Chinese Restaurant the week before and what my mother's fortune cookie had predicted, or what time Loretta Lasky said the dinner party would start next Saturday.

Remembering was never hard work for me. The names of each president and his vice president in sequence, endless baseball statistics, state capitals, dinosaurs, film casts, key historical dates, the flags and main products of foreign nations, song lyrics, travel in-structions—my brain was a sponge for useless information. If, as Emerson says, "We estimate a man by how much he remembers," then I was easy to overestimate. I knew the colors of Jay Gatsby's mound of shirts when asked on a grad school quiz. During my years with an acting company I was routinely the first cast member "off book." Sometimes, as I got older, such remembering actually proved useful. By the end of my first week as a program analyst for the Illinois Bureau of the Budget in 1972, I knew by heart the names of each of the state's 102 counties. Also their property tax rates, since I was working on the issue of school finance reform and it was tedious to look them up each time someone needed a number.

Memory was always a rushing river I could dip into at will. We worked together, my memory and I, delivering the goods. Its wa-ters shaped my landscape, nurtured and refreshed me, and served my needs even as it rushed on its own mysterious course, a trusted highway leading out of the past and into future. From observing my mother's father, Max, I knew memory could dry up eventually, but that didn't worry me; his great age seemed so far away when I was in my twenties or thirties and he was nearing one hundred.

It never occurred to me that the river could also be dammed in a flash. Suddenly the flow might stop, back up altogether, and the past become a flickering body of still water glimpsed just around the bend as time fell away. This is what happened to me on Decem-ber 7, 1988. My familiar river was turned by a viral explosion into oblivion's watery labyrinth, a maze of confusing reflection, becom-ing a place as riddling and perplexing as the harbor of dreamland.

Now, almost fourteen years after getting sick and losing the easy flow of my own memory, I am fading from my mother's mind. She is still living in the retirement hotel that overlooks the Atlantic, spending her days pestering management to do something about the rude clamor of the surf. Still spending her days with Irv, she also tries to seduce the few other surviving males that haunt the lobby. But she is steadily losing herself, and me, to the erasure of memory.

For most of my fifty-five years, I would have said that being forgotten by my mother was exactly what I wanted. There would be no more calls to harass me about living at the opposite end of the continent, or demand that I proclaim her The Best Mother in the World, or affirm that my childhood was blissful. There would be no more assertions that I owe every achievement to her genes and lifelong devotion. And I would no longer have to explain that selfishness isn't keeping my brother, Philip, from visiting her. It's just that he's dead.

I would have said that nothing but good would come from letting the current of oblivion overwhelm us. In much of my writing, in lifelong night terrors or years of conversation with Philip, it was never possible to forget what she did to us when we were growing up. I could remember vivid details even after brain damage tore through my memory systems like a hurricane. So could Philip, even after the toxins produced by end-stage renal failure had obliterated his cognition and sense of time. While brain lesions have disrupted the network that operates my short-term memory and swamped much of my long-term memory, down in the deep brain where survival instincts reign, I am still connected to the fears and associations formed by my mother's voice and fists and flailing feet, by her plots, her deceptive tendernesses. Even as a fifty-year-old grandfather, I dreaded the sound of my mother's dark contralto on the other end of the line. So did Philip, who for decades would not answer the phone at night, leaving that job to his wife.

But if my mother could forget the beatings and lavishly orchestrated humiliations, not just sublimate them but truly forget them, and if the violence of her fury and its consequences for us were no longer abuzz in her brain . . . if I were no longer in my mother's mind, then maybe some kind of essential circle would finally be broken. Short-circuited by Lethe, the connections zapped, the loop snapped—something like that.

She is almost tame now. Her rages have burned down to a heap of dying embers. She forgets to phone me. She has lost my father's name, my stepfather's name, most details of her own fabulations. It has become less necessary for her to lie about her ancestry or education, her travels, her suitors. She forgets the question she has just asked before losing the answer I have given.

"When did Floyd die?" she wonders. "Should I light a candle for him?"

I was named Floyd as a conscious act of remembrance. My name is meant to kindle recollection by honoring an ancestor. Unfortunately, by the time I was born in 1947, no one seemed to know anything about this person.

According to Isaac Klein in *A Guide to Jewish Religious Practice*, "The prevalent custom among Ashkenazic Jews is to name children after deceased relatives but never after living persons." This way, the Ashkenazis believed, the living would avoid being robbed of a full life by his or her namesake. Since my mother's parents were both alive when I was born, she reached one generation further back to find a name for me from Flora Lamensdorf, my great-grandmother.

For my mother, the name's sole meaning lay in its connection with her mother's family. She hoped to signify a carrying forth of the sweetness associated with my grandmother in the only way available to her, by honoring my grandmother's mother. She said she had no idea what my given name itself might mean, that people didn't think about such things, names were names, she just picked one that linked to a dead relative.

My mother didn't know anything concrete about Flora Lamensdorf, who never left Galicia and was recalled chiefly as a blurred, tiny image in a dresser-top photograph. The absence of specific details or associations connected with her grandmother, whether forgotten or never known, freed my mother to believe whatever she wanted. So Flora could be a friend of Chopin and muse for the aging Schiller despite having spent her life in the small city of Tarnow when neither the doomed composer nor the great poet was alive. Flora chose to remain in the old country when everyone else fled, forcing her husband to stay there as well, because of her great courage, or love of high culture, or pioneering work in the salon of Sigmund Freud. She was beautiful, devout, enlightened, sensual, gifted, loving, a housewife singer sculptress seamstress cook businesswoman inventor model diplomat actress.

Saturated by such fabrications, my childhood was stained by falsehood. My mother had been to the 1928 summer Olympics in Belgium and seen Jesse Owens win his medals, though Jesse Owens didn't compete in those Olympics, which were held in Holland. A cousin of my mother was said to have plucked his own mother from the sea after she escaped from Dachau and the British sank the ship she was on off the coast of England. Then the plucking was done by the cousin *and* his brother, who had not even known they were in the same place, and found each other while swimming in the icy waters. Then the cousin had become a Nazi, but when he saved his mother from the ship his submarine had torpedoed, he converted back and became a Jew again. I think Paul Newman played him in the film version.

It was never possible to know the truth or count on the present moment's version of reality. Peace transformed to war in an instant; laughter became fury, fiction became fact and vice versa, right became wrong, and night was day in the space of a breath.

Now, with enough distance between us and enough time elapsed, and especially with our memories separately teetering, it has become possible for me to imagine getting to the truth. An original kind of truth. I might assemble a coherent story by going back to the beginning, starting with my name. My mother's current confusion over the name of her dead son urges me to repossess mine. As her memory fades, I find myself searching among her earliest acts and gestures directed toward me, the ones I am most sure of, hoping to build a base of meaning from what can be salvaged from the rubble, encoding what I can know.

Since my memory was damaged a full decade before my mother's began to fail, we have reversed the customary generational sequence. For the last decade I have had to rely on her for verification of certain memories, which is a lot like testing your eyesight in a fun-house mirror. There is now a desperation about reclaiming whatever I can, even as my primary sources destabilize. I must work out for myself from surviving clues who she meant me to be and, from there, who I became.

My mother once told me I was conceived in a blizzard and born during the hottest summer of the first half of the century. The implication was that thinking about me always reminded her of the extremes of discomfort. I'm lucky she didn't name me Payne.

Conforming with the language of the country in which they live, modern Jews use naming as a way to celebrate the dead, to honor specific qualities or memories. "In the Jewish tradition," Rabbi Morris N. Kertzer says in *What Is a Jew?* "the name given to a child usually has some meaning." Well, mine didn't, other than sounding like my great-grandmother's, and I've often thought about this issue, wondering if, as in many traditional cultures, there might be a way in which my essence were incorporated in my name, even by accident.

One meaning of the name Floyd is "sacred" or "a holy glow." I am intrigued with the notion that my mother, however unconsciously, wanted me to be some kind of light in her life. Or that she was trying to bless me with an independence of spirit, a sense of inner sacredness, that she never subsequently encouraged. My naming, looked at this way, was hopeful, even if that hope came into being by luck, an odd stroke of fortune that carried my great-grandmother's name across genders and turned it into something with a meaning my mother hadn't planned.

I have never thought about my mother or my name in this way. Liberated from the constraints of pure memory, however, such a reading feels like deliverance. In *Understanding Media,* Marshall McLuhan says, "The name of a man is a numbing blow from which he never recovers." Maybe that's the case if you're named Marshall, but I'm thinking the opposite could be true for me. Having a relatively rare and strange name, one that suggests blessing, has begun to give me a place of haven, an enduring center during the chaos of long-term illness and brain damage. Further, exploring the meaning of my name helps to erect a shield against the insistent memories of my mother's blows. It is as though I have been given precisely what I need by the very person who seemed intent to deny it to me.

It gets even better, because my Hebrew name, Feivel, based on Floyd and derived from the Aramaic "Phoebus," also means light, or bright one. Few Hebrew names begin with the *F* sound, only Feivel and its variants Feibush, Fyvush, Feiwel. Having chosen Floyd, then, my mother found herself on a track that led straight to Feivel, a confirming light waiting there at the end of the naming tunnel.

While my names have taken on a load of symbolic meaning for me, I also must accept the idea that they came to me by sheer chance. No matter how I twist and turn my mother's unconscious intent, the truth is that I became Floyd because it was the only name that echoed Flora in a way my mother could tolerate. It was impersonal; I contracted my name the way I contracted the virus that scarred my brain—because I was in the right place at the right time, or the wrong place at the wrong time, and had the requisite genetic preparation for it to take hold. There is a meaning in this that is, I believe, even greater than the meaning of the name itself. Chance is in charge. The great challenge is to do something with what chance hands you, whether it be living up to a name that implies soft, sacred, inner light or with a virus that strands you in a kind of oxbow island of uncertainty at the heart of memory's watery labyrinth.

As people age, they often become distilled versions of themselves. They present a purer self, a stripped-down form of the person they had been before. Perhaps smaller physically, but intensified rather than diminished. This is especially true when the elderly live alone, freed from the corrective of companionship. A concentration of character occurs, a refinement through longevity, and their essence is laid bare. The former curmudgeon becomes malign, a beastly abuser; the kindly neighbor transforms into an angel.

In her early eighties, my mother had nearly everything she owned encased in plastic wrappings. Her pantry contained jars of Sanka and nondairy creamer shrouded in old baggies, a sugar bowl wrapped loosely enough in Saran Wrap to allow the lid to be placed over its hole, unopened cans of tuna and salmon in Ziploc bags. The contents of a box of Rice Krispies had been removed, packaging intact, and placed in a baggie before being restored inside the original box, which was itself then sealed in a larger baggie. The deeper I looked, the more her pantry mimicked a catacomb for mummies. Shrink-wrapped sets of gelatin boxes, packets of beef bouillon neatly bundled in produce bags sealed with clips, a few knickknacks in individual plastic sheaths closed with little wire ties. Her refrigerator was organized the same way; even her orange juice and milk containers were in plastic bags placed on a layer of waxed paper. The tiny kitchen in her apartment gleamed. Inside the oven, each pan was wrapped and nestled within a larger pan, and inside the topmost pan was a pink box of matzoh preserved in a baggie. Lidded bowls opened to reveal bags of individually wrapped licorice nips or a sack of Jujyfruits.

I recognized this as a condensed version of my mother's behavior when I was growing up. My mother needed to feel chambered at home, safe from external violation. From earlier vigilance to a totally Saran Wrapped world was a simple journey. My mother's life in her eighties became catered; dinners were delivered to avoid the dirtiness of cooking. What she did not eat was thrown at once into the incinerator down the hall, and a housecleaner arrived three days a week for the easiest fifty-dollar days imaginable since there was little actually to clean. She seldom left the apartment. The view was north, away from the beach, because a beach view brought with it blowing sand and a filthy ocean breeze.

My mother's character has continued its process of distillation until what is left is a dense, smooth jewel of self. She is who she is. Somewhere compacted inside is her body's knowledge of all the forces that shaped her, even if her ability to recall and relive the past at will is gone. That would hardly matter anyway, since her experience of the world was always so altered by distortion. I see her now, the small room she lives in more cluttered than she would have tolerated before, her dress more stained by food, and realize that this too does not matter. She has slowly been going blind, as though her system has by now been well trained at compensating for reality's distractions, and these things no longer bother her. She believes all is in order and has been in order for her full ninety years.

Memory is what connects us and memory is what has torn us apart. As a family, we long avoided naming the truth of our experience when we were all alive together, though the narrative had an energy of its own and defined us anyway. Now, for the two who remain alive, it seems essential to move beyond recollection. We need to live in an immediate present that is a genuine rebirth, shorn of the past. Or perhaps I mean a genuine renaming rather than rebirth. We have a fresh chance at the end of my mother's life, when the past is falling away. It is too late to say some of the things that never got said, to remember them for each other, but there is an opportunity to reimagine the story's end.

In his poem "The Old Fools," Philip Larkin writes:

Perhaps being old is having lighted rooms
Inside your head, and people in them, acting.
People you know, yet can't quite name.

I have begun trying to see my mother in this manner. The rooms inside her head are steadily growing dimmer and the people in them, names confused or forgotten, are fading from her view. This is a phenomenon I witness with my own eyes during annual summer visits to her hotel. I look enough like my father to be unsettling to her. Then she gazes at a desktop photograph of her beloved brother, Albert, dead fifteen years from cancer, glances back at me, turns toward the curtained window, and is clearly unable to organize the images or assign the proper names. Who are these men, all briefly illuminated in those darkened rooms? The next morning, I can tell that she wonders at first if I might be her brother after all, except that I am so short. Once I speak, though, she knows who I am. When my daughter comes up from Pittsburgh to visit her, my mother thinks that Rebecca might be her sister-in-law and wants to know how Albert is doing. After learning that Rebecca is her granddaughter, my mother offers condolences.

Her confusion suggests that the barriers of time have collapsed. She is time traveling. The psychologist Endel Tulving observed that "remembering, for the rememberer, is mental time travel," by which he meant that it permitted "a sort of reliving of something that happened in the past." He called the special brain system by which we retrieve information in the context of a particular time and place, with reference to ourselves as a participant, *episodic memory*. But what happens in an aging brain like my mother's is time travel of a different order, where past and present merge, the distinctions blur, and everything is experienced simultaneously. I *am* my father or my uncle. It *is* the autumn of 1938; that water out there beyond my mother's window is dangerous because Martians have landed in New Jersey, the radio said so, and the invaders are making their way to New York via the river.

She cannot travel backward to a place that makes sense, to a time of happiness or accomplishment. Most of her time is spent gaily in the present, playing bingo, trying to make the other girls at the hotel jealous of her power over men. But some of her time is spent in a mazelike timelessness that feels threatening, and it is possible to hear her fear, her despair, when she loses herself in that labyrinth.

My mother's situation suggests that true oblivion, at least while we are alive, is not so much about being completely forgotten as about completely forgetting. If no one else remembers us, or says our name, at least we can remember our selves, travel backward to relive the vivid parts or random parts of our lives. We can look into those lit rooms. We can say our own name. But when memory loses its grip, when the lights do finally go out, when neither our own nor our loved ones' names remain, that is when we are lost.

My job is once again to be my mother's memory bank. The process works differently now, since she forgets what I have helped her remember almost as soon as the images come clear. I can only illuminate the rooms in her head for a moment. But I can also fill one of the rooms with a light of my own, with my own dull gray glow, so she will sense that at least someone is at home. In doing this job, I find myself helping to stabilize my own memories, working past those awful ones that survived the viral damage to my brain because they were kept in a deeper vault. I tell her stories that she readily believes, elaborates on, then forgets. There is laughter. I am astonished to find in all this an opportunity for us to love one another. I am, in some ways, rediscovering my mother amid the rubble. I am trying to help her stay here.

Tomorrow Will Be Today

We are an hour behind schedule and still parked in front of the nursing home, but my mother is finally inside the rental car. Maureen, the nurse who has been a constant source of support during these three weeks of rehabilitation, leans in for one more embrace.

"I'll never forget you," she says, kissing my mother's cheek.

"Oh, me too." My mother smiles, kisses Maureen's cheek and then the air nearby.

The car door slams. I start the engine and reassure my mother that we'll be at the airport very soon.

"Excuse me, dear," she says. "Who was that lady?"

Bolstered by exact routine, using notes, staying close to home, relying on friends and well-meaning aides, it may be possible for people to disguise for a while the tightness of dementia's embrace. My mother knew where her clothes were, where the soap and her hosiery were; she could find and operate the elevators. She may not have remembered the names of her two dead husbands or recalled what she did ten minutes ago, but the age-related damage to her brain was in a different set of circuits than the ones that controlled her procedural memory, the ability to perform tasks. My mother had everyone fooled. Until leg infections sent her to the hospital, we didn't know how lost she really was.

More and more, she was forgetful and knew she was forgetful. She relied on to-do lists, cluttered as weedy gardens, which swarmed across her telephone table. But she forgot where her notes were and then forgot to look for them. She called me at six in the morning, forgetting the three-hour time difference, to ask what our phone number was. It was almost impossible for her to encode new memories, which vanished within a minute or two, or to track and hold a conversation in mind, to make sense of new information—all signs of increasing hippocampal damage associated with aging. Her vision, damaged by macular degeneration and other age-related conditions, was erratic. Life had shrunk to include only her boyfriend Irv and their tight routine at the hotel, me and Beverly, and sometimes my daughter, Becka, and her new husband, Gualtiero, who periodically drove from Pittsburgh to visit. Never leaving the hotel building except for a weekly appointment at the beauty parlor or the occasional doctor's appointment, she seemed to do fine. She was happy. We asked if she wanted to live closer to us, in Oregon, and she said, "No, dear, not now. If I need you, you can just walk over to the hotel."

It was the shoes that got her. No one could talk her out of wearing them because she feared that ungainly footwear would limit her attractiveness to men. The fluid buildup of edema had been a problem for at least a quarter century, making the tops of her feet puff and spill over the tight strap where her metatarsals ended. My mother's feet had long been asked to carry a considerable burden. They were now at least as high as they were long and conformed to the template of her shoe, which she had in varying colors. She could no longer wear any other style except the sort of orthopedic footwear she refused to consider.

It became difficult for my mother to walk. Beverly and I kept urging her to get appropriate shoes and so did Becka, who also offered to take her shopping or to go to the store and bring shoes back.

The hotel management, my mother's physicians, her friends—no one could convince her.

She was hospitalized on a Saturday morning, suffering from cellulitis in her feet, a spreading bacterial infection of the skin and the tissues just beneath the skin. Circulation had been compromised, the skin irritated; the swollen site created an ideal environment for bacteria. By the time the infection cleared, she had lost her tenuous hold.

On the drive to JFK, my mother is calm but confused and almost unrecognizably compliant. With no idea where she is or what we are doing, she remains composed, speaks without the familiar wrath, smiles, issues phrases of pure praise about my driving or my hair or my good fortune in having Beverly as my wife. I am, she says over and over and over, a fine son. Except for her efforts to figure things out, she is relaxed. It is a version of my mother I'd never dreamt of seeing.

"I'm going to Oregon?"

"That's right, Mother. You're moving to Oregon."

"Is it a very long drive?"

"It's too far to drive. We're going to fly there, the three of us."

She nods. She looks out her window, then turns to look at me. "I'm going to Oregon?"

"Yes. You're going to live there."

"Where do I live now?"

"Well, you've been living in New York all your life, but now you're moving to Oregon."

"I am? Oh, that's nice. I've always wanted to go to Oregon. My son lives there." She leans back in her seat and gazes through the front window.

"We're almost there," Beverly says from the back seat.

"Who's that?" my mother says, twisting herself in the direction of the voice.

Beverly leans forward so my mother can see her. "It's me, Beverly."

"Oh, hello, dear." She looks from Beverly to me and back. "She's gorgeous! You two should get married."

"We are married," I say.

"You're married? Congratulations. How long are you married?"

"Eight years."

"Did I come to the wedding?"

"No. We invited you, but you thought Oregon was too far away."

"Oregon? I'm going to Oregon?"

"Yes."

"Is it a very long drive?"

"We're going to fly there, Mother."

"We're going to fly?"

"Pretty soon," Beverly tells her.

"Then you'll have to go faster," my mother says.

When she was admitted to the emergency room, my mother became agitated. It was an unfamiliar setting, Irv was nowhere to be found, there was hectic activity, and the doctor barely spoke English. When I was finally able to reach this doctor later in the day, she told me that my mother was the most difficult patient she had ever encountered. During the crisis, another doctor—a stranger to my mother rather than the general practitioner who had treated her for the last forty-one years—was called in to consult. An intravenous line was introduced to deliver antibiotics for the infection. A urinary catheter was put in place. My mother, more distressed and confused, tried to pull out the various lines. Unable to communicate with her, the doctors administered a dose of Haldol.

Haldol is a powerful antipsychotic drug used primarily to control symptoms of schizophrenia and other psychoses, the tics associated with Tourette's syndrome and hyperactive behavior in children. Its use as a major tranquilizer—the way it was used on my mother—should only occur when there is no other pharmaceutical or behavioral choice. Haldol has well-known, potent side effects, particularly in the elderly, and especially among elderly women. In this group, it may cause an irreversible condition known as tardive dyskenesia—involuntary muscle spasms and twitches in the face and body. Though it was being used to control her agitation, it is also known to cause agitation as a side effect, along with psychotic behavior and hallucinations. Haldol can cause muscle stiffness and affect heartbeat—both areas of major concern in a ninety-year-old woman whose ability to walk has already been affected. It should be avoided in patients with glaucoma. It should be avoided in patients with thyroid disease, which my mother would be treated for—for the first time—in the following weeks.

This was not a patient who should have been given Haldol. Not even once, and my mother was kept on the drug for the next five days. I spoke with the nurses daily, who told me that my mother was doing well, was resting, and was still on Haldol to ease her agitation. Because it was easy to imagine my mother agitated, I did not become alarmed about the drug's ongoing use until a second day had passed. When I eventually reached the consulting doctor, he claimed to have ordered only one dose and only for the ER. By Friday, I had brokered an end to the drug's regimen.

Whether the Haldol was used punitively on my mother because she'd been difficult to manage, or was used for five days because of a breakdown in communication between doctors and nurses, when my mother emerged from its effects she was in cognitive chaos. Clearly, she had tumbled over whatever edge she'd been treading for the last few years. Her leg infections were better, thanks to five days of antibiotics, but her memory and awareness had been cut loose altogether; she had lost her head, had finally swooned into dementia's embrace.

Perhaps that would have happened anyway, without the drug, once she'd been removed from her familiar surroundings and routine, taken away by the need for prolonged emergency medical treatment. Regardless, everyone involved in her care agreed that my mother could no longer live on her own. This was confirmed by Becka and Gualtiero, who had rushed to New York once the extent of my mother's problem became apparent. She would need a few weeks of rehabilitation, but then it would be necessary to move her into a nursing home.

My mother is convinced that the airplane is a hotel. She hopes it isn't too expensive to be staying here.

The flight is scheduled for six hours. We sit in the terminal for two hours and on the plane for an hour; now we've been airborne for about an hour. My mother has not stopped talking for more than five seconds at a time, going over and over the same set of questions. Are Beverly and I married? For how long? Did my mother come to the wedding? Is Becka my daughter or my wife or my mother? Are Becka and Gualtiero married? Am I married to Gualtiero? Are we really going to Oregon? How far is it?

She looks out the window. We're sitting in the second row, as close to the bathroom as we could get. She can see the engine just at the edge of vision, but not the wing it dangles from. The huge engine hovers, moving neither forward nor backward, and my mother is convinced it is a car.

"Why doesn't it pass us?" she asks me, turning away from the window.

"It's attached, Mother. It's part of the wing."

"The hotel has wings?"

"This is an airplane."

"It is?" She looks out again. "There's a car right beside us. I hope it doesn't crash into us."

Her eyes close and I am elated, thinking at last she (and of course we) will have some rest. But then she leans forward, glimpses Beverly, and says, "She's gorgeous. You two should get married."

Our memories are encoded through a chemical process that, essentially, strengthens the connections among the brain's neurons. The more deeply we encode a memory—because it matters to us, because we need to refer to it frequently, because it was formed under traumatic conditions—the more powerful those neuronal connections are. But as we age, neurons are lost in the basal forebrain, where such memories are harbored. We can't remember because the chemical pathways have been wiped away. In aging brains, the frontal lobes are where the worst damage occurs.

In the protracted presence of someone whose dementia has progressed as far as my mother's, it can be difficult to sustain the understanding that she can't help or stop being as she is. No amount of repetition will enable her to remember anything; no logic or precision of presentation is going to stop her from asking the same question immediately. Beverly and I cannot ease her mind with words, though we can't ignore her questions either because that only increases her confusion. We can sometimes distract her by producing a sketch pad and pencil—she loves to draw but loses focus in a few minutes—or by singing songs with her. Her memory that no longer contains my childhood or her childhood or her fifty years of married life does contain a vast collection of song-lyric snippets and their melodies.

For a while, I believed that the changes dementia produced in my mother's personality might afford us a fresh opportunity to love one another despite the past and its harms. After all, my mother is now sweet and mellow. Everyone who worked with her in the nursing home raved about how delightful she was to be around. Whichever neurons and connectors are damaged in her brain, they must be where the anger once lived. Unlike some elderly people, my mother is not tormented by the content of her dementia. If, for those with dementia, reality becomes elusive and unreliable as a dream, at least for her the dream seems not to be a nightmare. But her condition precludes the sort of connection that I had anticipated with such misguided optimism. Her love for me seems honest and undiluted—at last—but it has no substance. She does not in fact know who I am or remember anything about me. Gazing at my face, she notes the grizzled hair that has covered it since the fall of 1969, then asks if I've always had a beard. I am her son, she sometimes recognizes that, but she has no sense of my age, my background, my life, my personality. And we cannot talk meaningfully. She gives voice to her whirling thoughts, mildly and with a sense of wonder at almost everything, and I respond to her questions and comments, and she forgets the entire exchange in a flash.

Beverly and I switch seats. We are taking hourly turns sitting next to my mother, responding to her monologue and questions, keeping her comfortable, helping her eat or sing or draw. A moment after settling down, she looks across at me and asks Beverly, "Who's that lady sitting next to you?"

Irv was not capable of visiting my mother in the hospital. Neither was anyone else from the retirement hotel. Hoping to provide her with familiar voices and faces, I tried to get in touch with the few people who remained part of my mother's life outside that place.

There weren't many. I got out her phone bills, thinking I might be able to reach my mother's routine contacts and alert them to her situation. For the previous two months, she'd placed twenty local calls, fifteen of them to the same number, none of those calls lasting longer than two minutes. That turned out to be the Verizon phone company's office in Garden City, which had no explanation for my mother's barrage. I imagined her picking up her phone, seeing the local office number on an old envelope or the cover of the phone directory, and dialing without further intention. Just trying to make contact with the world somehow.

There was another number that she had reached three times. It was located all the way across Long Island, on the north shore, and when I called a young woman answered whose voice I didn't recognize.

"I'm Lillian Rosen's son," I said.

"Who?"

"You don't know Lillian?"

"Is this a joke?"

"My mother's ninety and in the hospital in Long Beach," I told her. "I live in Oregon and I've been tracking down the people she's called in the last couple of months. Wanted someone to visit her before I get there in two weeks." I could hear what this sounded like.

Strange Lonely Man Makes Bogus Calls in Search of a Sympathetic Voice.

"Look, I'm really sorry. That's so sad. I don't know your mother, but I tell you what: if she was closer, I'd go visit her anyway."

When I called the fourth number, an elderly man answered and seemed unable either to hear me or to speak any word other than "Hanh?" I figured he might be an old boyfriend of my mother's, but he lived even farther away than my previous victim and didn't seem likely to visit.

The final number turned out to be my mother's ninety-three-year-old cousin Muriel. Her mind totally clear, she knew at once who I was and was sorry to hear about my mother. "I'd go see her, but I can't leave the house. I'm sick, don't ask me what's wrong because there isn't enough time in the world for me to cover everything. Take your mother's body and my mind, we'd have one wonderful old lady. Keep me posted."

My mother does not sleep, does not even close her eyes. She just keeps talking. I offer her a piece of her favorite coffee candy; she raises her eyebrows and nods but continues with what she was saying: "You two should get married."

"We are married." I unwrap the candy and hand it to her. "Eight years now."

"Eight years!" She puts the candy in her mouth, then spits it back into her hand. "Was I at the wedding?"

"You couldn't come. It was too far for you."

She reaches into her mouth, removes her upper dentures, cups them in her left hand, and reinserts the candy. "Did I get you a present?"

"You did." As she passes, I ask the flight attendant if we can have a headset for my mother.

"Tell the waitress I'd like more soda," my mother says. "This one's almost finished."

While we wait for the headset, I scan the in-flight magazine to see what the options are. No channel for old standards or show tunes, which are the bases of her repertoire. The only programming that's not for teens or younger adults offers opera; though my mother is not familiar with much of the canon, I think she will respond to the pomp and drama of it and perhaps recognize a few melodies.

She lets me slip the headset over her ears and smiles at the music. "They're singing to me," she says. She nods her head a few times. "Beautiful." Then she notices the cord across her chest. "What is this?" She pulls the cord, which tugs the earpieces out. "They're done."

As I reach to readjust them, she says, in a slightly deeper voice, "Will you come up to my room later?"

For a moment, I'm not sure if she's still thinking the airplane is a hotel or if she's wondering about the procedures when we arrive at the nursing home in Oregon. Then, remembering that she'd used the deeper voice earlier when asking if I was single, I see her look at me and smile, and I realize she thinks I'm Irv. Or maybe, zipping ahead, her soon-to-manifest Oregon boyfriend. She's flirting with me.

I lean back and ask, "Are you enjoying the candy?" She nods, looks in her left hand, and says, "What are my teeth doing here?"

Moved to the nursing-home wing of the hospital, my mother had received two weeks of physical and occupational therapy after her cellulitis disappeared. Her feet remained massively swollen, and she spent most of her time there in a wheelchair. Becka and Gualtiero bought her an entire wardrobe of brightly colored lounging clothes to replace the dresses, stockings, skirts, and blouses that are no longer practical. They also bought her a pair of surf shoes, rubber soled, flexible, and have cut the top to accommodate my mother's swollen midfoot. In terms of apparel, it was a fresh, sensible start.

We were told that she'd progressed as far as she can physically. But her memory impairment made it impossible for her to dress herself, use the toilet by herself, eat or use her walker without someone present to cue her at every step, answer a ringing telephone or place a call by herself. She could not remember how to get out of a wheelchair or side chair. She could not fend for herself. She was in an eternal present moment, with mere flickers of recollection showing themselves from time to time in the form of song lyrics or images from her early life.

That much was clear when I spoke with her. Though we'd arranged for my mother to have a bedside phone, the only way to reach her was by calling the nurses' station, where she would be wheeled and the phone would be handed to her. Once, I convinced a nurse to bring my mother to her room, put her in bed, and, when I called back, show her how to answer the phone. That didn't work well, because she dropped it, then leaned over and yelled toward the stranded mouthpiece: "Hello?" I heard the nurse give her the phone and heard my mother ask what to do with the thing they'd placed in her hand. I knew what to expect.

"Hello, Mother."

"Oh, Floyd!" Her joy at hearing my voice was extraordinary. Fleeting, but genuine and new. "My son. It's so good to talk to you."

"For me too. So do you know where you are?"

"I'm in bed."

"Well, I meant do you know where you're living now?"

There is a pause. "Apparently in my room."

"How do you feel, Mother?"

"I'm all right. But who are you, dear?"

Beverly and I found an excellent nursing home in Portland that was equipped to give her the required attention and care, made the necessary arrangements, then booked flights to and from New York. Despite what Becka and Gualtiero had told us about my mother's condition, despite what I'd heard over the phone and from the people taking care of my mother, I hadn't quite grasped the full extent of her dementia yet. So I thought the trip back to Oregon with her might be all right, maybe even fun.

Our two days in New York were devoted to lessons in how to help my mother make the long trip to Oregon, and to packing up her room at the retirement hotel. We brought along an empty garment bag, a suitcase, and a duffel bag. Since the fire and her relocation to the hotel, we had helped her sort through belongings and reduce the number of her possessions. This final packing, we thought, should only take a couple of hours.

But the room, though fairly neat on the surface, reflected the harrowing disarray of my mother's mind over the last year. The shelf on top of her closet contained only empty plastic bags she had stashed rather than throw away. Several drawers held abandoned envelopes, scraps of paper, loose photographs, old bills and statements, and canceled checks. Two drawers were devoted entirely to unopened packs of playing cards. Another held ancient, torn underthings. The familiar group of paintings, a few of which were her own work from years past—a floral still life, a busty Gauguin copy—and a few by friends, all hung crookedly above her bed. Notes taped to the back of photographs and written in my daughter's hand identified relatives my mother had trouble remembering.

At the small telephone table by her bed, I found my mother's pile of notes. Periodically, she would ask me to send notebooks and pens. Sometimes she would request another wristwatch as well, insisting that the last one didn't work anymore. I knew she was struggling to keep track of time and get herself organized. Whenever we spoke, she would ask me to give her my phone number, or Becka's, or to tell her what day it was, what month exactly. And she would write it down, tear the page from her notebook, and ask something else. I expected a jumble of notes. I had not realized what their content would reveal. *Tomorrow will be Wednesday,* one page said. Another said, *Today is Monday* and another, *Today is Friday. Get hair done.* Near the top, a note said, *Today is.* Finally, another said, *Tomorrow will be Today.*

More than anything else in the room—the dresses soiled as my mother would never have allowed her dresses to be soiled, the bathroom with its empty lipstick holders and little else, the wooden treasure box cluttered with tangles of costume jewelry, the uncashed insurance check for $1,264.82 dated February 1995—these notes suggested what it must be like now to be in my mother's mind. Not only had time fallen apart for her, but so had hope. Tomorrow will not simply be *like* today, it will *be* today. Again and again, in a roiling eddy, going nowhere but never still, nothing ever happened except what happened now and it never made any sense. Perpetual disorientation, disintegration.

And yet my mother, always so enraged, so aggressive and haughty, always plotting and scheming, was now so pleasant that those who spent time with her never failed to remark it. She was special to the nurses and aides because she didn't complain, didn't snap at them (my mother!). Now, of all times, she was mellow. She was reported to be accommodating, patient, even cheerful. It would not be possible to exaggerate how alien these characteristics sounded when applied to her. I was grateful, relieved for her, stunned, and sometimes felt that familiar glimmer of hope. Maybe now, near the end, we could have a time of warmth and love. But then I reminded myself that the kind of connection I fantasized would no longer be possible. All that was possible was the external form of it, perhaps, a time to come in which we behaved as though she knew and loved me. That would have to be enough.

Sitting on the chair by her phone, her possessions nearly packed now, I wondered if my mother had finally given up trying to control things and found, in that, genuine relief. Surrender as a kind of victory over this endless, unmanageable derangement. Then again, I wondered if my mother—the former Melody Girl of the Air on KBNX in the Bronx where she had a five-minute radio show in the early 1930s, the would-be star of stage and screen—might be giving the greatest performance of her life.

We reach the nursing home in Portland at 10:30 P.M., almost eleven hours after we left the nursing home in New York. My mother is tired but still has not slept or stopped talking. She no longer remembers that she lived in New York or that she flew on a plane; she still wonders if Beverly and I are married.

As promised, the staff is prepared for us, and my mother is welcomed like a returning member of the family. We lug the garment bag, suitcase, and duffel bag inside and find her in bed already, being checked over by a nurse and cooed to by an aide. Two aides help us unpack my mother's things, making a list of her clothes and personal items, being sure we've remembered the necessities.

"How do you feel, Lillian?" the nurse asks, recording blood pressure and temperature, examining my mother's body for signs of problems. Her blood pressure is remarkable for a woman who has just traveled across the country. I don't want to know how mine is. The attention she is getting is tender, professional, efficient. Beverly and I are glad to see what we knew we would see: a place that will be good to and for my mother.

"I feel fine, dear. A little tired. Who is that over there?"

"That's your son."

"My son? Where did he come from?"

My mother's photographs are placed on her bedside table. Candy is stashed in its drawer.

"We just came with you from New York, Mother."

"New York? I was in New York?"

"And now you're an Oregonian," the nurse whispers, kissing my mother's brow.

Within twenty minutes, we are all done. My mother's possessions have dwindled, as her world and her awareness have dwindled, and it takes almost no time at all to make her feel settled and at home. Which is the word she uses, though it seems ironic to me. All it takes to allow her this reflexive sense of home is for her to be wherever she is.

We lean down to kiss her. "See you soon."

"When?

"In a few days."

"A few days? How long will I be here?"

"This is where you live now, Mother. And there are lots of people to take care of you. You won't have to worry about anything."

She closes her eyes for a second only, then looks up at me, looks at Beverly, looks around. She does not seem to recognize anyone. Then my mother mumbles, "She's gorgeous. You two should get married."

As though telling her a bedtime story, I say we are married and—not waiting for the next line—add that we've been married for eight years, that she didn't come to the wedding because it was too far to travel from New York to Oregon, that she did buy us a present.

"And where am I now?"

"Oregon."

"Oregon? Am I in prison?"

I start to tell her she is not in prison, is in her new home, a place where she will be well cared for, but the nurse interrupts, stroking my mother's face, reassuring her, whispering. She also waves to us, signaling that the time has come to depart. Beverly and I are almost giddy with fatigue and relief. We still have an hour's drive before we get home.

Hand in hand, we leave the nursing home. We settle into our car and kiss. I think we both have the same sense of sadness at my mother's final confusion and the fear it seemed to reveal.

Of course my mother is in prison. She is incarcerated by the enfolding dementia, and it's a life sentence. However congenial and cooperative she may be, she is not free to be herself, has lost her self, and I am surprised to mourn the very absence I'd always hoped for. Can it be that I want her to be angry, volatile, and difficult? That I would welcome the barbs and accusations and outbursts? No, that's not it; but still there is a sense of loss at the same time there is consolation, a feeling of deliverance. Maybe, I think, it's right that there should remain such confused responses. But the balance has shifted, and I know I am content to have her close by.

We roll down the windows as we drive into the night.

In the American Lives series

Fault Line
by Laurie Alberts

Pieces from Life's Crazy Quilt
by Marvin V. Arnett

Hannah and the Mountain:
Notes toward a
Wilderness Fatherhood
by Jonathan Johnson

Local Wonders: Seasons
in the Bohemian Alps
by Ted Kooser

Turning Bones
by Lee Martin

Thoughts from a Queen-Sized Bed
by Mimi Schwartz

Gang of One: Memoirs of a Red Guard
by Fan Shen

Scraping By in the Big Eighties
by Natalia Rachel Singer

In the Shadow of Memory
by Floyd Skloot

Secret Frequencies:
A New York Education
by John Skoyles

Phantom Limb
by Janet Sternburg